A BOY IN THE GULAG

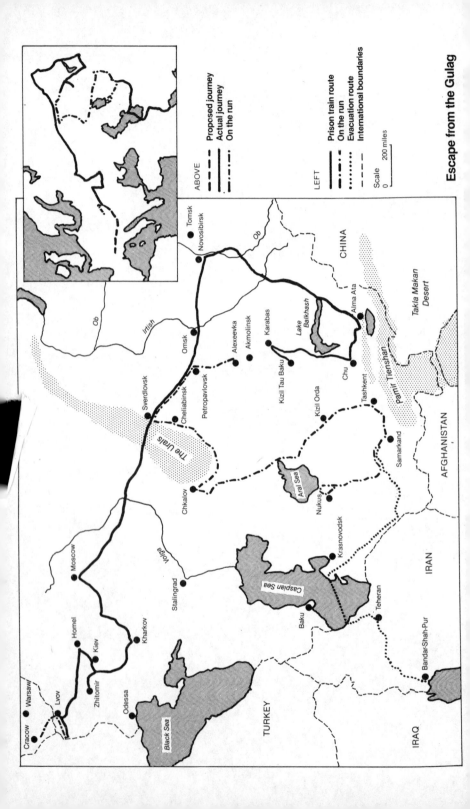

Escape from the Gulag

ABOVE
— — — Proposed journey
——— Actual journey
—··—··— On the run

LEFT
——— Prison train route
—··—··— On the run
············· Evacuation route
— — — International boundaries

Scale
0   200 miles

Tomsk
Novosibirsk
Ob
Irtish
Omsk
Alexeevka
Akmolinsk
Karabas
Lake Balkhash
Sverdlovsk
Cheliabinsk
Petropavlovsk
Kizil Tau Baku
Chu
Alma Ata
CHINA
Takla Makan Desert
Pamir Tienshan
Kizil Orda
Tashkent
The Urals
Chkalov
Aral Sea
Nukus
Samarkand
AFGHANISTAN
Volga
Moscow
Krasnovodsk
Stalingrad
Caspian Sea
Baku
Teheran
IRAN
Bandar-Shah-Pur
Warsaw
Cracow
Lvov
Zhitomir
Kiev
Homel
Kharkov
Odessa
Black Sea
TURKEY
IRAQ
Ob

JERZY KMIECIK

A Boy in the Gulag

Quartet Books
London Melbourne New York

To my son, Jan

First published by Quartet Books Limited 1983
A member of the Namara Group
27/29 Goodge Street, London W1P 1FD

Copyright © 1983 by Jerzy Kmiecik

British Library Cataloguing in Publication Data

Kmiecik, Jerzy
A boy in the Gulag.
1. Political prisoners—Soviet Union
I. Title
365'.45'0924   HV9846.5

ISBN 0-7043-2321-4

Typeset by MC Typeset, Chatham, Kent
Printed in Great Britain by Nene Litho
and bound by Woolnough Bookbinding
both of Wellingborough, Northants

CONTENTS

Foreword

It all happened many years ago. Most of the people who know my story told me that I should have written this book soon after the last war, when things were still fresh in people's minds, when the Iron Curtain fell.

This I could not do. For it is a true story, and had I written and publicized the truth thirty-odd years ago, the facts could easily have been checked by the NKVD, the Soviet Secret Police, now better known as the KGB. As a result many would have been shot, or condemned to a slow death in one of the many Eastern Bloc labour camps. Indeed, these are the same labour camps which the leaders of the Iron Curtain countries are still trying so hard to conceal from the free people of the Western world.

It is not generally realized that only a minute proportion of the citizens of the Soviet Union are members of, or have any interest in, the Communist Party. I have met individuals who joined the Party not for any ideological reason, but simply to better their standard of living.

It would be wrong also to address all the people as 'Russians', a word normally used in the West. Russians are only one of the many nationalities in the Soviet Union. And I found the majority of those I met good, honest, kind-hearted and hard-working, but very unhappy. Thus, when I refer to the 'Communists' or the 'Communist Party', I refer to that small band of highly disciplined, but blind or blinkered storm troopers who so ruthlessly rule the Soviet Union.

To a Communist, any non-Communist social system is automatically capitalist. I use that word simply to distinguish one system from the other, not for any other reason.

PART ONE

Bezhentsy

1

I was born in a small village in the Province of Cracow, on 1 April 1923. My father was the headmaster of the village school in which my mother taught. My parents, two brothers, Adam and Kazik, and I, lived in a small cottage by the school, close to the church which was surrounded by big linden trees. The church had a stork's nest on top of the roof, facing a small spire.

We used to await the coming of the storks because it meant we could run about barefoot from that time on. They came in huge flocks from the south, grunting like geese while spiralling down, before settling on a meadow on the other side of the vicarage. We knew they always landed there so we would steal across the priest's orchard next to our home and watch them gathering by a little stream and a pond.

They would stay there for an hour or more, looking for frogs, preening themselves and clack-clacking before dispersing in small groups. Our pair would immediately start repairing their usual nest, which was set on an old coach wheel from which the steel rim had been removed and which had been placed on top of the church a long time before I was born.

In time one or two young storks would become evident, and we would eagerly await their first flight. For days the parents would stand on the edge of the nest, flapping their wings, then stretching them as though soaring. Then the youngsters would try to do the same, to the accompaniment of much clack-clacking from their parents. After a day or two, the youngsters would push off from the nest in the direction of the meadow, and fly as though they had been flying for years.

My father owned about ten acres of land. Although he paid to have it ploughed and prepared, he would always sow the wheat,

3

rye and oats himself by hand. I remember his first effort. When the corn started sprouting it was obvious that he had never done it before. There were patches of green, and patches of nothing.

'Never mind,' he said philosophically. 'I'll know better next time. It proves my view that one must always try to do what other people are doing. One can appreciate their difficulties and become a better man.'

During vacations, when we were old enough, we were sent to work in the fields so that we too could learn to understand other points of view. I was ploughing when I was ten years old, holding the handles of a plough drawn by two horses, making sure that the furrow was straight and had an even bite.

'It looks better that way,' my father would say. 'Besides, it is more professional.' How right he was.

One year my mother made us a tent from old sheets. I was eight and Adam twelve, and with great excitement we packed our gear and trooped off to set up camp in the nearby wood. It covered about five square miles, and there was a pretty little stream flowing right through the centre. Some parts of it were very dense, others quite open with plenty of bilberries, raspberries, wild strawberries and mushrooms. When they were in season, we would get up at the crack of dawn to gather mushrooms to be dried for winter use: chanterelles, saffron milk caps and morels for eating the same day; the berries we would have with sour cream and sugar for dessert. Delicious! From our very earliest days we played hide-and-seek, tracking, or 'Tarzan' in these woods. We soon discovered that moss growing on a tree-trunk normally faces north. We also noted the type of terrain and soil where mushrooms and berries grew. Little did we suspect that in the not too distant future this knowledge was going to be of great assistance to us.

We erected the tent under a huge branch of an oak, so that when the dew started to fall, our tent would not get soaked. We gathered some wood for a fire which we set just outside the canopy of the tree, and made some coffee which, with some bread and butter, comprised our supper.

The moon disappeared beyond the distant horizon, the birds stopped singing and there was complete silence, broken occasionally by the very low-toned hum of the wind in the tree-tops. I'd heard it many times in those woods, so I wasn't worried. From time to time there was a slight rattle from inside the wood, but I knew it was a branch of an oak rubbing against the trunk of another tree, some thousand yards away.

Suddenly the blood froze in my veins. I heard a terrifying shriek, followed by a howl: 'yoo . . . hoo . . . hooo!' I took a deep breath, letting it out slowly. Then I remembered my father's saying: 'The horse has a bigger head than you, let him worry!' So I stopped trembling, and then nearly burst out laughing. 'You fool, it was only an owl making a kill!' I felt very grown up.

Soon the days became shorter and the leaves on the linden trees changed to yellow and began falling. A man used to sweep them into heaps before taking them away. We would climb the trees and jump on to the heaps. One day it occurred to me that I could use one of my mother's duvet covers as a parachute and jump from a much higher branch than the others. Unfortunately there wasn't a tree around the church with branches far enough apart for me to try it, but the idea stuck in my head.

'I am going to be an aeroplane pilot when I grow up,' I thought, 'I might as well start learning how to jump now!'

At first I thought of climbing on to the church roof and baling out from there. Since we used to serve at Mass, we knew the caretaker, so the next time he went up the ladder to grease the bearings of a bell, I asked him if I could have a look. He agreed, but advised me not to stay too long. He needn't have worried! One peep through the bell tower was enough to convince me that I had set my sights much too high. The view was magnificent; I had never seen so far before.

I decided to jump from the school roof. I fixed two sticks at right angles to each other, then tied the stick ends to the open side of the duvet cover, so that my parachute was already open when I jumped, and I had something to hold on to. The cover, like a big pillow-slip, was about six feet long and four feet in diameter at the open end.

The next time my parents went to the nearby town for their monthly shopping, my contraption was ready. It was quite windy, and when I climbed on top of the roof, the ground below seemed to be much further away than ever before.

'Pull yourself together!' I thought, 'don't be a coward!' I

inspected the area I was likely to land on and decided that it ought to be between the carrots and the onion bed of our vegetable garden. I crossed myself, lifted the open end of my parachute towards the wind, and when I couldn't hold it any longer I kicked off from the top. I descended much faster than I had expected, and the ride was rough. The wind blew me on to the side of the plum tree and the branches cushioned my fall. I was a little scratched on my legs but otherwise unhurt. I did not do it again!

Winter was soon upon us. We inspected our skis in case the snow fell early. We also became extra good, the incentive being 6 December, St Nicholas's Day. He always brought presents for good boys and girls. We would find ours under our pillows when we woke up.

Christmas was approaching and we were on holiday. We used to go skiing at daybreak, after a quick breakfast of coffee and bread and butter. Soon the best day of the whole year was with us, *Wigilia*. Our parents would be preparing dishes all day, while we boys would help with washing up by licking the pots that contained sweet things.

My mother was an expert at making apple strudel, which we boys called 'two table cake', as two tables were required to spread the dough. She pulled and pulled until it was as thin as paper. She would then sprinkle a layer of chopped apples, sultanas, orange peel and vanilla sugar with cinnamon on top of it, catch one end of the cloth on which the paper-thin dough was lying and roll the whole thing into a sausage about three inches in diameter. She would cut it into pieces about eighteen inches long and bake them in the oven.

Wigilia, the Polish equivalent of the British Christmas dinner, only much more elaborate, started with the sighting of the first star in the east on Christmas Eve. We all, including the servant, gathered in the dining room around the table covered with hay beneath the tablecloth to commemorate the birth of Jesus in a stable. Father would pick up a plate of Holy Bread, as used in Communion, break a little with Mother and wish her a happy Christmas and New Year. Then everyone did likewise with everyone else present. A glass of vodka would be drunk by all, even by us, except that ours was nothing stronger than weak, cold tea flavoured with raspberry juice.

There was always one extra place prepared for a 'traveller'. The idea was that should anyone call at that time, he would fill the place. No one was to be homeless or in want.

After offering a prayer, the marvellous feast would begin. It started with beetroot soup, clear and red as wine, with noodles filled with mushrooms that we had gathered in autumn; stuffed pike or perch in aspic with tartar sauce; carp in grey sauce; fish cooked in the Jewish style; cabbage leaves stuffed with rice and mushrooms; sauerkraut pasties; pasties with cheese and currants; noodles with poppy seeds; dried fruit *compote*; poppy seed cake; the delicious 'two table cake'; ending with dates, figs, crystallized fruit and all sorts of nuts.

Liberal amounts of wine would be consumed, all of it made by my father years before. Our vodka bottle would change to wine, by means of a rubber band and a strip of paper.

About ten o'clock the bells in the church would peal, to remind the merry-makers that Midnight Mass started in two hours. They would peal again at eleven and thereafter every fifteen minutes. We would leave the house just before midnight, each carrying a coloured lantern lit by battery or by a thick candle and see all the villagers coming down the snow-covered slopes to the church in the valley. Everyone carried a lantern, creating multicoloured ribbons, all ending in the vicinity of the church, while the more distant parishioners arrived on jingling, horsedrawn sleighs. It was a sight that no show on earth can possibly reproduce; nothing could re-create the feeling and the mood then occasioned.

There would be a short Mass with many carols, after which the whole congregation would go outside the church to greet friends, acquaintances and strangers. Even enemies would shake hands and let bygones be bygones.

In time the snow started to melt and the ice covering the nearby river began to crack. We cleaned and waxed our skis and skates and put them away. When the icefloes began to move with the swollen current, we would jump on the big ones and ride as far as 'Jew the Milkman', about 300 yards away. Great fun, but not so in the opinion of my mother.

That year she caught us at it, brought us home, and after pointing out the possible outcome of our stupidity, gave us two smacks on our bare behinds. I felt guilty and ashamed. Guilty, because I had made my mother unhappy, and ashamed, because I had never been smacked before. There was never a repeat performance.

However, life was not all play, and at school I progressed quite well. I particularly remember looking forward to St George's Day (23 April), which was my Name Day (in Poland, birthdays were not really celebrated). I woke up very early when the great day came and there, by the side of my bed, was a bicycle! I ran to my parents to thank them for it.

'Good work deserves a prize,' said my father. 'Keep it up or, better still, do better!'

I was then nine and my results did improve. When I was twelve I passed the entrance examination to the grammar school in Tarnow five miles away. That meant I had to leave home and stay in digs with my brother Adam. We had a bedroom, shared a sitting room and were given three meals a day, all for fifty *zlotys*, or just over two pounds a month for both of us. We used to go home on free weekends, either on our bicycles or, in winter, on skis. I worked reasonably hard at Tarnow, my best subjects being mathematics, physics, chemistry and geography. My worst were Latin and history – I just could not remember people's names.

At the end of that term, after four years at the grammar school, I had to pass an entrance examination to a mathematics and physics lyceum. It was for two years prior to going to university. By then, I had lost all hope of becoming a pilot.

'There was a pilot in our family,' explained my mother. 'He was killed when you were one year old. We do not want it to happen again.'

They wanted me to become a doctor or a surgeon but I had no enthusiasm for the medical profession. If I can't fly aeroplanes, I will make them, I philosophized, and so decided to study aerodynamics when at university. I passed the necessary examinations and went home to the village for the holidays.

It was a beautiful summer. My brothers and I spent much of our time helping in the fields, but we also found time to forage in the woods. The storks had two young that year. One day I found one of them on the ground and tried to put it back in the nest.

'Don't bother,' advised one of the villagers who happened to be passing by. 'It is going to be a long, dry summer, and frogs will be scarce. The storks know this, so that's why they have tried to kill one of their young rather than let both of them starve.'

It certainly was a long, dry summer.

2

On the political front, Poland faced enormous problems. Germany was pressing for possession of Danzig, and also wanted a corridor across Polish Pomerania to East Prussia. Some reservists were called up and schools were to remain closed for an extra month. A big anti-aircraft exercise was to be carried out on 1 September 1939, while Germany sent two warships on a goodwill mission to Danzig.

I woke up at 5 a.m. on the day of that exercise and went on my bicycle to fetch butter from a nearby farm, all the time looking at the sky for aeroplanes. Soon I heard one, but it was too high for me to spot it. Then I saw an aircraft, then another, and they looked very much like Dornier 17s. The radio was silent except for code announcements – LAR-MIA 27, LAR-MIA 27 – and I remember thinking these must have been connected with the exercise. How wrong I was. The truth was that Germany had invaded Poland in the early hours of that day. Soon more and more aircraft came over in groups of about fifty. The village became full of soldiers and cavalrymen. On Sunday 3 September 1939, first Great Britain then France declared war on Germany.

'With all that might,' declared one of the officers temporarily billeted in our house, 'it will only be a matter of time before the Germans are pushed back.'

'I don't know,' answered my father. 'I don't know, but I hope so.'

Soon we could hear the artillery. At night there would be a flash, then some time later a thunderous boom-boom! On Tuesday night the flashes were almost continuous, something like lightning, except that the colours were oranges and reds. That night our parents warned us that if the Germans came close to the village we boys would have to leave.

'I don't want you to be taken to labour brigades,' explained Father.

'You can go and stay with Uncle Stanley,' counselled Mother.

Next day there was no respite from the bombers and even more fighters appeared. The soldiers and the cavalrymen left the village that evening.

'You will leave tomorrow morning,' said my father. 'Be prepared to go at a moment's notice.'

My mother packed some food in one rucksack and a change of clothing in another. She handed me her wrist-watch, and Adam was given 100 *zlotys*. We went to bed and rose early to the sound of machine-gun fire in the west. We were given breakfast, but could eat very little. My mother's eyes were very red; she had obviously been crying for most of the night.

'Don't worry, Lusia,' I heard my father say. 'They will be all right.'

We picked up the rucksacks, and Adam took Mother's walking-stick (I had shaped one for myself the day before). Our parents led us slowly to the front door.

'Let God lead you,' prayed my father. 'Don't come back till Poland is free,' pleaded Mother. They both sounded as though they were going to break down.

'Let's go!' I barked. I knew if we didn't leave then we would all burst into tears.

The time was 5.20 on the morning of Thursday 7 September 1939. It was a beautiful day: the sun was up over the hill to the east; everything was peaceful. We didn't turn round until we reached the top of the hill about twenty minutes later, when we took the last, long look at our house. It stood shining white against the green of grass and trees. My parents – the most wonderful parents anyone could be lucky enough to have – were standing in front of the door, both waving something white. Kazik, who was not yet fifteen, began to cry; I had a choking pain in my throat but refused to break down.

'We'd better go!' ordered Adam in a very shaky voice. So we three went. Adam and I had to wait twenty-seven years to see our father again. We never saw our mother.

We went along the footpath we had walked so many times before; it led to a forest about four miles away, and the manager was a friend of my parents. It seemed so unreal to leave it all.

'I hope we don't encounter that boar this time,' I said, breaking the silence, trying to divert the thoughts of Kazik, who was still crying.

The summer before we had been to see the manager and on the way back were confronted by a big, steely-grey beast with long fangs. When he charged, we had to climb a tree and sat there for about four hours until a forester, hearing our shouts, came to our rescue.

'I hope we do,' replied Kazik, 'then we can run back home.'

'Grow up!' said Adam. 'You are a soldier now.' Mercifully he stopped crying.

After crossing the forest we met a long column of people, mostly boys, walking eastwards. Some of them had left their homes three days before because the Germans had rounded up all the able-bodied males in their village and taken them away in lorries. It was about 10 a.m. when we saw the Heinkel flying low. It suddenly started machine-gunning. Despite the fact that our home had been near a firing range, I had never heard such a fast rate of fire. We all fell flat on our faces, covering our heads with whatever we carried. The plane circled around for some minutes, then flew away. About twenty minutes later a lone fighter appeared, shooting at the thin line of refugees. We scattered in all directions. The three of us and another boy hid behind a small stone wall, the remains of a building. We seemed to be picked as a target. Every time the fighter passed over us, we jumped the wall to the other side. It was the first time in my life that I heard the striking of bullets and ricocheting. I was scared.

'What have we done to him?' inquired Kazik, tearfully.

'Nothing,' I answered, pulling him over the wall. 'The swine is too scared to pick on a Polish fighter plane.' Little did we know that there were no Polish fighter planes left! The invader flew away, and nobody was hurt.

At midday we stopped for a rest and lunched on bread and sausages. We lay on our backs, feet in the air to let the blood run down from them, a trick we had learnt from our early days of foraging in the woods. We watched artillery moving eastward; some of the horses pulling the guns were wounded, as were the soldiers walking beside them. Yet again the bombers came, dropping bombs and machine-gunning. When they flew away, we decided to stick to the cornfields rather than the roads, and marched eastwards. When night came, we asked a farmer for permission to sleep in his barn. Not only did he agree but he also gave us a couple of litres of milk. We washed by a well and went to sleep; we did not need any encouragement.

At dawn Adam woke us up. He rose yawning and stretching his arms, lost his balance and fell. At that same instant we heard the rattle of a machine-gun and several thuds on the barn doors. A few holes appeared on them, and had Adam not fallen he surely would have been hit by a bullet. We left hurriedly, and only minutes later we saw the body of a soldier lying in the grass with a bullet through his head. We were hoping to reach a road and cross a river we knew to be in the vicinity, using a bridge if it was still there. The river was quite wide and fast-flowing, and although we were good swimmers we didn't want to get wet so early in the day. We heard clonking noises to the west and south.

'Tanks,' murmured Adam. 'And I think they are German!'

We increased our pace and about half an hour later we reached a road. Rounding the bend we saw the bridge – it was still intact! We remembered it from our cycling tour the previous summer. Then we heard a motorcycle approaching from the other side, and when we were halfway across the bridge it appeared, advancing slowly, before stopping a yard or two in front of us.

The rider wore a dark blue uniform, with a badge similar to pilots' wings above his right breast pocket, and a cap on his head. I had never seen a uniform like that before. A rifle was fixed to a bracket on the sidecar and a steel helmet lay on the seat. The man was small in stature with blond hair and blue eyes. He looked at each of us in turn. Very slowly, he moved his right hand away from the handlebars of his motorbike. As it reached his thigh, it became painfully obvious that he was trying to locate the revolver attached to his belt, whilst fixing us with his eyes.

I looked at his holster; it was done up with a locking-pin across the slot. Terrified, I thought: 'I shall have to hit him any time now, and I hope Adam thinks the same.' He did.

'Now!' he screamed suddenly.

I let go of Kazik's hand and leapt forward. Adam hit the soldier's head with the walking-stick, breaking it in the process.

Mine, however, did not break as I had cut it from a tree only three days previously. The German slumped forward over the handle-bars, although I don't know whether or not we killed him. We lifted the body from the motorbike and threw it over the side of the bridge into the river. Luckily, the engine was still running. Adam swung the bike around, I sat behind him, with Kazik in the sidecar. We expected to knock on Uncle Stanley's door later that day! After all, what was 180 miles on a machine like that? Alas, it was not to be. After about five miles we were stopped by an army lieutenant.

'In the name of the Polish Army I requisition this machine!' he commanded.

We did not argue. He placed a heavily bandaged soldier in the sidecar, another sat behind him and they roared away. Adam cut himself another stick and we continued our journey on foot. At least we did not hear the tanks any more. We met more refugees on the way, some of them travelling on horsedrawn carts, and heard a rumour that the Germans had dropped a parachute divi-sion to the south-east of us, and another that they had pushed northwards from Slovakia. We decided to alter our direction to a north-easterly course, to take us away from any such incursions. Knowing only too well how close we were to the German panzers, we allowed ourselves no more than fifteen minutes' rest every two hours. By evening we were on the outskirts of Bilgoraj.

By now, we were very tired. How Kazik managed to keep pace with us was difficult to understand. In two days we had covered one hundred miles, walking sixteen hours daily. For the past four hours we had been walking with leaves between the cheeks of our buttocks, as we were chafing rather badly, and the town was still two miles away. It took us an hour to cover the distance.

Once in the town we went to the railway station hoping to find a train. We were in luck! There was one, loaded with long, thick logs, but it was only going some twenty miles. We could not care, we were extremely tired. We clambered on the topmost trunk, hoping that we would not go to sleep. We kept nudging each other every few minutes, to make sure that at least one of us stayed conscious. The train was quite literally covered with human beings as it moved slowly north-east, but at least it was better than walking. It stopped in the early hours of the morning in a wood and was evidently going no further. We let ourselves down gently, walked just a few yards and collapsed under a tree absolutely exhausted.

The sun was well up when we awoke. My legs were aching but the chafing had stopped. We breakfasted on wild strawberries and bilberries and pressed on in a north-easterly direction. The woods were mostly of silver birch and not at all thick. We kept an eye open for any sign of a stream or a spring as we were tiring rather quickly now, and a good wash would help revive us. When nothing had shown up after some time, we decided on a search.

The springs we had found near our village were never at the bottom of the valley, but some distance up the slope. With this knowledge in mind, we spread out, calling each other every few minutes to avoid being separated. It was not long before Kazik found one.

The spring was a beauty. It was only about two feet across and six inches deep, but the water was crystal clear, and a streamlet ran from it for a few yards before disappearing into the sandy soil. The sun shone through the leaves of some bushes surrounding the water and sparkled on the little ripples spreading from Kazik's mouth as he drank eagerly from the little pool.

We drank our fill, then stripped and had a really good wash. Kazik, who was never keen on washing back home, and always found a valid reason as to why he should not, did not bother to think of an excuse this time. After resting an hour we pressed on north-east, feeling as fresh as the day we left home. An hour or so later we emerged from the woods to see a farmhouse roughly half a mile away.

'Good afternoon!' called Adam to a man who was walking towards us from a barn, 'we are making for Zamosc, could you tell us the way?'

'Yes,' answered the man. 'Take this path until you reach the road, then keep turning neither left nor right and you will get there.'

I thought it was a funny way of putting it, but of course, we were now in eastern Poland, and the language was bound to differ.

'It will be good three *versty*,' continued the man.

'How many kilometres to a *verst*?' I inquired sheepishly, not having the faintest idea how long the *verst* was.

'Well, some say it's three, some say eight of them kilometres,' advised the man, 'myself I always reckon it's a good three *versty* to town.'

We bought bread, butter and some milk from him, consumed them on the spot, then departed along the path. A good three *versty* later we arrived in Zamosc.

The town was full of soldiers and refugees. There was no hope of a train so we walked right through, heading for Hrubieszow. At sundown we bought some food from a Ukrainian farmer, stayed the night in his barn and rose early.

At about 8 a.m. we came across a cavalry unit some two or three hundred strong, but dismounted, moving eastwards. Some of the men had bandaged heads or arms, while most of the horses walked with their heads down, showing their exhaustion. Then the bombers came. It is impossible to describe the screams of those dying animals. We lay in the ditch by the roadside, praying for our lives, and the moment the planes flew away we leapt up and ran away from the massacre. Many of the horses were still alive, some of them lying on their backs, feet in the air, hooves clawing, as though trying to gallop to safety. It was a terrible sight. We must have run a mile before leaving the road and the inhumanity of it all. Back in the woods once more we felt safe.

We were now heading due east. The sandy soil slowly gave way to a heavier loam, much easier to walk on. We struggled for miles without seeing anybody or anything except an occasional aircraft. In the afternoon we entered a thick forest, which afforded even greater protection.

We made camp in the clearing by a stream just before dark, lit a fire, and discussed the plan of action for the next day, our fifth since leaving home. We had no idea of the distance we had covered. One thing we were certain of was that we could not walk too far and thus end up in the Soviet Union, for to do this we had to cross a main road running north to south. We decided we would turn south on reaching it.

We plodded on all the next day, reaching the edge of the forest by evening. We stayed for the night just there; we at least had food for the picking. At about 10 a.m. the following day we reached the main road. We turned south as planned and shortly afterwards came across an army convoy parked by the roadside. An army captain was sitting on a stone looking at a map. We looked at him in disbelief. He lived in our village and his wife was my godmother.

We were delighted when he told us that we had only twelve miles to go. After a chat we bid him God's speed. What we didn't realize then was that we were the last people from our village to see him alive. His body was one of the 4,250 subsequently dug up in Katyn Wood, near Smolensk, USSR.

It was 3.40 p.m. on Wednesday 13 September when we passed through the gates of our uncle's house. It was a much larger dwelling than our cottage, with four bedrooms, a lounge and a kitchen. Outside there was a stable where he kept his three horses, and a shed for a carriage and a cart. Before he retired he had been manager of a big estate; now he owned a small vinegar factory and employed four men. We used to work there occasionally when visiting him, washing bottles and sticking labels on them. My aunt opened the door when we knocked.

'Jesus and Maria!' she exclaimed. 'How did you get here?'

While we talked, she prepared a meal for us, our first proper meal for a week. Later we had a bath and went to bed. Not surprisingly, we slept for fourteen hours. We spent the next few days helping with the ordinary domestic chores, chopping wood or mucking out stables. According to the radio, Warsaw was surrounded by the Germans but fighting gallantly. Then suddenly everything went dead. Rumours spread that the Government, with the remnants of the Polish Air Force, had crossed to Romania *en route* for France, to carry on the fight from there; also that the Russians were coming to help the army to push the Germans back.

It was about 6 p.m. on Wednesday 20 September. I was looking towards the lake, about half a mile away, when I saw four riders on horseback. I ran to the house to tell the others. We all came out and recognized them as Polish cavalrymen from their diamond-shaped hats and white bands. They trotted behind a clump of trees, disappearing for a moment. When they emerged, they were galloping at full speed, rifles at the ready, yelling. Their hats were now round, with red bands.

The Red Army had arrived.

We all rose early the next day, and strolling to the nearby

factory I saw a notice pinned to a tree headed 'Soldiers!', followed by a lot of nonsense about 'Annihilation of the Polish Army; the officers who hate you and your families'. What really turned my stomach, though, were the words: 'The officers and the generals are your enemies; they want you dead. Kill them!' The leaflet was signed: Timoshenko.

I tore it down from the tree in disgust.

'How can this General put his name under such a lot of rubbish?' I shouted. 'Either he is very simple in the head, and ill-informed – in which case he should not be a General – or he is a liar.'

My uncle intervened. 'You must not talk like this any more, Jurek. We have been invaded by a country which has a different culture and very different ideas. People who talk like you in their country go *pod stenku.*'

'What does *pod stenku* mean?' I inquired.

'It means against the wall,' he replied, pointing two fingers at my head, as though shooting me with a pistol.

I had had my first lesson in the Russian language.

That afternoon 'visitors' arrived at our house, in company with a civilian on foot wearing a Polish Army coat with a red band on the sleeve. He was a local man sentenced to six months in jail for theft, but obviously released by the Red Army. We called him 'The Commissar'. While one of the soldiers took particulars of everyone present, the rest searched the house. I don't know what they were looking for, but whatever it was they didn't find it. The Commissar locked the scullery and the soldiers went to the stables and took the horses away. My uncle pleaded with the leader of the troop to leave one horse behind or we would starve, but he shrugged his shoulders saying: 'We have plenty of people.' I remembered the phrase but I need not have bothered. I was to hear it, and others like it, many times in the future.

In the morning my uncle went to town to see if anybody there was in charge of the mob. He returned in the evening without his boots. On the way back he was stopped by two Red Army 'heroes' who pointed their rifles at him and ordered him to hand them over.

Later that evening he went out and returned with a radio. 'Paris calling,' said a voice in Polish. 'Warsaw is still fighting . . . the Polish Army is re-forming in France.'

I looked at Adam as he looked at me. To us it wasn't a question of 'do we?', but 'how soon?' In a family discussion it was decided that since Kazik was well below military age he would stay behind. Later he joined the Polish underground, returned home, survived, and is still living in Poland. I have not seen him since.

Of course the 'visitors' called on our uncle again and this time ordered him to report to the *Kommandantura* in town. He returned a few days later saying that he had been asked a lot of questions about the estate he used to manage, and suggested that it would be wise if we moved on as soon as possible. We had left home in our school uniforms, with only a change of underwear. It was now the end of September and we needed overcoats for our trek to France. Adam had no problem, he was tall and was given Uncle's half-coat. With three girls in the family, I had no option but to accept one of their coats. The plan was to cross over the Carpathian mountains into Hungary, then travel through Yugoslavia and Italy to France. From the radio we knew that both Romanian and Hungarian authorities interned the refugees, so the idea was not to get caught.

A day or two after my uncle returned from questioning, two Soviet soldiers came to the house. Uncle opened the door and was asked what his name was.

One of the soldiers ordered, 'Get your things!' Their gorget patches and the bands round their hats were magenta. We didn't know then that the colours belonged to the NKVD (the National Commissariat of Internal Affairs). And we were to learn later that the NKVD, in effect the Soviet Secret Police, the mainstay of Communist dogma, was responsible directly and indirectly for the deaths of millions of human beings. In the eyes of the ordinary citizens of the Soviet Union the letters stood for *Nikogda vyernishsya damoy* – 'You will never return home'. My uncle packed some things – he was only given a few moments – and went with the soldiers. He, too, never returned home.

3

Adam and I left our uncle's house early on 4 October. On arriving in the nearby town, we saw a gigantic portrait of Stalin fixed to the wall of a building with a man kneeling under it watched by two Red Army soldiers. He performed a kotow then began to pray in Polish, but with a strong Ukrainian accent: 'Thank you, *batyushka* Stalin, for liberating me and my family from my house, now occupied by your army; for liberating me from the food I had to leave behind, and my two cows. If I could strangle you, I would do it with pleasure.'

The two Red Army goons clapped their hands in obvious agreement, clearly not understanding a word. We had to leave in a hurry, or we would have burst out laughing! We caught the train, arriving in Lvov later the same day. Since we had several hours to kill, we strolled round the town which Adam knew so well, having studied at the local polytechnic. The town was full of Red Army men. They were ambling about in groups of three or four, a number of them showing off their newly acquired watches which they wore on top of their shirt sleeves, so that others would see them. Luckily we were able to board another train that evening, the plan being to leave it three stations before the border, on the opposite side to the platform, so as to have a better chance of slipping away unnoticed. After some hours I looked at my watch: it was 11 p.m. and time to go. Just before the train stopped, we jumped off.

'Where are you going?' bellowed a hoarse voice in the darkness.

We saw a bayonet glistening in the dim light, scarcely two feet away. It was fixed to a rifle pointing straight at us, at the other end of which stood a big man with a red band on his sleeve. We were caught! He took us to the station master's office.

'*Vy bezhentsy?*' he inquired.

We did not understand. He lifted the telephone and jabbered away. There were two other men in the office, also with rifles and armbands, laughing, obviously satisfied with the night's catch. Then another man came in wearing railwayman's uniform and a red armband. He spoke Polish with a Ukrainian accent.

'What are you doing here?' he asked.

'We are fugitives from the Province of Cracow. We have been on the road now for a month, hoping to reach our Aunt Mary in Stanislavov. We overslept at Stryj, where we should have changed trains. We left the train as soon as we realized that.'

He put this information down on a piece of paper, murmuring to the man on the phone: '*Bezhentsy.*' I asked him what it meant; he searched for a word, then explained: 'People who are running away from something.'

Bezhentsy – the fugitives.

At about four in the morning a soldier of the Soviet Border Army arrived. The sole purpose of these troops was to prevent anyone leaving or entering the Soviet Union without permission. As permission to leave was almost never granted, the only way out was to do it illegally. As for entering, no sane man would ever apply for permission unless, of course, he was naïve enough to believe the propaganda.

'Let's go!' he ordered, pointing to the door. On the train, he tried unsuccessfully to buy my watch.

On arrival in Stryj we were taken to a school commandeered by the Border Army. The ground floor was used as offices, while upstairs housed the *bezhentsy*. The classroom was stripped of all furniture and the occupants sat on the floor. Most of them were young people, and some had been there for the past ten days. We were allowed out twice a day to go to the toilet, but if you couldn't wait that long you were allowed out if you banged on the door for a lengthy enough period. We found it more convenient to perform through the window. Those were not barred when we arrived, but this was remedied a day or two later.

We went through our story very carefully, and we were not going to veer one word from it under any circumstances. We learned from someone in the classroom that there was an office close to the school operated by NKVD, where one could get a permit to board a train to return home. If only we could somehow say goodbye to the school.

We agreed that if either of us got a sporting chance to escape, he must take it without thinking of the other.

Early next morning a militiaman (that was what a man with a red armband was officially called) opened the door and asked for two volunteers. We sprang to our feet and were taken out to sweep a yard which used to be the school playground. It was surrounded by a high wall with barbed wire freshly cemented on to the top. On the side attached to the school building was a wooden gate in two halves, fastened together with the biggest padlock I had ever seen.

There was a knock, the guard walked slowly towards the gate, looked through the peep-hole and opened one side. He placed a brick against it to stop it from closing, then opened the second half, holding it open. We watched in amazement, then both carried on sweeping as though not at all interested in the procedure.

We watched the lorry passing slowly through the opening, which was just wide enough for it to scrape through. We didn't miss the fact that there was plenty of room for a man to go under the side of a lorry! If we could volunteer next day, if we could position ourselves closer to that gate . . . I looked at my watch: 5.30 a.m.

'What were you doing?' we were asked on the return to our classroom.

'We swept miles and miles of corridors,' we lied. It might have been selfish of us, but then we didn't plan to stay in that school for any further education.

Each morning we volunteered, and each time we were given other tasks until the seventh day of our imprisonment. As 5.30 approached, we were within easy reach of the gate. When the lorry arrived, and the driver knocked, we started sweeping away from the gate as though not at all interested in the proceedings. We heard the brick being dropped, but we didn't even look in that direction. When the lorry revved up to move forward we waited a few seconds, looked up to see that everything was fine, a few long paces and we were under the overhang of a lorry and out in the street!

Left turn, first right then right again. We half-ran, half-walked, and in no time at all we were in the NKVD building, sighing with relief. About 8 a.m. an NKVD man appeared, shouted something, and a queue began forming. We joined it, hoping that if the search for us had begun, they would never think of looking in the office of the Soviet Secret Police!

Our turn came some three hours later. The NKVD man spoke reasonable Polish, filled in a small form, stamped it with a big five-pointed star and told us to use it instead of a ticket. We thanked him and found our way to the railway station. To our joy, the train was already on the platform. The man on the gate told us that there would be another one in two and half hours.

Our plan was simple. At one point the railway line ran some twenty miles from the border, at a place called Dolina. We would get off there and walk the rest. We arrived there about 2 p.m. on 12 October.

'Where are you going?' asked a militiaman as we alighted.

'Actually, we are going to Stanislavov,' replied Adam coolly showing him the NKVD pass, 'but we have heard that the food situation there is not very good. We thought of looking around here to buy some. There is another train passing through in two and half hours.'

The militiaman studied the form, handed it back to Adam, and told us how to find the market place. We thanked him, and walked in the direction he had indicated.

We both felt we were being followed. We strolled nonchalantly, stopping from time to time to look at the shop windows, as though we did not have a care in the world.

There was only one solution if we couldn't shake off our pursuer in the market; there was little we could do except go back to the station and catch the train. We could not risk being caught again. We bought apples, cheese and a cabbage, the latter for the benefit of the snooper who was watching our every move. Then we saw him getting interested in some beetroot. That was our chance.

Our problem was that we did not know the town. We wanted to be out of it and into the woods as quickly as possible, yet not by an obvious route. Clearly, he suspected us of being *bezhentsy*, so there was no point in heading into the sun and south. It had to be east or west. We wanted to run, but reason told us otherwise. We could see woods in the distance now. If only our luck held!

It did. We had never felt so happy and safe. It was then 4 p.m.

The sun was shining through the canopy of the trees, the birds were singing and somewhere in the distance a woodpecker was hammering at a tree-trunk.

We walked silently southward using the sun and a watch to maintain direction. We came to a forest road, covered with footprints, so decided to leave it well alone. We then heard distant chatter coming from the south and hid in the undergrowth until the intruders passed by. We decided to stop more often, listen longer, and talk only when necessary. We must have wasted an hour, but we were still free and much wiser.

We made camp before it got dark, using my coat as the roof of the tent tied neatly under a fir tree. We had some cheese and cabbage for supper and went to sleep. Our main concern, however, was navigation. The map we had brought from our uncle's house was of such a large scale that it was of no use, and so we came up with an idea of counting our steps, two steps to a metre. Whoever was counting would give the other a nudge every hundred metres, and that one would stick his finger out. When he ran out of fingers he would make a notch on a stick, and that would be a kilometre.

Next day we covered the first kilometre in half an hour. It was a little slow, but safe. After a second kilometre, again covered in half an hour, we abandoned the idea of counting steps and assumed our progress to be constant at two kilometres an hour. At around midday, we came across new tracks. Following them for a time we came to the conclusion they belonged to people like us. However, just in case we were wrong, we decided to stick to our 'stop, listen, go' technique. When the tracks suddenly turned down the slope we left them, and continued in our own direction.

Sometime later during our listening period we heard footsteps and an occasional rustling of leaves. We hid under a spruce with branches down to the ground. We felt a little apprehensive since the tracks we left behind us could betray our position, yet there was nothing we could do. The noise was coming from down the slope and getting louder; it stopped occasionally, then started again. In due course a head wearing a beret popped up about thirty yards below us. The man stopped for a moment, then waved his hand as though calling somebody. In a couple of minutes another head, this time covered with a school cap, appeared near him.

They were both about twenty years old.

'Pssssst,' I hissed. The heads ducked and a voice asked quietly: 'Who is there?'

'Poles,' I answered. The heads popped up once more, the apprehension gone from their faces. We came out of our hiding-place and shook hands.

'To Hungary?' the four of us asked at the same time. There was no need for an answer.

They were also from Cracow Province, and like us left home when the Germans approached. Originally, they had planned to cross over to Romania, but had discovered that the border was heavily guarded. Thus, they had decided to try their luck over the mountains to Hungary instead. So we joined forces and by the afternoon of the following day, we judged ourselves to be no more than two miles from the border. We could see the tops of the mountains lit up by the evening sun, and on the other side, we hoped, was our initial goal, Hungary. We ate the last of our cheese and apples and had our final conference, then retired with a plan to attempt the border crossing at midnight. We had heard rumours that the Soviets had cut all the trees along the border, therefore it would be madness to attempt crossing in daylight. We couldn't sleep and the time dragged. I tried not to think about anything but it was impossible to relax.

When the time came, we picked a couple of stars in the opposite direction to the Pole star as our guides, and started out in silence. We walked slowly, as far as possible avoiding open spaces. We could hear the barking of a dog to the south-east but nothing else save the murmur of the trees.

After a couple of hours we changed our guiding stars, as they had moved too far to the west of south and we continued walking silently and steadily.

Suddenly there was an almighty crash which sounded like a tree breaking in half. One of us must have stepped on a dry, half-rotten branch. At the same instant there was a thud, then lights, powerful torchlights, shone at us from all directions. A voice roared in Russian: 'Hands up!'

There was little we could do. We were surrounded by eight men we had hoped to avoid; soldiers of the Border Army. They stood there rifles at the ready, while their leader, yelling his head off, pointed at the ground with a big revolver. We lay on the ground face down, while the men closed in on us, their bayonets almost touching our backs. The man with the revolver, still barking loudly, came to each of us in turn and spread our legs and hands apart.

My heart was thumping madly but I wasn't really scared. I kept saying to myself: 'Don't worry, the horse has a bigger head than you, let him worry.' It helped. After the initial shock of being caught, I was quite relaxed, since I reasoned that there was little I could do. I had no doubt I was going to get out of it somehow, some time. I decided not to worry, but to treat the whole episode as a grand adventure, to be enjoyed if at all possible.

It was not that I gave up. It didn't even enter my head to do so, but for the moment I put my mind into neutral. It might have been a childish type of philosophy, but it worked. So it was here, not far from the border, lying on the ground with the bayonet of a Soviet soldier almost touching my spine, that I sowed the seeds of my survival.

4

After a thorough search we were instructed to sit down with our backs to each other, hands resting on our knees, and forbidden to speak. When the leader and three others returned from a patrol, he spoke to us for a couple of minutes, but we didn't understand a word. We were then told to form up, one behind the other. Our return journey had begun.

The sun was well up when we arrived at a lonely farmhouse and were told to sit down as before. I was called inside.

'*Kak vasha familiya*?' inquired the leader.

I thought it was decent of him to start the questioning by asking how my family was. I shrugged my shoulders and answered in Polish: 'I don't know, I haven't seen them for six weeks.'

'*Kak vasha familiya*?' he repeated angrily.

It was clear we were not on the same frequency.

At midday two militiamen arrived. The Polish-speaking one took our statements, one by one, while the others waited outside. Our story was simple. We left home as the Germans were approaching, taking to the fields soon afterwards as we were being strafed. We had entered the woods some two weeks earlier and had lived off the land, or what we could buy from the hamlets. We hadn't seen anyone for the past four days, we were lost and out of food. We had met the other two lads the day before, and we knew nothing about them. We were trying to reach Stanislavov where we had some relations.

The militiaman took it all down, then said: 'You were lucky that you were found. Three hundred metres further on is the Hungarian border. You would have been arrested and sent to the concentration camp. As it is, we shall take you to Dolina and you will be sent home.'

I tried to look very shocked, but I couldn't help thinking how close we had been to Hungary. Had we not walked into an ambush, we would have been there. Had we not changed the guide stars, we would have missed the ambush. Had we . . . and my father's words came springing to mind: 'And if my grandma had a moustache, she would be my grandpa!' So I stopped thinking about what might have been.

At about 3 p.m. a woman appeared with bowls full of porridge. It tasted a little sharp, there might have been some goat's cheese in it, but it was very welcome; after all, we had had nothing to eat for eighteen hours. We left the farmhouse soon afterwards, accompanied by the two militiamen and a sheep dog. We reached a big village before dark, and were taken to a militia post. Adam and I were separated from the other two, and shown to a room. As soon as we entered, the guard slammed the door and locked us in.

For a few seconds I couldn't believe it. There was no handle or a knob on the door, so I tried to grasp the edge with my nails. I felt sick and my whole body shook with anger. I started kicking at the door, then walked to a small window and tried the iron bars. They were solid. Then I got hold of my senses. 'You fool!' I told myself. 'You are ruining your nerves and playing into those thugs' hands. Calm down and go to sleep. This is supposed to be a grand adventure, remember?'

I was back to normal, but very tired.

The cell was of stone, and was about nine feet long and six feet wide. On the right side of the door there was a wooden surface six feet long and two and a half feet wide, our bed. It was pitch black by then, and there was no light in the cell, so we lay on the wooden platform, rucksacks acting as pillows, and went to sleep. It was still dark when we woke up. The grim facts of the situation we were in startled me for a second or two, but I soon dismissed them from my mind.

'I slept like a log,' I said cheerfully to Adam. 'What about you?'

'It's my fault,' he replied, shaking his head. 'I led you into that ambush.'

'Look, Adam,' I retorted. 'It's nobody's fault; the only guilty ones are the Border Army, they had no right to be there. Besides, you could have been shot, being up front. Would you have wanted me to worry that I killed you? So stop crucifying yourself, it doesn't help you, and only can make matters worse.'

That seemed to have the desired effect, and he became quite cheerful.

We heard footsteps and a militiaman presented himself at the door, a big bowl in one hand and some bread in the other. The bowl contained warm water. This just did not make sense; first of all they locked us in without light, bedding, or any toilet facility, now not only did they seem to care about our ablutions, but as an incentive, gave us warm water to do it with. Since it was quite obvious that the comrades didn't care a hoot about our well-being, the logical answer was that the water was not to wash with, but to drink!

I then became aware of a white speck on my shoulder, standing out clearly against the navy blue uniform of my grammar school. I came closer to the window and discovered, to my horror, that the speck was moving. It was a louse, a big fat louse. I didn't like the idea of touching it with my fingers, so I yelled for help from Adam. He didn't fancy the idea either, but the battle of the louse had to be won. I put my shoulder as close to the window as I could, Adam pressed his forefinger against the thumb and flicked it out. We stripped and searched for more, but we couldn't see any. Poor, naïve, inexperienced me! One louse created such havoc.

We were still looking for the vermin, when the militiaman opened the door and called us out. We were joined by the others and by midday we were back in Dolina. We passed the market place where we had been only a few days before, and stopped outside a new-looking building with big, but barred windows.

It was the local jail.

We were taken to the office, searched and registered, then led along the corridor to the second cell on the left and shown in. The cell was about five yards square with a wooden floor, and a large barred window. There was no furniture of any kind, and the occupants, about a dozen of them, sat on the floor. We stopped in silence by the now closed door, surveying the situation.

'Tourists?' inquired a biggish man sitting close to the window, when the footsteps of the guard could no longer be heard. We made no reply.

'You can speak freely here,' continued the man. 'We are all tourists here, or as our liberators from the east call us *bezhentsy*,

29

and we are all Poles. Welcome to the boudoir. Find yourselves a spot and sit down, you must be tired.'

The men near us moved a little to make room and we took the hint.

'What's the news?' asked another man with a balding head.

'We don't really know,' replied Adam. 'We have been in the woods for the past three weeks or so.'

They were all officers or NCOs of the Polish Army Reserve called up two or three months before. They wore uniforms with epaulettes cut off, or torn off, and in civilian life they were mostly professional men. There was a barrister, a doctor, a dentist and two schoolteachers. Some of them had been in the cell for the past twelve days.

We settled in slowly and after a few days of monotonous prison life I was called for an interview which took place at the public school ten minutes away.

The interview room itself was a classroom, divided by wooden boards so that two prisoners could be questioned at the same time without either seeing the other. The interviewer wore the uniform of an officer of the Border Guard. When he discovered that I did not speak Russian, he spoke Polish with just a trace of accent. Having established my name and patronym, he explained that in Russian the question for all that was '*Kak vasha familiya*', then asked me to repeat it.

'Very good!' he exclaimed. 'Soon you will speak my language as well as me. We have a saying in the Soviet Union: "Prison is the best university". I think you will do well!'

'What a strange saying,' I thought.

'Which party did you belong to?' he asked.

'I did not belong to any party. In Poland we went to school to learn, not to play politicians.'

'Your politicans did play,' he snapped, 'and look what they did to Poland. In the Soviet Union politicians are workers like anybody else. Children are prepared for Party work from the beginning. They join the Pioneers when they are very young, even before they start going to school. When they are older, say fifteen or so, they join the Komsomol, then when they grow up, and are good enough, they are permitted to join the Communist Party.'

30

I tried to look interested. 'What is the Komsomol?'

'Oh, I beg your pardon. It is an abbreviation of *Kommunisti-cheskii Soyuz Molodyozhi*, *Kom-so-mol*, the Communist Youth Union.'

'Do you belong to the Communist Party?' I inquired.

He hesitated for a moment, then said: 'Yes.' To me he didn't sound too convinced.

The officer wrote down all my answers in longhand, and when the interview ended he read it back to me sentence by sentence, each time translating to Polish. I was then requested to sign a sheet full of hieroglyphics. I hesitated. Should I sign? Was what he told me on that sheet of paper, or was there something different? I came to the conclusion that he couldn't possibly have remembered the story so exactly. He must have been reading my thoughts.

'Don't worry, Yurie,' he called me by the diminutive of my Christian name in Russian. 'What I've just translated to you is on that paper.'

He looked quite honest, so I signed.

'Where is my brother?' I asked the inmates on my return to the cell.

'In an interview,' replied the teacher.

'What was it like? What happened?' everybody asked. I told them the story.

'Some of them are quite nice fellows,' said the dentist, 'but some of them are real bastards!'

'You did the right thing by signing,' advised the barrister with a knowledgeable look, 'at least it shows that you have nothing to hide.'

When Adam returned, I had never been so pleased to see him. He had a different interviewer, was asked the same questions, and the whole exercise was conducted in a polite manner.

More people arrived in prison, five of them coming to our cell. They were about twenty, and obviously *bezhentsy*. When they settled in, they told us their story. They had engaged a guide to take them across the border. Four hours later they were picked up by the Border Army. The guide was not detained. At least they didn't have to remember their cover story!

However, the interviews were to continue. Although Adam was shouted at on one occasion, the sessions were carried out in a civilized manner. My Polish-speaking examiner kept dropping hints that we would be released soon.

Before long our cell, originally built to house three people, contained twenty-four. Then, without warning, the evening porridge ration was discontinued, the guards became stricter, and the cell lights burned all night. Lice began to appear in the cell, and mornings and afternoons were spent searching for, and killing, the unwelcome intruders.

Late in November I was called out for another interview. The examiner was the Polish-speaking man I had originally. He looked sad, and that gave me an uneasy feeling. He kept sorting out the papers as if he didn't know what to do with them. I looked at his face, trying to discover what was in his mind.

'The NKVD is taking over your case,' he finally muttered. Then looking straight in my eyes continued: 'I am sorry, Yurie, but it has nothing do with me.'

He called a guard and that was that.

Next time I was called out, the guard was a Soviet soldier with magenta gorget patches and the hat band. The militiaman had allowed me to walk rather slowly, as I had neither shoelaces nor braces, and I had to keep my trousers up with my hands, while trying to keep my shoes on by screwing up my toes. The soldier was too dim to realize my predicament and kept saying something, which I took for 'go faster'. I increased my pace. Immediately my shoe went flying ahead, while I hobbled on one leg in a vain attempt not to get my sock wet. I lost my balance, let go of my trousers which promptly obeyed the law of gravity, and ended up prostrate on the pavement. That seemed to amuse him. I got up, lifted my trousers, retrieved my shoe and proceeded at half my original pace. After a number of promptings from the guard I stopped, turned about, and in my best Russian announced: 'No!' To my great surprise this had the desired effect, and we arrived at the school without further incidents.

I was taken to another part of the school, and told to wait, while the guard reported my arrival. I was shown to a room which had a huge desk instead of an ordinary table. The NKVD officer, about twenty-five years of age, sat behind it reading some papers. He completely ignored me. After I had been standing by the closed door for at least twenty minutes, he acknowledged my presence by pointing to a wooden stool on the other side of the desk, and telling me to sit down.

'*Kak vasha familiya*?' he asked. I told him. The usual preamble followed, all in Russian. Then, instead of asking me to make a statement as was usual, he leaned back in his chair staring at me without saying a word. He looked very amused about something. After what must have been three or four minutes he asked quite gently: 'Who are you?'

'*Ya biezheniets.*'

He started to laugh, then he suddenly stopped. As he leaned forward over the desk, his face changed, his eyes narrowed and he started telling me something in a hissing voice, the volume rising until he ran out of breath.

Since I understood only three words, spy, saboteur and anti-revolutionary, I shook my head and told him as calmly as I could: 'I don't understand, Comrade.'

That upset him. He stood up, banged the desk with his fist and bellowed, 'I am not your comrade!'

The feeling was mutual. He rattled on, waving his hands, for a few more minutes and again I told him that I did not understand.

He walked to the door and called a guard. I was taken outside, and told to sit by the Duty NKVD man in the corridor. It became clear to me that I was not going to be released for a long time.

While I waited I thought I would try and and find the muscles controlling the movement of my ears. The task was not as simple as all that: each time I tried to move them, my forehead moved up and down instead. I found it fascinating, but before I discovered the secret – and I tried for some two hours – I was called back to the room.

The same officer was there, and he must have just had his lunch, as he was picking his teeth with a sharpened matchstick. There was a knock, and an interpreter arrived. His Polish was adequate, but he had a heavy Russian accent. The first question was to the point.

'Who sent you to Hungary?'

'I wasn't going to Hungary. I am a fugitive from Cracow Province.'

'Do you know where you are?'

'Yes, in Dolina.'

'I mean this room, this building.'

'No.'

'This is the investigating centre of the NKVD. We ask simple questions and we expect simple, but truthful, answers. Who sent you to Hungary?'

This kind of questioning went on for about twenty minutes. My stomach was rumbling, and he must have heard it.

'We have both had our lunch. If you want yours, you had better answer my questions truthfully.'

'I want my lunch and I gave you the answers to your questions.'

After a short pause, he asked me quite politely: 'What is the address of your relatives in America?'

'As far as I know, I have no relatives there.'

'You know as well as I do that there are millions of Poles living in America. You are not telling me the truth!'

'I am telling you the truth. I don't know of any relatives in the USA.'

'Look, boy, I want to help you. If you tell me where they live, I can send them a message. They then can telegraph money here, and as soon as this investigation is completed you can go and see them!'

'I told you, I have no relatives in the USA.'

His tune changed.

'Which partisan gang do you belong to?'

'I don't belong to any gang.'

He stood up, narrowing his eyes, and said slowly: 'You are challenging the might of the Soviet Union. I will get the truth from you even if I have to suck the last drop of your white blood!'

I felt very honoured by his remark. There was I, a sixteen-year-old grammar school boy shaking the foundations of the Communist empire, and the Comrades were so worried that they were prepared to suck my white blood (whatever that was) to prevent me from toppling it.

However, I was getting more and more hungry. I had eaten only half of my bread ration in the morning, saving the other half for supper, but that was seven hours ago. Naïvely, I again asked the interpreter if I could get something to eat.

'In the Soviet Union,' responded my inquisitor, 'he who doesn't work, doesn't eat. Not only do you do no work at all, but also you refuse to co-operate. Show me your hands!'

I showed them to him not knowing what to expect. He turned them palms up and remarked: 'These are not the hands of a worker, but of a capitalist swine!'

I looked at his; they were softer than mine. By his reasoning he was a capitalist swine, too, but I did not tell him so. I did not get any food, but he let me go about half an hour later.

Many inmates were called out for questioning, including Adam, and they were all asked about their relatives in the USA. The ruse was obvious: the NKVD had instructions to get names and addresses for possible future blackmail of innocent persons by threatening the lives of their relatives in jail. This, we learned later, was standard procedure.

St Nicholas's Day, 6 December, was approaching, and I decided to put the crust of my bread ration, the best part, under Adam's rucksack, since we always found goodies under our pillows back home on that morning.

'Do you know what day it is?' asked Adam, when we woke up early that morning.

'No,' I replied, trying to look astounded, 'is it any special day?'

'Yes, St Nicholas's Day, and he always brings presents for good boys.'

'Let's have a look then.'

We both put our hands under our rucksacks and both retrieved a top crust of a bread ration. Neither of us had expected it, yet both received a present. It was really touching, and I had to wipe a tear from my eye.

From two newcomers to our cell we learned that some three weeks before the Soviet Union had invaded Finland. We decided to make a break-out attempt on Christmas Eve. As the date of the attempt approached, tension in the cell rose dramatically. Things that would have been too trivial to bother about became major issues. But, it was all for nothing. On 24 December the guards were increased, and not only was the inner door locked, but also there were two guards present each time the cell door was opened. Early on Christmas Day we were told to pack our things, given one kilo of bread each, and were then taken outside. We were counted as we went through the inner and outer doors then counted again after we had lined up in fours.

Each time any of us turned his head, the guards yelled. When we entered the railway station, an ordinary goods train was just arriving from the direction of Stryj. I noticed each waggon had a guard box at one end, the bottom part of which was above the floor level of the cattle truck, while the top was overlooking its roof.

The doors were slid open and we were herded inside. Right in front of the door, and in the middle of the floor, was a small stove. At each end of the truck were two shelves stretching from side to side, and about seven feet deep. I jumped on the top one urging Adam to follow. I thought the air might be foul there, but at least it would be warm. When the last of the forty-two prisoners were pushed in, the doors were closed shut and locked.

Our waggon had two small windows diagonally opposite the two corners, but they were crossed with bars, two vertical and one horizontal. I inspected one thoroughly, but there was no possibility of escaping through it.

We took stock of the situation. We were being taken somewhere, most probably to the USSR. None of us liked the idea, so the thing to do was to break out. Several suggestions were offered, but were rejected as impracticable, impossible or simply suicidal. Then someone proposed burning a hole in the side of the waggon. After a short discussion, my plan of burning a hole under the guard's box was accepted. I felt very proud. We were still missing one very important ingredient in our escape recipe, a poker, or an iron rod to burn the hole with.

The door slid open and the guard doled out the 'boiling' water which was only tepid. It must have come from the locomotive as it tasted oily. Still, it was better than nothing. Soon the train rolled gently in the direction of Stanislavov. Any concern I might have had about accumulation of foul air at our level quickly disappeared. The draught created by the train's movement sucked out all the warmth that our bodies produced, and it became progressively colder.

The train stopped about half an hour later, apparently in the middle of nowhere. Snow was lying thickly, and the branches of the trees were bent with the weight of it.

Darkness fell and we were still in the same place. The guard brought us an oil hurricane-lamp, and the little light it produced lifted our spirits. We lit the stove. It was a small one, perhaps nine inches in diameter and eighteen inches high. The pipe rose straight up, disappearing through a square hole cut out in the roof. To prevent escape that way, the hole was rimmed by four iron bars bolted to the roof. But the bolts had the nuts inside the waggon!

Our spirits rose even higher. The idea was, of course, to undo one of the bars and use it as a poker to burn the hole. Then a man took his army boot off and started tapping the side of the bolt with the steel bit surrounding his heel. It worked! It was a very slow, yet agonizing job. The train started to roll again about midnight, and still in the same direction. The man was still tapping.

When I woke up we were stationary. The stove was stone cold, and day was just breaking. The internal walls of the truck were covered with hoar frost up to three feet from the floor. There was nobody tapping the bolt, the noise was too great. I couldn't see anything through the window as it was covered with ice. Nobody had any idea where we were, but we all knew that it was very cold.

As the chattering began, the man with the boot stood up on the stove and started tapping again. But it was all in vain. About half an hour later the door opened, and we were told to get out. We were in Stanislavov. The sky was clear and there must have been twenty degrees centigrade of frost. We were loaded on open lorries and taken to a local jail.

Very early the next day, Adam and I and a few others were called out 'with things'. It was still very dark and very cold. In due course we were driven to the station, the goods train arrived, and we were back in the ice box. Adam and I climbed on to the top shelf with ten others, all keeping close to stay warm. There was no coal, coke or lamp. About an hour later we left the station in a westerly direction. When we passed Dolina, the optimists were certain that we were going to be handed over to the Germans, which seemed quite possible, since all the inmates in our waggon came from the west side of the Bug river, the boundary between the two invaders. However, when we arrived in Stryj, we were told to get out.

We were taken to a local prison and put in a ground-floor cell. There was just enough room for all fifty of us to lie down, provided we were on our sides. Every so often a shout was heard: 'turn around!' and the whole mass of bodies would lift for a moment, only to collapse again on the other side.

On 1 January 1940 about ten of us were told to get ready 'with things'. After the usual search and issue of a kilo of bread, we knew we were on the move again. In due course we were loaded in cattle trucks, Adam and I managing to get the top shelf. Out of forty-four men, twelve were Ruthenians from Romania who had come to Poland when the Soviet Union invaded. Still hailing the glories of Communism, they were promptly imprisoned.

One thing was very clear, we were not going home, and as soon as we settled down, we talked about escape. Adam explained our previous try which was approved. Quick inspection revealed that one bolt was not properly tapped in, which would make the job much easier, but this time we were going to do it in the presence of Ruthenians, people we did not trust, and who would have no hesitation in denouncing us to the guards at the first opportunity. We decided on a strong line of action. Anyone who tried to get close to the door would be stopped, anybody attempting to shout would be throttled.

In about three hours we arrived in Lvov, but to our surprise, we were not told to leave. Now it was quite obvious that we were on our way to the Soviet Union. The next morning when the doors were opened, I saw two bodies lying on the ground outside an adjacent waggon. The sight made us even more determined to escape. One of the Ruthenians began to shout but before he could finish, a big hand closed his mouth.

Apart from the cold, the biggest discomfort was the lack of drinking water. After the morning ration, the guard would not give us any more, unless we hammered on the door long and hard, and often that didn't work. We used to scrape the ice off the inner walls of the truck to quench our thirst.

We increased our efforts to undo the bar, but it was an uphill struggle. The Ruthenians were kept quiet only by threat of murder. Now two men were working on the bar; one tapping, the other trying to undo the other nut. By evening, one nut was free.

We made contingency plans, in case the guard heard the tapping, and came to investigate. We had to relieve ourselves through a four-inch hole drilled in the floor. A number of people were suffering from diarrhoea, and the hole was now surrounded by a frozen mound of excreta. That evening we had to use our emergency plan.

We heard a sudden unlocking of the door, and when the guard

looked in to investigate the tapping, he saw 'the tapper' peacefully standing near the mound, trying to dislodge it with a heel of his boot! The guards brought a spade, and our excuse was gone. We could not tap any more that evening.

Four days after starting, the job was complete. We lit the stove and went to work. Alas! To our great disappointment, the fuel ran out before we had burned half the square. The distance to the wall was too great, and the bar had lost most of its heat by the time the burner got into position. By lunchtime next morning we had the solution.

The door was kept closed by a big lock inserted between two lugs of U-shaped bolts, one on the door and the other on the side of the wall. All we had to do was to burn a square hole round the bolt in the wall, and we could slide the door open at will.

The idea was to burn a hole just deep enough, so that when the time came, a sharp kick would break the remaining wood, and at the same time keep the outside wall intact. As soon as we were issued with coal, we lit the stove and went to work. By about nine o'clock that evening, 5 January, the job was done.

The evening dragged on. Suddenly, at about eleven o'clock, there was a great commotion some distance from our waggon. In minutes, hundreds of guards surrounded the train, some of them tapping each truck with small hammers, inch by inch. We learned later that in one of the other waggons, the inmates also managed to get an iron bar, and burn a hole. A guard happened to see the red hot iron penetrating the wall and sounded the alarm.

They didn't find our hole, but it didn't matter. About midnight, we were told to leave the waggon, and were taken under heavy escort to what we thought was an ordinary passenger train. It was painted olive green on the outside, like any other passenger train in the Soviet Union. On the platform side, it even had ordinary-looking windows. But it was not an ordinary train at all! For, as we were later to discover, in the Soviet Union the business of transporting human flesh was a highly developed enterprise.

To 'commemorate' Commissar Stolypin who introduced the prison waggons which could be attached to any passenger train, the prisoners called them *stolypinki*. The inmates could be taken to their destinations without fuss or bother and with very few passengers ever being aware of the contents of the other carriages.

Once inside the *stolypinka*, the difference between it and the passenger version became apparent. Basically, it was a coach with a corridor on one side, and compartments on the other. The windows in the corridor were barred, but since the bars were some distance from the glass, they could hardly be seen from the outside. Each compartment was separated from the corridor by iron bars with sliding doors, also made of iron bars. In the centre of the door was a small hatch, through which food was given to the inmates.

In the compartment, there were two benches on each side of the wall, and an extra wooden plank which, when fitted between two benches, converted them into a platform. Above that, there were two more platforms, slightly shorter in length, so that the inmates could climb up or down them with the door shut. Those two were split in the centre and hinged to each wall. Theoretically, during the day, prisoners could store these two upper shelves flush against each wall, and sit on the benches below. In practice, this was impossible. With twelve people and their belongings crammed into each compartment, there was simply not enough room for such comfort. There was no alternative but to lie four on each shelf with our heads towards the corridor. The distance between the shelves was not great enough to allow one to sit up. As I walked along the corridor to my compartment I had a little chuckle. The whole thing looked so bizarre, so much like a menagerie, except that the animals had human faces. 'Oh well,' I thought, 'we have plenty of people.'

Early in the morning the train moved. It was impossible to assess the direction in which we were going, although in our hearts we all knew that it wasn't westward. There was silence, except for a slow and rhythmical thump of the bogeys as they jumped the gap in the rails.

Three days after boarding the train, late at night, we saw the lights of a town. It was one of only two or three official crossings along the 750 miles of the Polish–USSR border. What we had felt all along, we now knew for sure. We were being deported to the Soviet Union.

The news spread like lightning throughout the waggon. Everybody started talking loudly, and the guard's shouts fell on deaf ears. He must have called for help because a gang of guards entered the carriage with Nagan revolvers in their hands, looking as though they meant business. The leader of the troop shouted loudly waving his pistol. We quietened down.

'Welcome to the Soviet Union!' I thought.

We moved off about four hours later, stopping again after a few minutes. It was 5 a.m. Central European Time, on 9 January 1940.

I was now in the Soviet Union.

The station was very drab and poorly lit by paraffin lamps with dirty glass. As dawn broke some locals appeared on the scene, slowly walking about. They were dressed in padded coats, many of them patched generously, and some wore long boots reaching to their knees. I shall never forget my first impression of that strange land. It was a fact which stood out a mile: nobody smiled. More and more locals could be seen going about their business, all in slow motion. Some of them came to within a few feet of my waggon, but none looked up to see, which would only have been a natural reaction. Perhaps they had seen it all before, or perhaps they were told not to look up. I shall never know.

At midday, some guards entered the waggon with big wooden bowls and thick wooden spoons. Food! I was introduced to *shchii*, the soup which was going to be my staple diet for months ahead, the soup which only varies in density or stench or the foulness of its taste. Basically it was made of sour cabbage and as such should have been delicious. There was nothing delicious about the muck dished out to the prisoners. I am certain it was made either from the sour cabbage that had gone bad, or the top layer of the pickle, normally thrown away, or given to pigs mixed with oats. It tasted vile. So vile, in fact, that it was impossible to eat it, although we were half-starved already, without holding our noses. Later on I developed a technique of eating it without tasting, or smelling it, and without holding my nose.

Again I saw bodies lying on the snow, face down. By the time the journey ended, I must have seen about fifty such bodies and concluded that the death rate must have been about ten per cent.

It wasn't until 17 January 1940 that for the first time in twelve days I breathed the fresh air of the outside world. Twelve days in the cages of the prison train and seventeen after leaving Stryj, we stepped down on to the snow of the Soviet Union.

It was a bitterly cold day. So cold that sometimes our breath turned into minute snowflakes, but mercifully there was no wind. As we stood outside the train, I took stock of my physical and mental state. To my satisfaction I had suffered no ill effects of any sort, except for a slight weakness in my legs. Mentally I was as alert as ever but then I did not allow depression to enter my thoughts. I spent the time either sleeping, talking, trying to move my ears back to front, or simply with my mind in 'neutral'.

We were loaded on to open lorries, twenty-five prisoners in each, sitting down tightly packed with knees against our chins, facing forward. On each corner of the lorry sat a guard facing inwards. They wore long army greatcoats that almost touched the ground, long felt boots called *valenki*, and funny hats with small turrets on top, the sides let down to cover their ears and buttoned under their chins, and the usual red star above a small peak. They, too, were complaining about the bitter cold, and no wonder. According to one of them the temperature was forty-three degrees below zero!

The lorry started up and wound its way round some sheds and on to an empty road. Although we were in a small town, there were no pavements or kerbs as far as I could judge from the way the snow had fallen. We left the town and turned into the country. About half a mile further on there was a drab-looking, rectangular box of a building which had obviously been painted white many years before. It had no windows, but what appeared to be wooden planks where the windows should have been. There were two tiers of those and the whole building was surrounded by a tall dirty white wall.

The big gates swung open with a lot of banging and screeching, and we were counted both before and after passing through them. Then we were counted again as we climbed down from the lorry. By this time we were all frozen stiff, and hungry.

PART TWO

'Prison Is the Best University'

5

We were led inside the bluish white building through a small gate. Coming from brilliant sunshine into that dingy hole we could see nothing, but at least it felt warm. The smell inside was of sweaty, sweet stale air. We descended below ground level through a wide corridor and into a cell quite empty of any furniture and unpainted. There was a small window almost touching the ceiling, and it was nearly totally covered by snow. That was our only source of light. The dungeon was quite large, but with some seventy-five people crammed inside there was not much room to move, certainly not enough for all of us to sit down. The floor was made of stone slabs.

When our eyes became adapted to the meagre light, we saw graffiti, some in Polish, some in Russian, covering every square inch of the walls. Simple statements of facts: name and date, or name, address and date. There must have been thousands of them.

Although reading them passed the time, it did not fill our stomachs. By my watch it was nearly 11 a.m. and still no bread. We decided to act. While some of us kicked the door hard, the rest of us, except the Ruthenians, chanted loudly: 'Food! Food!' The guard blew his whistle, the door opened, and a big man with a revolver asked us what we wanted. Somebody who spoke Russian replied: 'We have had nothing to eat for almost twenty-four hours; this treatment is inhuman.'

'Inhuman': the word that deflated the most arrogant, the most staunch Communist in a second; the word that turned the biggest Communist bully into a little lamb; the word that achieved what hundreds of argumentative words could not do. Why it should be so, I never discovered. Unless of course, they knew at heart that

45

the system they were pursuing was not, in fact, human.

'*Khorosho!*' said the big man – good – and the doors were closed. About a quarter of an hour later, a huge oval wicker basket with a handle in the middle was carried in by a man and a woman in uniform. It was full of bread portions. The man left the cell while the woman shared out the bread. The portions were small in size and heavy, and some of them had an extra bit of bread pinned with a wooden skewer to make it up to the proper weight. As soon as a man received his portion he tucked into it, chewing each bite a thousand times before swallowing, to prolong the enjoyment of eating.

The pain of hunger slowly diminished and we became tired. Some of us sat down on the stony floor, some continued reading the scribblings on the wall. A number of people recognized their friends or relatives. There were about a dozen from Cracow Province, two from Tarnow, the town where I went to school.

About midday the door opened and five people were taken out. No names, just any five. Adam and I decided to go with the next group. Fortunately, we were the last two in the group, or I would not have been able to do what I did. We walked a short distance along the corridor, and were taken to a well-lit cell. There were two guards there and a table. The first two men were told to take their clothes off. The guards meticulously searched each garment, paying special attention to the seams. They took everything out of the pockets, even small pieces of paper which those lucky enough to have them could use in the toilet. They took all belts, braces and ripped off metallic buttons. Anything of value, they put in a brown envelope with a code scribbled on the front. The first man had a pocket-watch which was greatly admired by the guards, before they put it in the envelope amongst words of protest from the loser.

I, too, had a watch, my mother's wrist-watch, and I was determined not to let them have it. It was easier said than done. The first man was now completely naked, his clothes about three feet from him, while he was told to stand astride with his hands up and fingers apart. The guard proceeded to search his body, looking between his fingers and toes; he told him to open his mouth and had a good look there. Then he ordered him to bend down and looked in his anus.

My brain was working in top gear, searching for a solution. Adam was being searched, and in a few moments it would be my turn.

'Take your things off!' commanded the guard.

I took my greatcoat off. 'Where do I hide it?' I thought. I took the watch from my wrist, clutching it in my hand. Thank God I didn't slip it behind the lining of my greatcoat. The guard had ripped the bottom part and poked his greasy hand inside.

'Aaaah!' exclaimed the guard. 'What is that?'

My heart stood still. He was pointing to the maroon shield on the sleeve of my school coat, with three numbers embroidered on it in silver thread, the number of the Lyceum where I was going to study.

'Are you an officer or a corporal?' inquired the guard.

I had never been asked that question before. I learned later that to be one or the other was the biggest crime in the eyes of our captors.

'No, I am not an officer or a corporal,' I answered in halting Russian. 'I am a schoolboy.'

'Isn't that a badge of rank?' he continued, still pointing at my shield.

'No, this is the number of my school in Poland.'

'Don't you lie to me, you bourgeois mister! If that isn't a badge of rank why do you wear it?' There was no point arguing. If it had been a badge of rank, it would have been cut off long ago.

'We in the Soviet Union are all equal,' droned the guard. 'We have no corporals, no officers and no badges of rank.'

He was obviously lying, as I had seen several ranks already, and there was an officer rank, however camouflaged. He himself was sporting two triangles on his olive green shirt, while his mate had none. He came close to me, and after a struggle, managed to cut off the shield.

'Yes, we are all equal now,' repeated the guard. 'All the people who thought that they were better than the others were sent *pod stenku* a long time ago. They are all equal now, all dead!'

He was telling the truth.

'Your trousers!' demanded the guard.

While he was examining them I struggled with the problem of my watch.

'Your pants!' said the guard. Down they came. Only a few seconds remained and I still could not find an answer.

'Your vest!' That was it. It was now or never. I gave him the vest. He stretched it to look inside, exploding almost instantly: 'Lice! Look at that! Lice!'

'Where?' I inquired, as though I did not know they were there. I had had no time that morning to carry out the usual louse-killing operation, and the cell I had just left was too dark to see the vest, never mind the lice. He handed me the vest. Without much concern I set about killing the vermin with the nails of my thumbs, still clutching the watch in the palm of my right hand.

'Throw it over there!' ordered the guard, pointing to my clothes lying on the floor. 'No time for that now!'

I obliged willingly. I screwed the vest into a ball, carefully placing the watch inside it, and threw it on the heap of my clothes. I wanted to jump with joy, but instead I had to look innocent.

'Raise your arms and separate your fingers!'

He looked me over as thoroughly as he did the others, but of course I had nothing to hide.

We were led to another cell where our particulars were taken. Not only names but also any peculiarities, like a wart or a deep scar. They did not believe us, of course, so we had to undress again. Fingerprinting followed, three examples each of fingers, thumb and palm. When all the formalities were completed, we were taken up two flights of stairs to the first floor and halted at the first door on the left. The corridor guard produced an enormous key, and opened the door. The cell smelt of stale air, felt damp and cold, was about five yards wide and four deep, and contained fifty-one prisoners. Most of them had arrived only a few days before, except for some twenty locals. There was a window on the far wall, about two feet high and three wide, with thick iron bars. The walls were about four feet thick. At about five o'clock by my watch, which was now two hours slow by local time, the guard called for two men. They came back with a big drum. It was called the *parasha*, and served as a urinal, which was emptied each morning and brought back in the evening. In cells containing more prisoners, the *parasha* was at the inmates' service twenty-four hours a day. It stank to high heaven.

Adam and I settled for the night, our feet cuddled up to the *parasha*. We were woken up, frozen, at 5 a.m. by a hard knock on the door by the corridor guard. The wall with the window in it was covered by hoar-frost, and there was a free space two feet wide all along it. The door opened and the first batch of prisoners, Adam and I amongst them, carrying the almost full *parasha*, went to the toilet. It smelt worse than the urinal. There were four taps there, without handles, but one of them dripped and the more experienced men made a bee-line for it for the morning's wash. The toilet itself was a wooden plank with a narrow slit behind it, and the temperature was well below zero. Before we could get to the tap we were called back, so we decided to be much wiser next time.

When we returned to the cell I noticed a young boy walking past me, clutching the hand of a man wearing a sheepskin coat. He was just nine years old and named Vanka. He had crossed with his father from Romania to the USSR, was arrested on the border, and parked in this filthy hole.

At about 7 a.m. breakfast was served: 500 grams of bread and a mug of warm liquid tasting of dried bark. The bread was violet-coloured, soggy and did not taste like bread at all. Gradually, the temperature in the cell rose a little and the hoar-frost began to melt. The sky was blue and the sun must have been shining outside, but we couldn't see it because of those wooden shutters, known as *yezhovki*. Not only did they prevent our looking at the outside world and gave the surroundings the appearance of a subterranean dungeon, they also cut the already meagre light entering the cell.

We stripped, looking for lice as we waited for lunch which arrived at 12.30 p.m. We were served the usual *shchii*, cabbage soup with some fish roes in it. One day I counted the eggs in my bowl; there were twenty-three in all. After lunch we had another battle with the lice – there were usually just as many of them – then came the call to the toilet at about 5 p.m. Adam and I went straight to the dripping tap, managing to wet our hands sufficiently to soften the dirt on them. We wiped the resulting grime on the back of our coats. That was the first wash since Christmas Eve back in Dolina, the first wash we'd had in twenty-five days!

It started to become cold again, and one after another the men sitting by the wall with the window in it inched themselves away from it. Then came the call for two men to bring the *parasha*, and my first full day in Gorodnia prison came to an end.

The next morning we were called out for a walk. Another guard took us down to the yard, a specially constructed compound, a high-walled area of about twenty yards square. Although we were in the shade, the light was so strong for our dark-adapted eyes that it caused pain at the back of the eyeballs, as though someone was poking at the back of them with a number of blunt pins.

We started to throw snowballs at each other.

'This is not a playground!' yelled the guard. 'Walk round in a circle in a single file, hands behind your backs and don't talk!'

I tried to take deep breaths of fresh air to purge my lungs of the stale, prison air, only to discover that it dried my throat so much that I began to cough. I heard similar coughs in the adjoining compound. The reason for these partitions was that several cells could be exercised at the same time, without the inmates seeing each other.

Unknown to us, some of the elderly Poles decided that it was barbaric enough to keep adults in a cell like ours, but to keep youngsters as well was positively inhuman. One of them called the guard, told him that he wished to speak to the prison governor, explaining the reason at some length.

'*Zavtra utrom!*' replied the guard – tomorrow morning.

I tried to plead with the elders not to mention me as I wanted to stay with Adam, but they would not listen. They told me it was for my own good. The next morning came, but not the prison governor. What I did not know then was that *zavtra utrom* was synonymous with the Spanish *mañana*; it very seldom came.

It was about a week later when Vanka and myself were removed from this adult cell. I nearly choked when I heard this news as I badly wanted to cry, but I knew it would help neither me nor Adam if I did. I gave him a hug and left the cell. We were led a short distance along the corridor, and stopped outside a cell roughly halfway to the toilet. This was the children's cell. The room was quite light and felt warm. The brown painted door had a hatch in the centre like any other cell, and in the centre of that was the Judas, the peep-hole through which the guard would look every half an hour. We were hoping to get better food but it turned out to be the same as in the other cell. On rare occasions, one of the guards would serve our cell last. That meant that there were

50

more fish roes in the bowl, and once or twice we actually received a bit of a fish carcass with small pieces of flesh on it.

We were given books from the prison library. Slowly I deciphered the title of mine and the author. It was *Das Kapital*, by Karl Marx! Not exactly the book I would have chosen, certainly not to start learning the language, but it was better than nothing. The others did not fare any better, their authors were V.I. Lenin and J.V. Stalin.

It suddenly became very quiet in the cell, the silence being only occasionally broken by questions like: 'How do you pronounce a big X with a small X in the middle of it?'

I was slowly ploughing through my *Kapital*. Very often if I could not understand a word, I could deduce it from the others in the sentence. If not, and the others did not know either, I would knock on the door and ask the guard. In general they were quite helpful, but not all of them.

After much effort, I came to the word *vo-oruzhyonnyi*. No matter how I looked at it, I could not arrive at the meaning. There was nothing else for me to do but knock at the door, and ask the guard. He was the unco-operative one, young and strict. When he opened the hatch he barked, as usual: 'What?'

'*Vo-oruzhyonnyi* . . .' I said, but before I could utter another word, he slammed the hatch in my face, blowing his whistle as though there was a fire.

Then we heard the thundering of guards' boots as they ran up the stairs and along the corridor, stopping outside our door. After a moment, the door suddenly opened, and there was the usual semicircle of guards with fixed bayonets. The leader, his Nagan revolver pointing towards us, sternly demanded: '*Kto vo-oruzhyonnyi?*'

I marched to the door with my book, pointed out the offending word to him and asked what it meant. They all burst out laughing. They were absolutely in stitches! The guard who had called them out did not laugh, he did not even smile. I wished I knew what the joke was.

'Well, little Pole,' mumbled the leader, trying to stop himself from laughing. He thought for a moment, handed his Nagan to the unsmiling guard, whose face was now the colour of a beetroot, and pointing at him said slowly:'*On vo-oruzhyonnyi.*'

Then pointing to himself, showing me the palms of his hands: '*Ya nye vo-oruzhyonnyi.*' It was our turn to laugh; the word obviously meant 'armed'. Clearly the guard on hearing the word 'armed', assumed that somebody in the cell was armed and called the alarm.

He took his revenge soon after. When we returned from our so-called walk, the cell was dark. We did not think much of it, as it always seemed dark on return. After some ten minutes I picked up my *Kapital* and tried to read; I found it a little difficult.

'Hey, fellows!' I remarked, 'don't you think it's much darker now than before?'

'Yes!' they replied in chorus.

We all looked towards the window, and there was the answer. While we were away, somebody, most probably our unsmiling and humiliated guard, had closed the *yezhovka*. Bartek lifted me up and I went to the window to investigate the problem.

Our *yezhovka* was only half closed. I tried to push it open, but I could not reach it. The iron bars were cemented well inside the half thickness of the wall, and my arm was simply not long enough.

'Psssst! He's coming!' hissed Janush in his normal position by the door.

I came down and we all sat on our beds, reading, as though nothing worried us. The guard tiptoed to the door and looked through the Judas. We all looked at him, waving our hands. He walked away, but we sensed that he would be back soon. Bartek, who was tall enough to look through the Judas without standing on his toes, tiptoed to the door, positioning himself just to the left of the spy-hole. In a few moments he pointed to the side of the door, as though saying he is just there!

The guard started to open the peep-hole very slowly and noise-lessly. Bartek was no fool, he was watching the lid and could see it moving. When the guard put his eye to the opening, Bartek leaned over, putting his eye to it as well, and they were both looking at each other, eye to eye, to coin the phrase. The guard did not like it. He opened the hatch and delivered a lecture.

'Detainees are not allowed near the door, or to obscure the spy-hole. Any further acts like this – *kartser!*'

Kartser was a punishment cell. He saw Zbyshek sitting on his bed, leaning against the wall.

'Leaning against the wall is forbidden! If I see any of you doing that again, I'll see to it that you will be prohibited to sit on beds for twenty-four hours!'

He closed the hatch and walked away.

It suddenly occurred to me that Karl Marx was a good chap. In his folly he wrote a book which I was now holding in my hand. His book plus the length of my arm should be long enough to open the *yezhovka*. Janush to the door, Bartek to the window wall, leg up for me, *Kapital* through the window at the end of my arm, a mild creak from *yezhovka* as it opened fully, and I announced: 'Let there be light!'

We were all sitting upright on the edges of our beds, reading our respective rubbish, when we heard the Judas being opened. We ignored it. In a moment, the cell door opened with great gusto, and our 'friend' came storming in, looking very annoyed. He suddenly stopped, thought for a moment, looked round at nothing in particular, then withdrew as quietly as a lamb. Clearly the cad was going to admonish us for opening the *yezhovka*, then realized that would show him up as the culprit responsible for its closure.

We persevered with our difficult task of reading in a foreign language, often discussing a particular statement by one author or another. We came to the conclusion that they all had one thing in common: narrow-mindedness and a marked misunderstanding of human beings. We all particularly noticed Lenin's obsession for violence, destruction and dictatorship, and Stalin's insistence that he was nothing less than a God and therefore could never make a mistake. In fact, that last misapprehension was common to them all. They never gave it a thought that they could be wrong. Anyway, that was the light in which we saw them.

After about two weeks in the children's cell, the door opened, and the guard announced: '*Banya!*'

We could not believe our ears. A bath? We had visions of a large warm, white-tiled bathroom with copious hot water, where we could enjoy the pleasant feeling of removing the grime from our stinking bodies. But this was all degenerate, capitalist, bourgeois, anti-revolutionary and provocative thinking. When we arrived at the bath we stripped, and all our garments were taken away to the lice-killer, which was a huge oven filled with wire baskets in which our clothes were cooked at 150 degrees centigrade for half an hour. During this time, we were waiting, naked, shivering with cold, shut up in a wooden enclosure, while another party was having a bath. At last our turn came.

As we left the compound, we were given a sliver of soap each. It was greyish-brown in colour and smelt of very bad meat. There were no baths in the room, just eight showerheads all the worse for rust.

We positioned ourselves under those roses and stood there, now really frozen, waiting for the water to flow. After some five minutes a man appeared, opened a valve and a few drops of tepid water trickled down from almost totally blocked roses, and the few that were not blocked sent the water in all directions.

The 'wetting' time lasted only some thirty seconds, so we did not get very wet, but our temperature had risen slightly from bobbing about trying to catch the elusive liquid.

Another wait, and our clothes were brought to us, steaming and burned in many places. Those who had no towels were out of luck, for the establishment provided none. There was no real need for them, except to remove the soap which got stuck in unreachable places and the stink that went with it. Our bodies were quite dry by the time our garments arrived from the lice-killing machine. The lice unlucky enough to be on the outside were duly destroyed. Those inside? Well, my diagnosis was: stunned, but otherwise unharmed. The clothing suffered badly. It was not long before mine started going to pieces. I tried to get some from the prison authorities. '*Zavtra utrom*,' said the prison governor, but tomorrow never came.

The following day a bucket of water and a stiff brush were brought to our cell. We were ordered to scrub and sweep the floor; it was nice to be in a clean cell for the first time, but it took the rest of that day and part of the night before the floor dried. Clearly, there was something afoot, but what? We were not so naïve as to think that it was all for our benefit. We did not have to wait long. A day or two later we heard a lot of footsteps. Our door opened and a group of officers, or whatever they were officially called, entered our cell, escorted by the prison governor.

'Detainees, stand up!' he called.

The group consisted of the *Oblastnoy*, or the Commander of all jails in the Chernigov Province, and his assistants. They talked amongst themselves in subdued tones. I happened to be closest to them, and in due course the Commander turned to me and barked something which I did not understand, ending his dialogue with: '*Ye . . . tvoyu mat*!' ('Go and fuck your mother.')

I had done nothing to offend the *Oblastnoy*, yet he offended me. Furthermore, he chose to offend my mother, a person he did not even know. Where I came from such behaviour required only one action. So without further ado I stepped forward, and unceremoniously slapped his face. I was immediately grabbed by one of his assistants, and the prison governor, and taken outside.

'*Kartser*!' he yelled.

I was immediately taken down two flights of stairs, to the punishment cell below ground level. I was not allowed to take my greatcoat, indeed, when I stopped outside the *kartser* door, I was ordered to take my jacket and my shoes off. I was pushed inside a very dark cell, and immediately felt my feet getting wet. I nearly tripped on something solid standing in the middle of the floor; I sat on it with my feet in the air. The cell stank of foul air and was extremely cold. As my eyes adjusted to the darkness, I surveyed my new abode. On the right there was a metal contraption consisting of three bars, about six feet long by two inches wide and four inches apart. At right angles to them, and about six inches apart, there were eight similar bars. The whole thing was surrounded by a metal frame and supported on four legs. A bed?

The object I was sitting on was a trunk of a tree cemented into the floor. I could not see any water, but when I touched the ground with my fingers it was there all right. On the wall opposite the door, touching the ceiling, was a window, about two feet wide and a foot and a half high, with half of the glass missing. Mercifully, it was almost totally covered by snow. Immediately to the right of the door was the *parasha*, chained to the floor. There was nothing for me to do but await developments. I did not know how long I was going to be in that hell-hole, or whether I was going to be charged with assault. One thing was certain: I was going to be very cold! I could not walk up and down the cell because of the water. I could not really sit still, either, or I'd freeze.

My legs were going to sleep, so I had no option but to get up from that post, cross over to the 'bed' and give the blood a chance to flow freely through them. To my satisfaction and surprise, the iron bars were not as cold as I had anticipated. I walked to and fro, my hands folded to keep as much heat within the body as possible. I could only take three steps, turning back on the third one. This little exercise reminded me of my visit to the menagerie, a few years back. I had watched a wolf in a cage exercising his legs; he too took three steps.

Lunchtime had long passed and I was getting hungry. I knew that I was not going to eat anything until morning. I also knew that I must conserve all my energy, or I would have none to provide the necessary heat to prevent me from freezing. It was during one of those walks on the iron bed that I noticed dark smudges on the grey walls. They were anything from one to three inches long, and there were many of them. Closer examination revealed that they were most probably smudges of blood. Whose? I had an answer later that night.

It became clear to me that sooner or later I would have to get some sleep, and the only place for it was the iron bed. I thought that later they would bring a mattress, or a wooden board. When the door opened, I really thought it was for that reason. Alas! The guard just handed me a mug of cold water, and that was the end of my dream.

It was soon after that that I heard the spine-chilling howl of a woman. She was crying for some time, then started to sing. It was a very sad, oriental song, consisting of just a few bars, which she repeated time and time again. I remember the tune to this day. The guard ran to her door, banged at it with what sounded like a boot, yelling, 'Silence! Silence!'

She did not care a damn. She carried on singing for about ten minutes, then suddenly stopped. The silence was occasionally broken by her sob, or a short howl. It was terrifying.

It was much later that I learned that she was a Russian Jewess of about thirty. I never discovered why she was in prison, but she spent many days, indeed weeks, on and off, in that *kartser*. We could hear her howls, sobs and singing, although we were two floors above.

I curled myself on the iron bars, closed my eyes, and started multiplying a four figure number by another, in the hope that it would make me sleep quickly. A very low wattage bulb, covered by a wire mesh, shone in my face. It was fixed just above the door, inside the wall, so that prisoners could not get at it. I was soon fast asleep.

I woke up in the middle of the night with a feeling that I was being eaten alive, not by lice, I was used to that, but by something else. The bite was much more stinging. I caught whatever was crawling along my ankle and squeezed it. I immediately became aware that my fingers were wet with something. It was blood! I got up in horror to discover hundreds of bedbugs crawling all over the 'bed' and walls. I started crushing them with my fingers; I knew then what those smudges were, I added many more myself. My fingers stank after the battle, but I did not care; I wiped them on the back of my trousers and sat, satisfied, on the wooden post. They were there too, but I slept nevertheless.

I woke up frozen stiff, with swollen legs and arms where the bugs had bitten me. The door opened and a guard handed me a miserably small piece of bread, and a mug of cold water. I learned later that the ration was three hundred grams of bread, and a litre of water per day.

I spent the time multiplying figures, or trying to move my ears. On the fourth day of my incarceration, I discovered how to do it. I can still move them now!

The next day I was called out. As far as I could make out, I was being released on the instruction of the *Oblastnoy*, to whom I should offer my apology when I saw him. To my enormous relief I was taken back to the children's cell. As it turned out, the whole episode was one big misunderstanding. Stalin, it was generally known, swore loudly and often. His disciples, trying to emulate their teacher, swore in sympathy. That particular phrase, which the *Oblastnoy* used, nasty though it was, meant nothing at all. It was just a phrase which a speaker used while thinking what to say next. The whole thing was cleared up some two months later.

I was in another cell when the *Oblastnoy* came for his periodical visit. He must have known I was in that cell, because he brought a bucket of thick soup with him, a soup most probably cooked for the guards. In comparison to the muck we were getting, it was absolutely delicious. It also contained half a potato. That was one of the two potatoes I ate during my whole stay in the Soviet Union.

By that time my Russian had improved enormously, and the

Oblastnoy did not swear once. We had a very pleasant conversation lasting some twenty minutes. I apologized for slapping his face, while he admitted that he ought not to have said what he did, in case of misunderstanding. I also told him about some mathematical problems I had solved while in solitary confinement. He was interested. 'We have a saying in the Soviet Union: "Prison is the best university". What you told me proves the correctness of the statement.'

I could not help reflecting that if to gain knowledge in the Soviet Union one had to go to prison, there must have been something radically wrong with their educational system. On the whole, I thought, the honours were even, and we parted friends.

When I entered the cell, I was greeted with pieces of bread which the boys saved for my return. Only a person who has existed on such meagre rations can imagine how much those boys sacrificed by saving the bread they gave me. I showed them my ear-moving trick; they were amused.

The library arrived, and we changed our books. To our great satisfaction, they were not by any of the previous authors. Mine described a flight of a Soviet four-engined bomber to the North Pole. The other books were about a future war between the Russians and yellow races, and short stories by A. N. Chekhov.

After about six weeks, the book-lending stopped. By that time I had become quite proficient in reading the cyrillic alphabet, and learned a lot of words. I still had great difficulty in expressing myself in Russian, although I understood almost all that the guards were telling me. The time was dragging, the only diversions being mealtimes and the occasional walk.

On Zbyshek's suggestion we decided to make a chess-set out of bread. We saved small pieces of bread each, then proceeded to knead it for hours, until the resultant mess became almost white. With a tiny piece of wood, no more than a splinter, Zbyshek began shaping the figures, starting with a king. In a couple of hours he finished it; it was a bust of Stalin. The queen became Lenin, bishops Molotov, the Foreign Secretary, the knights were Voroshilov, the Cavalry Commander, and the rooks were Beria, the boss of the NKVD. The pawns were simple soldiers, although uncannily like the guard who shut the *yezhovka*. Considering that Zbyshek did all that from memory, the likenesses were startling. We obtained two pieces of brick, and by rubbing them patiently together, we made enough powder to make the second set red. That boy was extraordinarily talented.

One morning early in March the hatch opened, and the guard informed us that *lavochka* had arrived. This was a prison shop which visited the cells once a month. Those who had money could buy items like soap, boiled sweets, tobacco, matches or cigarette paper. Since we had no money, we had no problem in choosing what to buy. In my whole stay in Soviet jails, I met only one man who bought anything other than tobacco; the rest could only afford the tobacco. At a guess, the people with money in a prison account constituted perhaps one per cent of the community.

A few days later, Zbyshek and I were called out, with things. We were taken to a cell similar to the one I was in originally, but the light was better, and there were seventy to eighty people in it. We found a spot where we could sit together, settling down as best we could. We spent a lot of time playing chess watched with amazement by the other inmates. They made a simple set of draughts, but it was confiscated during the first search. These occurred once a month, usually during the walk, and the cell was thoroughly combed for things like glass, needles or pieces of wire.

One day the door opened, and the guard commander handed eight packets of tobacco to every Pole who smoked. I did not smoke then, but I went to get mine as a matter of principle. If anybody offers one anything in prison, especially if it also helps to ease the pain of hunger, one grabs it with both hands. Who the Good Samaritan was we never discovered, but the rumours were that it was the American Red Cross.

The *kuroshki*, the staple smoke of a great majority of the citizens of the Soviet Union, was made of the stalks of a tobacco leaf. Each vein was cut into pieces about an eighth of an inch long, then tightly packed in a thick brown paper bag. To smoke it, one found a piece of paper, usually a newspaper, preferably *Pravda* or *Izvestiya*, tore a piece the size of a cigarette, then poured *kuroshki* on it directly from a bag. This would then be rolled into a cigarette, the end of paper chewed to provide a good seal, the ends screwed tight to prevent tobacco from falling out, then lit.

It was for this reason, and this reason alone, that the two main newspapers were selling so well. Much, much later, when I was 'free', I asked a man if he had the latest newspaper. He replied quite seriously, 'I do not smoke'. True, cigarette paper could be bought, but it was of a very poor quality.

One day I was introduced to racing, louse racing, that is. A space was cleared on the floor, and a thin line of water drawn. The individuals taking part in the race would then produce their own competitors, not a very difficult task, the lice would be placed at the end of the lines, head first of course, the lines sealed with more water, and the race was on. Each owner would back his personal hope with a stipulated amount of sugar, the first past the post receiving agreed prizes.

There were a number of locals in the cell. At first we did not fraternize with them in the belief that they were planted there. It soon transpired that we could trust them more than we could ever trust the Ruthenians. They were a mixed bag of peasants and factory workers of all ages. It was from them that I first learned about the atrocities committed by their Communist rulers. It would require another book to relate it all so I shall quote only a few examples.

Early in the life of the new State of the Soviet Union, the leaders decided that the only way to feed the town dwellers was by requisitioning peasants' crops. They sent 'brigades' of thieves into the country, with orders to take all except the basic requirements of a family. It never occurred to them that if the peasants had no corn to sow, there would be no harvest, and nothing to collect next year. The peasants, however, had more brain that the leaders of the Communist Party and they concealed as much as they could, often with tragic results.

'I was about twelve then,' said a man whom I will call Grisha, 'when one of those brigades came. Days before, I heard my Dad telling Mum that if he gave all that was required, not only would we have none to sow the next year, but would not have enough to last us before harvest. He told her that he would hide some in the barn under the straw.

'When the requisitioners arrived and heard that we didn't have enough because of a poor crop, they went mad with rage and started searching for it. They even made us remove the straw from the barn. When they found the hidden grain, they took Dad outside, and shot him.'

'We had to pay taxes before the Communists came,' said another man aged about fifty-five, 'but they were nothing in comparison to what those people demanded. When the rumours came that they wanted not only crops, but livestock as well, we had a meeting and decided to chase those thieves off. We met them with shotguns, old rifles, sickles and forks. They retreated, only to return with a troop of Red Guards. Many of us were killed, together with wives and kids, who tried to attend to the wounded. We killed many of them, but in the end they took what they came to collect, and more. There was hunger in the village, I lost my wife and a daughter. It was usually the women who died first, as they would try and give food to the kids and their menfolk.'

It sounded like a bad dream, but it was not. Those men were real, and I had no reason to disbelieve them. They were too decent, too good.

It was in this cell, too, that I met a very interesting man. He was a Pole from Silesia, a miner. He was also a Communist, a very unusual occurrence. He was about forty, well built, tall with dark, almost black hair, and had a blue scar under his left eye. He joined the Polish Communist Party in 1924, and spent eighteen months in a Polish jail for his activities. On release he went to Germany on instructions from the Party, to continue his work there. He was arrested in 1938 and sent to the notorious concentration camp in Dachau. Somehow he got out of it at the end of 1939 (I believe he was exchanged for somebody) and found his way to the USSR. To his astonishment, instead of being greeted with open arms, he was arrested, and that was how I met him.

He was a very disillusioned man, to say the least. He never told me what he was charged with, but what he did tell me was this: 'Had I known what awaited me here, I would have stayed in Dachau.'

I do not know what happened to that man. He was taken out, with things, and I never heard of him again.

One day the guard opened the door, and told us that it was bath-time again. I had no more illusions about a white-tiled bathroom and plenty of hot water. When we received our minute portions of soap, one of the Ukrainians asked me: 'Do you know why this soap stinks so much?'

'No, I have no idea,' I replied.

'Because it is made of the fat of the people those bastards murdered in Vinnitsa,' he replied. 'A few years back, the Katsaps rounded up thousands of innocent people, and shot them in the town of Vinnitsa, not far from Kiev. They shot about 25,000 there, and a further 20-30,000 in Babii Yar, between Kharkov and Poltava. The bodies were thrown in a ravine and piled up one on top of another to such a height, that the bottom ones began to ooze a liquid, forming a rivulet at the bottom of the ravine. It stank to high heaven, contaminating the surrounding area. The soap we get smells the same, hence the suggestion that it was made of those bodies.' To say that I was shocked to hear the explanation would be putting it mildly. I heard the same story on several occasions, the only significant difference being in the reported position of Babii Yar.

A day or two later, shortly before my seventeenth birthday, Zbyshek and I were transferred to another children's cell, about twice the size of the first one. It was here that I had a chat with the *Oblastnoy* about our misunderstanding. He was shown Zbyshek's chess-set by the prison governor who knew all about it. Some two days later there was a phoney search, and our chess-set was gone. I do not think it is difficult to surmise who might have become its new owner.

On 15 April I woke thinking of a dream I had had that night. As a rule I did not dream much, but the one I had that night I had had a few times before. It was about a horse, a beautiful black horse, which I did not recollect ever seeing in my life. It stood quietly to the left of the 'picture', bridle on, and the reins leading from its mouth to the shoulders. After a few seconds, he turned his head towards me, looking at me with his intelligent, but very sad eyes. That was the end of the dream.

The interesting part about it was, that each time I had that dream, I also moved the next day, either from one cell to another, or to a different jail. I told Zbyshek the story, but he was a little sceptical about it, although I tried to convince him that I had no reason to lie to him and the day might prove, yet again, whether the dream would work or not. I told him that I did not believe in dreams, but the facts of that particular one did require some sort of explanation. Later that morning, Zbyshek, two others and I were taken out, with things!

We were taken to the dungeon below ground and stripped for a search. I put my watch in my mouth at the last moment, and it was not found. We were loaded on lorries, and I was back on the top shelf of a *stolypinka*, this time with Zbyshek. We stopped in Homel for a time, and by early afternoon, we were in Chernigov prison.

6

Chernigov was a huge jail, and like the one in Gorodnia, plastered with the infamous *yezhovkie*. Unhappily Zbyshek and I were separated. I went to a children's cell on the first floor, containing four beds, but there were only two boys in the cell. One was a Ukrainian pickpocket, the other a German Jew.

His story was entirely different from mine. He came from Berlin, where his family were very well-known. His father owned a big factory manufacturing, among other things, ersatz cloth. Just before the outbreak of war, his father decided to send him to the USA, where he had some relatives. The boy, I shall call him Max, wanted to see other relatives in Poland before his emigration, so he spent two or three weeks there. He had the visa, and the boat ticket from Constansa to New York.

Max was a tall, thin boy of about eighteen, with a small face full of freckles. He could not speak much Russian, and since his Polish was much worse than my school German, we conversed in German. At least, he conversed while I struggled. It did not take me long to get into the swing, and by the time we parted, I was quite proud of my German.

He was in eastern Poland when the Soviets came. When it was time to leave his Polish relatives, he caught the train to the border near Cernauti in Romania. The train did not go any further, so he got off and was stopped by the Soviet Border Army. He showed them the passport, the American visa, and his dated ticket to New York. The border troops duly examined his documents, arrested him, and that is how I met him five months later. He told me that he was charged under Article 16/80 of the Ukrainian Penal Code, with an attempted illegal exit from the Soviet Union!

Poor Max tried to see the German consul, and the American,

but to no avail. He was told that he could do so only with his prosecutor's permission, and that he should write and ask him. Since he had no paper or pencil he could not write, and when he asked for it he got the usual reply: *zavtra utrom*.

The unusual comfort did not last very long, and by the next afternoon five more boys were brought into the cell. Sleeping two in a narrow bed was still better than on the floor. I started developing ulcers, mostly on my legs and thighs, ulcers that would not heal. Some of them were an inch in diameter, perpetually oozing yellow pus. There was usually a crust on top, but this was easily dislodged, either in sleep while scratching, or when the matter stuck to some part of the underwear. When this happened, the next few days were not very pleasant. The raw flesh would stay raw, oozing fluid from the hollowed centre.

About once a month we were visited by a nurse, a shapely blue-eyed blonde of about twenty. She would sprinkle the ulcers with some white powder and suggest that the best way not to have them was to stay out of prison. I am certain that with a brain like that, she must have gone a long way in the Communist Party.

It was not long before my idyllic life in the Soviet prison came to an end. At about 10 p.m. I was called out for an interview. A short ride in a 'black raven', a contraption for ferrying prisoners to and from the investigative building, and I found myself in a small room, being handed over to another guard. Forbidden to move, I must have stood there for an hour before he looked at his watch and took me to a big door, padded outside and inside. The room was large and contained a desk with three lamps. Two big ones were facing away from the man standing on the other side of the desk, and converged on a square-topped wooden stool in front of it. The window had a black curtain drawn right across it.

'Sit down!' ordered the officer. He used the familiar '*ty*' instead of the formal '*vy*' of the other inquisitors. I lost sight of him as soon as I sat down. The lamps were pointing straight at me, producing not only a glare, but also a lot of heat. Rather than look for him, I lowered my sight towards the floor to escape the blinding light.

'Do you know where you are?' he asked in Russian.

I had a fair idea, but I was not having any of it.

'Russian no speak,' I replied, although I was capable of a much better effort.

'Go and fuck your mother, you son of a prostitute!' he shouted as he went to the door. He told the guard to fetch the interpreter. He came in a few minutes, sat just to the left of me, so I turned towards him, away from the lamps.

'Always face the examiner when you answer the question,' advised the interpreter after a prompting from the man behind the lamps.

'How can I face him if I cannot see him? I do not know where he is,' I complained.

'Just face the lamps,' he demanded. 'You are in the Investigation Centre of the NKVD. You must answer the questions promptly and truthfully! *Kak vasha familiya*?'

I told him. I could just see the inquisitor as he put it all down, but not his face. The deadly white snake and sword looked even more deadly on his gorget patches. Judging by his hands, he was not very old. He shouted at me on a number of occasions, but by and large, it was not a bad interview. I was back in the cell by two in the morning.

I was called out in the afternoon. My examiner was the same fellow I had in Gorodnia. He was the 'easy' one, never shouted at me, or swore. He just tried to play on my feelings. He would ask me about my parents, always dwelling on the subject of how much they must worry about me and miss me. Once or twice I nearly broke down crying during the many sessions I had with him but I survived.

I was called out once more in the evening. The lamps were switched off, and I saw my inquisitor clearly in the light of the solitary writing lamp. He was a big man, with a round Mongol-type face, long arms, and fat, hairy hands with short fingers. His eyes were small and looked cloudy; he was the big bully. He acted as though he had no nerves left, and anything he did not like aroused his fury. Each time he went into a frenzy I put my mind in 'neutral', paying little attention to his antics, until the storm passed. He kept calling me a spy, with all the possible adjectives imaginable. He flashed his Nagan revolver in front of my face, and continually told me that I would end up *pod stenku*. That first interrogation lasted about two hours. He was still in one of his tantrums when he called the guard to take me away.

'Take this spying rat and shoot him!' he told him. The interpreter did not translate it. I took the order with a huge pinch of salt, but it scared me out of my wits only a few moments later.

We were walking along the corridor, when the guard, who always walked just behind me, pulled me up by my almost non-existent coat, barking: '*Pod stenku!*'

My heart stood still for a moment, and I automatically turned my head towards him. He grabbed me by my shoulders, man-handled me against the wall, so that my face almost touched it. He then placed my hands on my eyes and stepped back.

'Why do they want to shoot me?' flashed through my mind. My adrenalin glands were working at a fantastic rate, but nothing happened. Then I heard two men approaching. Firing squad? I tried to take my hands off to see my executioners, but the guard barked sternly: 'Don't you look!'

I was conscious of the fact that my legs were getting rubbery as the steps came closer. They came, and they went, and I was still alive. When they could not be heard any longer, the guard said something which sounded very sweet indeed: 'Let's go!'

I did not require any prompting. I took off like a hare, although my legs were still feeling a bit funny.

I discovered the secret of that exercise before we left the building. This time I was the one making the noise, while some inexperienced, innocent soul stood by the wall, shaking with fright, expecting anything, and wondering why.

The isolation in Soviet prison was total. If during the walk along miles of corridors in the investigation centre, another prisoner approached from the opposite direction, one or the other had to face the wall and cover his eyes and face, so that he could not see, or be identified by the other.

When I returned to my cell, I could not sleep. That episode really shook me rigid.

One morning we had a surprise. Instead of our normal bread ration, we received two small pieces, one the usual stodge, the other nearly white. It tasted absolutely delicious. We were still wondering about this special treatment, when the pickpocket produced a simple enough explanation; it was 1 May! He assured us that the same would happen on 7 November, the anniversary of the October Revolution. He ought to have known, he had been in prison twice before, and he was only sixteen.

A bucket of water was brought into the cell, and we scrubbed the floor clean. Then a long rod, with a piece of cloth tied to one end, was given to us to get the cobwebs out. Obviously, somebody of importance was coming. The prison governor inspected the cell and we had a search. On the prison telegraph operated by the pickpocket, we obtained information that the Commanding Officer of all the prisons in the RSFSR, Ukrainian SSR and Byelorussian SSR – in short, the whole of the Soviet Union bar a prison or two, was the visitor.

He came in the afternoon, after a much better lunch, which we expected. The soup was thicker and had some oily mess floating on top. The inspecting officer was a big man, and according to the pickpocket, a general. He looked around, then asked if anyone had any complaints. I certainly had: 'Citizen Inspector, I am always very hungry. This ration might be sufficient for the mature people, but I am still growing and I need more food. I have no money. Is there any chance of more food?'

The answer came promptly and without thinking. He obviously had been asked that question before many times: 'This is the ration on which a man who does not work, does not die.'

The inspecting officer did not wait for any more complaints. He turned on his heels and left. Poor Max never had a chance to ask for a pencil and paper.

The lack of sunshine and the perpetual incarceration within the cell clearly showed on our faces. The skin was greyish white in colour, and the flesh looked waterlogged or like a ripe yellow plum, with the bloom still on.

Soon the inquisition started in earnest. It began with one or two sessions a night, augmented with another one during the day. I saw the face of my first examiner, the one who hid behind the lamps. He was aged about twenty-five, with blond hair, but there was something about his mouth that I did not like. I called him 'the Lip'.

One morning, after a stormy interview with the Lip, instead of being taken back to the jail I was escorted to a room where the guard pointed at a high stool standing in the corner, but away from the wall, and told me to sit down.

It was a four-legged stool with a round top, but so high that my legs did not reach the floor. There was no crossbar where I could rest my legs. This did not occur to me till later, when they began to weigh a bit. After a couple of hours, my guard was relieved by another, while he went for his lunch.

My legs were getting heavier, and started developing pins and needles. If I could touch the ground for just a moment it would all go, but unfortunately the floor was about four inches below my toes. I tried to sit on one part of my backside to help the circulation; he saw me fidgeting.

'Sit still!' he shouted disapprovingly.

It became very clear to me that I was not sitting on that confounded stool waiting for the examiner, but that it was part of the game. Later on I heard of many such exercises. Standing to attention, standing with hands raised, standing in the corner of a room facing the wall. There were other methods as well, much worse than those.

In about an hour the original guard returned, and while they were busy talking and exchanging places, I lifted both my legs in quick succession.

'I told you to sit still!' roared the outgoing guard, jabbing me with the butt of his rifle on my right shin, about three inches below the knee.

It was a short, sharp pain. I screwed my toes up several times, grinding my teeth. In a few moments I could feel the blood tickling down my leg, like a louse walking down it. I looked him straight in the eye without saying a word. I thought he knew what was in my mind.

The wound was not as bad as I feared, but it did not heal for four months. I still have the scar now, about an inch in diameter.

Soon afterwards a man came with a bowl of soup. As far as I was concerned, he was late. I gobbled it up, not even realizing that it was very salty until I finished. That was part of the game too.

About 4 p.m. a man came to fetch me. My legs weighed a ton by then, and my spine was aching. I got off the stool, but did not feel my legs touching the floor. I picked myself up as though it were an accident, I did not want those bastards to enjoy my misery. I must have sat on that stool for seven hours.

My examiner was the Polish speaker I had before. I called him 'the Father'. He was most apologetic about the delay. I did not believe a word he was saying. What I did believe, though, was that he was part of the game too.

'You are accused of some grave charges,' murmured the Father. 'To be perfectly frank, I do not believe you are guilty of any of them. You are young and easily led. Forget the uniform I am wearing, I am a Pole, too, and to do what I am doing, I have to produce some information. Tell me all about it, I will see what can be told and what cannot, and you will get away with it. You are not what they are after; at the most you will get a year, or less, which would mean an almost immediate release. You can go back to your parents, who must be worrying about you.'

He was getting more and more sentimental about it, trying to bring tears to my eyes. The thought of my parents did upset me a little, but I was determined not to show it.

'You are charged,' continued the Father, 'under Article 16/80 of the Ukrainian Penal Code, with an illegal attempted exit from the Soviet Union. This is nothing, it carries a penalty of three years. The others are much more grave. Article 54/6 – spying for the enemy power; Article 54/8 – commission of terrorist acts; 54/10 – anti-revolutionary propaganda; finally, 54/14 – anti-revolutionary sabotage. The penalty for those is death by shooting.'

I knew that I had attempted to go to Hungary, but I was not in the Soviet Union when I tried to leave but in Poland, therefore Stalin and his mates had no civil, or any other right to charge me with that 'crime'. As for the others, they were simply idiotic. There was no point worrying about something that I could honestly deny, without having to remember the minute details.

I did not know then, that the Article 54 of the Ukrainian Penal Code was the notorious Article 58 of the RSFSR, which sent millions of the innocent citizens of the USSR to their deaths, either by shooting – which at least was quick – or by a slow disintegration of the human frame in the numerous labour camps through undernourishment, overwork and cold.

'This is ridiculous,' I told the Father. 'Any man, or a group of men who thought up those charges must be of very low intelligence. When the Soviet Union invaded Poland . . .'

'We did not invade Poland,' he interrupted, 'we came to liberate the Polish people from the clutches of the bourgeoisie.'

70

I could not help thinking that he missed his lines. A man who professed to be a Pole, certainly came to the defence of the USSR rather quickly. He had an honest enough face, but his eyes were false.

When a man is imprisoned in conditions as I was, he slowly develops an animal instinct. One look is usually enough to assess a person, whether he is trustworthy or not. As far as I know, my animal instinct never failed me.

I was taken out and waited for a while in the corridor, while the guard had a chat with another. It suddenly occurred to me that I was a very selfish chap, without an ounce of Communist ideals. On the wall by which we were standing, there was a fitting where many inquisitors hung their coats. It was reasonable to assume that the coats were lice-free. It was really not fair, certainly against the teaching of Marx and Lenin, that I should hog the lot, while those overworked guardians of the Revolution had none. The Communist ideal of share and share alike suddenly ran through my brain. Unselfishly, I decided not to kill the vermin, but at the first opportunity to collect enough to fill a matchbox, which I might be able to deposit on the louse-starved coats of the comrades.

That was for the future. For the present, I was more interested in getting something to drink. I waited patiently until the guard had stopped talking, then asked him for water, but no, we had to go back to prison now. When we arrived there, the answer was that other cells were using the toilets, and I would have to wait. I decided to collect some lice and store them in a box, I had a feeling that I would be called out again that night.

I had a red and yellow woollen scarf given to me by my cousins, this was usually a good hunting ground. I had inspected about two feet of it, collecting eighty-four lice, when I was called out again. I asked for a drink of water, but no, the examiner was waiting. So I had no drink. I was getting a bit desperate now, my mouth was hot and I had no saliva left. When we entered the investigation building, I asked the guard if I could go to the lavatory, hoping that there might be a tap there. He agreed readily, but I was out of luck. I thought he knew about it too.

I waited for my 'waiting' examiner for about an hour. The guard took me to the door of my examination room, knocked, but there was no reply, so he opened the door and looked in. That was my chance; with a quick movement of my wrist I emptied the contents of the matchbox over the hanging coats of the inquisitors, hoping the present would not be appreciated. Minutes later, a huge man, looking like a bear, with long arms, ambled towards the door. I had no difficulty in recognizing him, he was my third inquisitor. I called him 'the Mongol'.

I was glad to see him switch the room lights on instead of the searchlights on the bureau. He sat down behind it, turning the portable lamp on. Without saying a word he pointed at the stool, then searched for something in a file. The interpreter arrived, and the inquisition began about eleven in the evening.

'*Bezhenyets*; he says he is *bezhenyets*. I will tell you who he is; he is a spy, a capitalist, bourgeois spy.'

'What is he saying?' I asked the interpreter, as though I did not understand a word.

'Don't interrupt!' he snarled.

I did not want to interrupt, or hear his translation, I just wanted to take my mind off the jug half full of water. The Mongol must have read my thoughts. He picked it up and poured the water into a glass, raising the jug higher and higher, spilling some of the water on the floor. He took a swig, spitting it out immediately.

'It's warm!' he moaned as he emptied the glass, then the jug, into a bucket standing on the floor. I could not help licking my lips watching the precious liquid being thrown away. I had seen that room, and others like it many times before. The whole scene, it was clear, was prearranged.

The Mongol lifted his huge frame from the chair, picked up the now empty jug and left the room, coming back a few minutes later with a fresh supply of water. He spilled some on the desk, poured himself a glassful, and slurped some through his teeth. '*Kak vasha familiya?*'

At last we started. The whole performance till now must have lasted an hour. I really thought it was bestial; starve a man first, then feed him with very salty soup, next take water away from him and follow it with the water pouring act. All very simple, and not a mark on his body. If the brute thought that after all that I would sing the tune he wanted me to sing, he was going to get a nasty shock.

'How long were you following the Red Army unit before you

72

were apprehended by the Border Army?'

'I wasn't following anybody. My brother and I were running away from the advancing German Army. We didn't even know where we were.'

'What did you say was the name of your leader?'

'I didn't say anything about any leader. Nobody was leading anybody. My brother and I were trying to find a way out of the woods.'

'At three o'clock in the morning?'

'*Tovarishch* Examiner . . .'

'I am not your comrade!' he yelled like a wounded bull. 'There are no comrades in any of the jails of the Soviet Union, there isn't a single Communist Party member in any of our prisons, only ruffians like you.'

He stood up from his chair, banged the desk with his fist, leaning towards me each time his fat, hairy hand hit the table. He really hated me for the use of that sacred word. I knew that the proper word was 'citizen', but speaking Polish to the interpreter, I had momentarily forgotten the Polish equivalent, and had I used the Russian word *grazhdanin*, I would have admitted that my Russian was not non-existent.

'The riff-raff!' he murmured as he sat down.

Visibly shaken, he poured himself another glassful, this time to cool his nerves perhaps, then offered some to the interpreter. He went through the same routine as before, but I was not looking. After some time, the questions began again. Soon they were coming thick and fast. The examiner started to lose his head again, and I knew he was going to explode at any moment. The veins in his temple thickened, and his face became redder with each question. He drew his revolver out of its holster and waved it in front of me, occasionally pointing it straight at me which gave me the opportunity to inspect the drum. It was empty. At least it gave me an assurance that the ogre would not shoot me accidentally.

After about half an hour of those antics, the Mongol replaced the Nagan in the holster, paused for a minute or so, then asked me quite sweetly: 'How much did Mr Churchill pay you for the information?'

Before the interpreter had time to translate it, the examiner rose, the veins in his temple thickened again, and he started to bang the desk with his apish fist.

'How much did Mr Churchill pay you for the information?' he repeated, this time roaring like a wounded bull. Froth started forming in the corner of his mouth, and he kept hammering on.

The truth of the matter was that I had never heard of a Mr Churchill, so I asked the interpreter. Before he could repeat the question the Mongol came storming round the desk, drawing his pistol.

'If that son of a prostitute, that capitalist spy does not tell me the truth, I shall kill him before the morning!'

I would not have been worried had he pointed the gun at me. Unfortunately, he held the gun by its barrel, as though he were ready to club me. He moved it up and down, inches from my nose, grasping it so hard that his knuckles became white with stress. 'Don't worry,' I said to myself, 'in ten years' time you will know what happened that night.'

'Who is Mr Churchill?' I asked the interpreter again.

'He wants to know who Churchill is,' said he to the Mongol.

'Take that *svoloch* out of here, or I will smash his head against the wall!' bellowed the examiner, his voice hoarse.

I was taken out. On the way back to my cell, I pondered who that Mr Churchill could be. The name sounded English, so I decided that he must have been some fellow in charge of the British espionage organization.

It must have been three in the morning when we arrived back in jail, and I was taken straight to my cell. I noticed that the guard did not walk away after locking the door. I went to bed in my clothes, as usual, and was just about to close my eyes, when I happened to look at the Judas hole. There was the eye of the guard watching me, so I turned on my side, showing him my backside. A few seconds later I heard the key being inserted in the lock, and I was called out again. I tried to get a drink, without success.

I waited for my inquisitor for about an hour. It was clear to me that this was part of the softening-up process, and I wondered how long it would last.

As I entered the examination room, I saw the now familiar searchlights, signifying that the Lip was in the chair. The jug was still there, and on the other side of the desk there was a two foot long, two inches square piece of wood, looking like a leg of a chair.

My stool was without its top. I pointed it out to the examiner, but he did not take any notice.

'Sit down!' he barked.

I sat carefully down, placing my posterior so that it rested on the front left join of the top of the frame. With one swift movement of my hands I folded the back of my coat, so that I was sitting on three thicknesses of it instead of one. I had practised it just in case as I had once before seen the stool without its top. The Lip never noticed it. In due course the translator arrived, and the interrogation began. The same old questions, the same old answers, and the usual string of swear words from the Lip, of which he seemed to have an endless supply.

After about an hour, the Lip stopped for a moment and poured himself a drink with the same ceremony as the Mongol. He then poured another glass and handed it to me. I did not believe my eyes. Somehow I sensed a trap, but still that glass of water looked very tasty. I began to get up, and had just started lifting my hand to collect it, when he suddenly threw the contents of the glass in my face.

'You bourgeois spy! If you think I am going to waste any of this good Soviet water on you, you must be out of your mind, you enemy of the people!'

He suddenly picked up the wooden chair leg and started waving it in my direction as though he were going to hit me, or throw it at me. It did not seem to worry me at all. I was sure that he was not going to harm me: even when he came round and performed the same repertoire in the vicinity of my right ear, my stomach was at ease, although my heart was beating a little faster. The person I sympathized with was the interpreter; the poor man did not know what to translate and what to leave. In the end he gave up, until the rage of the examiner abated. He let me go three hours later.

I was taken down to a small cell in the basement, with nothing but a cement floor. I sat with my back to the wall and was just drifting to sleep, when the usual bread and a mug of water was handed to me. I took a small sip, rolling the precious liquid round my mouth before swallowing, to make it last longer. When I had drunk half of it I ate the bread, finishing off with the drink. I felt very tired and was about to lie down when the door opened, and I was taken to the toilet, then back to the examination room.

75

Mercifully, the guard did not tell me to sit on the stool. I was in quite good shape, but my legs felt a little stiff. There was a change of guards, indicating to me that it was eight o'clock. I had now been without sleep for twenty-seven hours. I was called out some two hours later.

I expected the Father, but it was the Mongol again. The stool top had been replaced, but the black curtains were still drawn, and the inquisitor was soon on my side of the desk, waving his pistol in all directions. At one point he actually placed the barrel at the back of my skull, sending a chill right down my spine.

At about midday, I was taken to the cell in the basement and given soup. I tasted it before eating, in case it was as salty as the day before. Fortunately it was not, so I ate it lying on my stomach, to give my legs a chance to relax. As soon as I had finished, I rolled over on my back to snatch some sleep, but I was called back. After a short wait in the corridor, an officer appeared and spoke to the guard in a whisper. I noticed he was of a superior rank to my three examiners.

I was led a few paces towards a wall connecting the two corridors. The wall had a number of doors and the guard opened one of them, revealing what looked like a cupboard. It was only two feet wide and just as deep, and the seat was the same distance from the ground. I was told to enter, but I hesitated, so the guard encouraged me by a firm push in the back. I turned about, and was just in the process of sitting down, when the guard slammed the door. I had a nasty surprise. It was not an ordinary cupboard where the prisoners were occasionally kept waiting, but another contraption to help the softening-up process.

As the door closed, my feet were swept backwards under the seat which pressed against the back of my knees, so that I was half standing, half kneeling. What I had not noticed on entering the cupboard was that the door had a wooden plank fixed at the bottom, at about ankle height, so that as the door was closed, it pushed the occupier's legs back. The front edge of the seat, pushing against the back of the knees, prevented the unfortunate prisoner from falling on the floor, thus keeping him in that un-natural position. In addition, the back of the wall was heated slightly, making the atmosphere stuffy, to say the least.

I started banging at the door with my hands as hard as I could, then shouted, but nothing happened. After some minutes I got hold of my senses. 'You fool,' I thought, 'this is precisely what those Communist bastards want you to do. They want you to panic, or go out of your tiny little mind. This is supposed to be an adventure, remember? In ten years' time you will know what happened, so pull yourself together and go to sleep.'

How long I stayed in that cupboard I had no idea. When I came to, I was lying on the floor being shaken by a guard. I tried to get up, but my legs would not carry me. After some minutes the feeling returned and I stood up. My knees hurt a bit, but otherwise I was unharmed. I was taken to the toilet, then for another grilling.

Later on I learned that that confounded cupboard was called 'the intestine' by the prisoners. It certainly was narrow, and very dark. I was in it on two other occasions, but I was no longer a greenhorn. As soon as I entered, and the door was being closed, I supported my body on my hands while lifting my legs off the ground. Whether a fully grown man could do the same, I would not like to say; there was very little room to manoeuvre.

The Father was in the chair. As always, he was most apologetic about keeping me waiting, inventing yet another excuse for being late. He was full of sympathy and advice.

'I am the only friend you have. I have a boy of similar age, and I know how I would feel if he were in trouble; it would break my heart.'

I was feeling very low, and I knew if he carried on like that much longer I would break down in tears. I tried not to listen to his quiet, fatherly voice, but without much success. I tried deep breathing to stop myself from crying, but in the end he succeeded and I broke down and howled.

He came round to my side, put his hands round my shoulders, saying: 'There, you have a good cry. Nobody will ever know about it, only you and I, and I am your friend. You have nothing to worry about.'

He started stroking my head with one hand, while tapping my shoulders with the other. After some minutes, he whispered softly in my ear: 'Tell me, my boy, who sent you to Hungary?'

Still sobbing loudly I whimpered: 'But I was not going to Hungary, we were lost in the woods.'

The Father stopped being fatherly, swore filthily in Russian and

77

returned to his side of the desk.

'I tried to help you, but you did not want my help. We have enough evidence to convict you on all counts. I am washing my hands of your case, and now you have nobody in this world to help you. You are absolutely alone, you are a fool, and you know it. Now get out!'

He called a guard, and I was out of his clutches. He certainly was a dangerous man. I never saw him again.

I was taken to the same basement cell as before but I barely had time to lie down when I was called out again. I was brought to the room with the stool and told to sit up. I clambered up it, hoping for a quick and occasional nap, but I could not stay upright, while the guard kept yelling at me to sit still. After about an hour, I was escorted to the interrogation room. The searchlights were on, and I could see three men behind the desk. One, I thought, could have been the officer who sent me to the cupboard. The interpreter sat in his usual position, signifying that the inquisitors did not speak Polish.

They fired questions at me, one after another, for two or three hours without a break. But it was all in vain. What the comrades never scented out was that I spoke a fairly good Russian by then, and I had a reply ready a long time before the hard-pressed interpreter finished translating.

When I was taken out of that room it was daylight. I was wondering how much longer I would have to undergo that relentless questioning. How much longer could I hang on, before collapsing through sheer exhaustion and lack of sleep. My brain was working very slowly, I felt tired, sleepy and sticky. The lice were crawling all over my body, and I had no time to do anything about it.

I was taken down, yet again, to the basement cell, given bread and water, then called out again by a different guard. It must have been eight o'clock then, and I had been without any sleep for forty-eight hours. He marched me along a pale green corridor and out into the safety of my cell. The questioning was over.

'Where have you been for the past two days?' inquired Max as I entered the cell.

I told him all about it briefly, then we˗˗t to the top left corner of the cell, sat down with my back to the wall and went to sleep. I could not lie on my bed, as the guard would reprimand me immediately. That left corner was the only spot invisible through the Judas.

The next day I explained to the lads how to beat the 'intestine', and the mistake of gobbling up food dished out in the investigation centre without first testing it for salt content. Personally, I thought it was easier to starve than to suffer from thirst.

Later I learned that the prisoners called that particular method of interrogation the Conveyor. I was lucky, I was only on it for two days and nights. Some of the more unfortunate spent a week or more, being grilled incessantly with hardly any sleep or water, until they confessed to the crimes they had never committed.

Two or three days later I was called out, with things. I said goodbye to Max and the others, and left. Max and I arranged to meet on the fifth anniversary of the ending of the war in Cracow, outside Mariacki Church, at twelve noon. I could not keep that appointment. It is doubtful that Max was there either. By then, the rule of the 'dictatorship of the proletariat' stretched far beyond the boundaries of that lovely and ancient city.

I was escorted to the basement, to the end cell on the right of the corridor. When the guard opened the cell, I shuddered; it was almost pitch black inside. The guard gave me a push in the back, and I was in. Seconds after he closed the door, I was thrown on the floor by invisible hands, more hands took my rucksack from me, while yet more hands thoroughly frisked me. I heard my coat and my jacket being torn, then all was quiet. I lifted myself from the floor trying to look around, but it was too dark to see anything. In a minute or so, I felt some sort of material landing on my head. It was my empty rucksack. Moments before, I had in it a very dirty and scorched pair of pants and a vest, both full of holes, the remnants of my towel and a packet of green tobacco; now I had nothing. I put my hand inside my pocket, but my watch was gone, too. For a moment I felt helpless, insecure and downhearted, then my blood boiled.

'If I find the thug who has stolen my mother's watch,' I thought, 'I will kill him!'

Very slowly my eyes adapted themselves to the darkness. It was a big cell, about eight yards square, and full of boys. There must have been a hundred of them. They were all speaking Russian or Ukrainian, swearing badly. In the top right hand corner of the cell, a large boy was lying on the only mattress, cleaning his nails with a matchstick. He was obviously the leader of this particular pack of wolves. They were, I learned later, the second generation of *bezprizornye*, the unsupervised ones, the offspring of parted parents. In his wisdom Lenin decided that what was required in the new regime was, more or less, free love. A licence to marry cost five roubles, and the divorce just as little. All that one of the spouses had to do to obtain a divorce was to go to the office, pay five roubles, collect a form, fill it in and send it to the other by post. From the moment of the receipt of that form, they were divorced. It was all very simple, very nice and very revolutionary. Except that the 'thinkers' did not think what to do with the children of such marriages. When they finally realized there was a problem, they began building special baby care units, where the children were put while their mothers went to work. By then it was too late. The streets were full of those unfortunate children, abandoned by their parents, living on their wits. Most of them did not even know in what part of the Soviet Union they were born, let alone who their parents were. They survived by stealing during the late spring, summer and early autumn, then either by getting picked up by the militia and spending the winter in prison, or by migrating to some southern part of the USSR to carry on the trade. I should know, I migrated with them.

I had a good look at the boy lying on the mattress: he was bigger than me. At first I thought I would go and ask him for the watch, I was not really interested in the other things. I quickly discarded the idea. Not only would he do nothing about it, but probably would send his guard dogs to rough me up. So, with my heart thumping, I slowly pushed my way forward to his corner. I was absolutely certain that he knew where my watch was, and I had to get it back. When I was only a foot or two from him, I changed my mind. Against the urge of my half animal instinct, I decided to give him a chance, and ask him for my watch. I could see, just above his right shoulder, my towel and the tobacco, under which, half hidden, was my watch.

'Please, may I have my watch back?' I asked him politely. 'It was a present from my mother, and is very dear to me. You can keep the rest.'

'Hey, boys!' he bellowed, with a bored look on his face. 'This riff-raff says that somebody has nicked his watch and he wants it back!'

They all jeered, while he continued cleaning his fingernails. My instinct took over. In a flash I fell on him, kicking him in the crotch with my knee, at the same time grabbing his throat with my hands. I bashed his head against the wall, squeezing his windpipe with all my meagre strength. When his eyes started coming out of their sockets, and his tongue was almost totally out of his mouth, I released my grip on his throat.

'My watch, you dog! My watch!' I snarled.

The fool did not budge. I repeated the dose, and that time he pointed to the side of his head. I let him go. I retrieved my watch and kissed it. The lad rolled on his knees and quit the mattress, indicating that I should move in. I did not really want it, but since he offered it to me, I accepted.

I felt very tired, but I had learned a simple truth. Violence was best cured by a violent reaction, something I had never believed in the past but it was what the *bezprizornye* understood.

The boy I roughed up became my best pal during my short stay in the cell. He was not a bad lad really, all he needed was a proper upbringing, but he had nobody to do it for him.

After some minutes, he handed me a neatly torn piece of paper saying, 'Have a smoke'. I obliged willingly, and we smoked a peace pipe. Before I rolled mine, I had a look at the print. It read: 'London, TASS. English premier Churchill . . .' and the piece of paper ended just there. That was how I discovered who Mr Churchill was!

The next day I lost my watch; somebody reported to the guards that I had one. I was taken out, with things, and thoroughly searched. I never had a chance. As soon as they found it I was told to get dressed. I was taken to the office, and the watch included among the other items on the list, then dropped into the brown envelope together with the rest of my things.

I saw my watch only once again, before it disappeared forever. I was taken to the office for the routine examination of my property. My watch was not there, so I inquired about it, pointing to the wrist of the official. His watch was very similar to mine.

'Oh, I beg your pardon,' he said apologetically, his face now as red as the flag of the Soviet Union. 'I only borrowed it while you are here.' He put it back in the envelope, and that was the last time I ever saw it.

I was taken back to the cell of the jackals, feeling my way to the mattress because of the darkness. I told the bad news to the ex-leader. Without much ado he and a few others went to the far corner of the cell, and beat the hell out of a poor wretch who was a known stool-pigeon.

I stayed in that cell for about five days, then was transferred to a normal one on the second floor. It was about the same size but full of light by comparison. According to the unwritten law, I found a spot close to the *parasha*, shifting away from it as people were moved out from the cell. The fraternity was a mixture of Poles, Romanians and locals. The four sitting closest to me were Red Army officers. They had fought in Finland and had found the life there not at all as it had been described to them by the all-knowing *Politruk*.

Politruk was the abbreviation given to *Politicheskii Rukovoditel*, (Political Guide). He was a man of great power, although usually of inferior rank to the Unit Commander, and was generally accepted as an official spy of the Party. His sole purpose in life was the spreading of official propaganda, and seeing to it that the Party line was strictly adhered to. On returning to the Soviet Union, the four officers told their friends and neighbours what they had seen in Finland. They were soon arrested, charged with the spreading of anti-revolutionary propaganda, and accordingly sentenced to eight years of forced labour.

'For what?' they kept asking each other. It was obvious for what. They had told the truth, and truth was a forbidden word in the Communist state. Slowly, as the days went by, I progressed further from the *parasha* until I reached the spot occupied by the Poles on the right side of the cell, by the wall. My neighbour on my left was a university professor, and to his left was a retired judge. On my right was a student of about eighteen, and on his right a Jewish lad of around twenty.

I discovered the professor was 'sitting under' Articles 54/14 and 16/80. That phrase was a literal translation from Russian, and was used by everybody for its simplicity. It merely meant 'to be in prison accused, or be convicted of, a crime contrary to the Article . . .'. The judge was accused of trying a Communist thirteen years before and sentencing the man to six months in jail. The judge did not remember the case at all since he dealt only with common criminals, thieves, robbers or fraud experts. It was possible, he said, that one of them could have been a member of the Communist Party, hence the arrest. The Jewish lad was a *bezhenyets*. Before the war he had lived in England for a while, and therefore spoke good English. He started to teach us but it soon transpired that it was impossible, without paper and pencil, to teach a language which is written in one way and pronounced in another, so we gave it up.

The student next to me was also a *bezhenyets*, and had been picked up on the way to Romania. He suffered from fits, and was offically certified as an epileptic. He was also our 'official stool-pigeon basher'. What normally hapened was this: the lad, I shall call him Stefan, could imitate the attack rather well. As soon as one of our two stool-pigeons – both Ruthenians – started shuffling towards the door, Stefan would begin his 'dance'. The inmates, knowing the ritual, would make way for the rat, so that he had to pass fairly close to the spot where Stefan was performing. Once there, he was trapped. A queue would form to use the *parasha*, or people sitting nearby would decide to get up and stretch their legs, and he could go no further. He could not go back, either, because for one reason or another, but always a very valid one, the people he had just passed by would decide to get up too. Somehow or other, but always without fail, a broom would suddenly appear in Stefan's hands, by now in the full fury of his St Vitus's Dance.

Regrettably, the professor and I could hold Stefan no longer. He would jerk and jump, his eyes rolling in all directions. From time to time the broom would ascend to a great height, only to descend at a fast rate a split second later. It was truly unfortunate that the stool-pigeon was, invariably, in its downward path, again and again!

There was nothing we could do, as Stefan's strength during the 'attack' was much greater than ours, or at least it looked like that. The shouts for help would, sooner or later, bring the *chasovoy*. Before he even opened the door, the people queueing for the *parasha* would realize that they did not really want to use it. Those who got up to stretch their legs would suddenly feel tired, and would sit down again. The broom, as if by magic, would appear in its usual position by the door. The professor and I would attend to the now miraculously recovered Stefan.

'They are beating me,' the stool-pigeon would cry.

'Nobody is beating anybody,' a bored voice would reply from somewhere near the door, 'he just happened to be passing by, as Stefan was having one of his fits. He might have touched him with his foot, or something.'

Citizen Guard would look around, and seeing everything quite normal, would walk away. The stool-pigeon would return to his nest, his ego pricked and his hide sore.

It was in this cell that I learned more about Communist schemes that were not allowed to fail. Misha was a well-built man of about fifty, with an honest face, and sad blue eyes. He had a farm of about twenty-five acres when the Communists arrived. At first he was allowed to farm as though nothing had changed. Then he was made to join a collective farm. In a year or two the production steadily dropped, and there was a great famine in the Soviet Union. People were dying like flies. The figures I heard mentioned were five million dead. Lenin asked the USA and Canada, his ideological enemies, for food. They sent millions of tonnes of wheat to the USSR, to feed the starving nation. Lenin then produced his famous New Economic Plan, part of which gave peasants their stolen land back.

'We went to work,' related Misha, 'without interference from those who very often did not know the difference between a carrot and a cabbage, and had never heard of rotation. I planted what I thought was good for the soil, and not what the town magician wanted me to pull from the ground.

'To encourage production, the authority established a new title, the Red Farmer. My farm flourished, not that I was after a title, it meant nothing to me or anyone else for that matter, it flourished because we were working for ourselves, and not for some good-for-nothing townsman. It wasn't long before I was given a title, with much ceremony, since I was the first to receive it in the area. According to the speaker, the workers and the peasants of the Soviet Union were winning their historic struggle against the oppression and the exploitation of the bourgeoisie, and the achievement on my farm showed the wisdom of the Leninist-Stalinist policy on agriculture.'

Misha's face was happy and contented as he was telling us about it. He even looked younger, and his blue eyes were focused far beyond the grey walls of our cell, on the green fields of his beloved Ukraine.

'I had a wife and two kids, with a third on the way,' he continued. Suddenly, his face tightened, and thick veins appeared on his temple. 'Then the bastards realized that what we were doing disproved the theory they believed in. All the peasants with the title of Red Farmer were arrested, peasants who only a short time before were hailed as the saviours of the country. Then other peasants, without any titles, were arrested, our common guilt being that we worked too hard.

'I was tried, and given eight years, that was twelve years ago, and I am still in. Since my arrest I have not seen, or heard from my wife, or the kids. I don't even know whether they are dead or alive.'

A single, small tear appeared in the corner of his eye, a tear on the face of a simple, but very tough man who survived it all, and whose only crime was that he worked too well.

'We were taken to some God-forsaken spot in the north, only to find that there was nothing there. We cut trees to build sheds so that we could have a roof to sleep under, then we cut more trees, and built more sheds, only to be moved to do the same again. After about a year of that we were given pickaxes, shovels and barrows and told to dig. We were told that we were building a big canal which was going to be named after Stalin and that it was going to connect the White Sea with the Baltic through the lakes Onega and Ladoga.

'We called that ditch the White Sea Canal, and for most of us it spelled a death sentence. I've heard it said that half a million prisoners died digging it. On some days so many died, that the bodies would have overfilled the stretch of canal we dug up that day. We reckoned that a year, or for a strong man a year and a half, was as long as anybody could last. I was there two years. Out of the original twenty men in my brigade, only two survived.

'In 1933, I was transferred to the Distant Camps. We went by train to the far east, then were loaded on a boat like cattle, although I would not have allowed my cattle to be transported under such conditions. We were put in the holds, and there we stayed until we arrived at a place called Magadan. Those who survived were taken out first, then the dead were brought up and neatly placed in lines. Then we were all counted together. About a quarter of my shipment did not make it.

'Next we were taken to a place by a river called Kolyma and put to work looking for gold. We were not the only ones doing it; I heard stories that the Americans and the Japanese were looking for it too, except that they were doing it for themselves.

'We worked every day, rain or snow, the only respite being a very hard frost in winter. As we formed up in the morning to be counted, we would always spit on the ground. If the spit turned to ice by the time it hit the ground, we would be sent back to the sheds. That was our only thermometer. It could have been worse, I could have been sent to dig coal in Novaya Zemlya. I heard about it from a couple of fellows who did a stretch in Vorkuta. Those sent to Novaya Zemlya were often taken across the sea in open barges, and those barges had a nasty habit of sinking on the way. Strange, but I have never met anyone who had been to Novaya Zemlya, and returned, in twelve years!

'A few weeks before my release date, I was brought in to the office of the Camp Commandant. He told me that I had got an addition, another three years. He didn't say why, or for what, but I was not released. I started on my way back last year. I was in good spirits, hoping that it was the end of my stretch, but I am still here.'

Misha's face suddenly changed, he clenched his fists so tight they became white. He ground his teeth so hard that I thought they would crack, then hissed: 'If ever I got hold of Stalin, I would tie him to a tree and strip his back naked. Then I would cut his back into thin strips, and tear each one from his back, right down to the bottom. When he cried for mercy, I would rub salt in the exposed flesh and leave him, in the hope that the wolves would find him and tear him apart.'

I listened to Misha with horror. I could not believe that he, normally a very placid and kind person, would be capable of such an act. But then, I had not seen what Misha had seen, I had not been through what he had been forced to undergo. He should, by rights, have been dead long ago; it was only because of his toughness that he was still among the living.

Soon rumour spread that a stage was being formed. This was the name given to the prison train taking convicts to their various labour camps. Misha was one of those called out. I only hope that he survived.

One morning, the door opened for more prisoners to be admitted. I looked towards them and suddenly my heart started thumping harder: one of them was Adam, my brother! When he was next to enter the cell the guard put a hand in front of him and closed the door. I made sure that he saw me, and smiled, but he looked very old and pale. He went to the next cell. Moving swiftly, I wove my way towards the door and tapped. I had become an expert telegraphist but unfortunately he was not; nevertheless I was glad to hear that he was in good spirits and, most important, had stuck to the story.

Once more I was transferred to another cell, where I was the only Pole amongst Ruthenians and others.

When we went for our monthly bath and received the tiny pieces of smelly soap, I asked one of the other inmates whether he knew why it stank so badly. He did not, so I told him. The guard overheard and immediately called me over to him and said: 'Sonny, if you want to see the sun again, forget that you have ever heard of Vinnitsa or Babii Yar.' I understood, but did not forget.

When I received my clothes I nearly wept. My jacket had one sleeve missing, and the rest of it was so badly burned that it crumbled in my hands. The underwear and the remnants of my towel I could not find at all. The trousers escaped most of the punishment, but they had more holes than material. My school cap was missing too.

I reported the fact to the guard who promised me new garments *zavtra utrom*. I was really surprised when they did arrive in the morning. Black cotton trousers and a black cotton shirt with buttons right up to the neck. Now I even looked like a *bezprizornyi*.

One day I was called out of my cell by an NKVD non-commissioned officer, with four triangles on his collar instead of the usual two.

'Walk,' he said.

I became suspicious. For a start, I had never before been taken for a walk on my own so why employ a high-ranking NCO to do so now? When we arrived in the walking-yard I had another surprise: the NCO, instead of waiting in one corner as the others did, proceeded to accompany me on my way round, becoming quite chatty. I did not know what to do: whether to speak as I was capable of doing in Russian, or plead, as hitherto, that I did not understand. I decided to speak with some hesitation. He pointed to the windows of the cells occupied by the *bezprizornye*.

'Jackals, human waste,' he said. 'There is no hope for them, but you are different.'

'Thank you,' I replied.

I could have told him that they were the jackals. I saw them occasionally passing goods from one cell to another, by swinging a length of rope tied to a broomstick.

'You are an intelligent boy, and you must not let yourself go the way they went.'

'I don't think I will.'

'I am glad. The Soviet Union is a good place to live, you will see. It won't be long before you come out, and you will be able to study whatever you want.'

Clearly he was after something, and whatever it was, I had to be on the look-out.

'There is everything in the Soviet Union,' he continued, 'wheat and barley, sugar-beet and potatoes, coal and gold. Our factories are working continuously producing goods, and soon we shall have everything we want. It will even be better than it is now.'

This was not the story I had heard from people only recently arrested. It seemed there was a general shortage of everything and many things were rationed, including bread. Some of the shortages were caused by the distributional chaos. For example: one set out to buy a few items, including a box of matches. There were no matches in the shop, and one was obliged to accept a pencil instead of small change. In another town, say ten miles away, one would get a box of matches in lieu of change, although the main reason for going to a shop was to buy a pencil which was not there!

It became very plain that I was in for a spell of indoctrination. After a further twenty minutes of claptrap I was taken back. The next day he called me out again. It was a lovely day, I could hear people singing outside the prison walls.

'Do you hear that?' droned the NCO. 'The workers of the Soviet Union love the life so much that they sing while they work. Have you ever heard people in your country doing that? Of course not, they are overworked, and receive little money for their toil. I know this is so in the capitalist world.'

'You are very wrong, Citizen,' I replied. 'I ought to know, I lived there. Very often I worked in the fields when on vacations, and I took part in the singing. Sometimes when harrowing on my own, I would whistle, or sing to myself.'

The truth of the matter was that the Ukrainians were very fond of singing, it was a national characteristic, and had absolutely nothing to do with Lenin, Stalin, or Communism.

'How old were you when you first started working in the fields?' inquired the NCO.

'I don't really remember, eight or nine.'

'A typical case of exploitation of child labour that would not be allowed in the USSR.'

'I wasn't exploited by anybody,' I interrupted, 'I was only helping my father. If my neighbour wanted some help, I would help him too. Don't you do things like that in the Soviet Union?'

'Of course we do, we are one big Communist family.'

'Well then, what you are saying is that if you help your father in the USSR it is a good deed, but if I help mine in Poland, that is exploitation. Do you really believe in that kind of foolish philosophy?'

Citizen NCO obviously did, because he calmly passed his judgement.

'You see, you lived in a capitalist country, and by definition, capitalism is the exploitation of man by man.'

'It therefore follows,' I intervened, 'by that definition, Communism must be the other way round!'

'No, it isn't,' replied the NCO, missing the punchline completely. 'To quote Lenin, Communism means public ownership plus the electrification of the whole country.'

The next day he came again.

'My brother is a carpenter, he earns about 900 roubles a month. How much would a carpenter get in Poland?'

'The one I knew earned about 100 *zloty*,' I replied.

'You see, here you have a good example of capitalist exploitation. The rate of exchange is one for one, so the worker in the USSR gets nine times more for doing the same job.'

I did not want to tell him that the rate of exchange was established by the Soviet rulers on their arrival in Poland. So I used another method of comparison.

'How much do you pay for a kilo of *salo*?'

Salo, pork fat, was either eaten smoked with a piece of bread, or cup up in small cubes and fried.

'Oh, about eighty roubles,' he said.

'In that case your carpenter can buy about eleven kilos for his monthly wage.'

'That is so,' he agreed, after a short pause.

'One kilo of *salo* in Poland was two *zloty*, so the Polish carpenter could buy fifty kilos, or about four and a half times as much as his Soviet friend.'

Citizen NCO did not say a word, so I carried on.

'How much would you have to pay for those boots?'

He stopped for a moment, lifted one of them to have a better look, and suggested about 800 roubles.

'In other words, he would have to work almost a month for his pair.'

'That is so,' he agreed.

'I can't say exactly how much a pair like that would cost in Poland,' I continued, looking with interest at his canvas footwear, 'but I would say about fifteen *zloty*. In other words, the Polish carpenter could buy, let's say, six pairs a month.'

He stopped for a moment as though he were going to tell me something, shook his head, then carried on walking in silence.

For three weeks Citizen NCO came to take me for walks. As the days went by, he asked more and more; about holidays, travel, schools, even about trade unions. In the end we both had our facts right, the difference being that I had them straight in the first place. I have no doubt that the whole, and only reason for the daily, twenty-minute walk, was an attempt by the Soviet authority at my indoctrination. They did not succeed. In return, I should like to think, that in a boyish way, I succeeded in removing one, if not both blinkers from the eyes of the Citizen NCO and that he, at least, started to see daylight in the abyss of Communism.

At the end of our last walk together, we stopped just outside the door leading to the prison proper. He made a movement as if to shake my hand but he stopped himself at the last moment.

'I shall not see you again,' he said, looking rather sad. 'This is our last meeting. I enjoyed it, I hope you did, too. Don't worry, Yurie, you will survive. You have hope and faith, something I do not have, at least I didn't have. Don't worry, you will survive.'

I did.

In a day or two I was transferred to another cell, and a day or two after that I was called out again, this time to sign the 'two-hundredth'. According to Article 204, a prisoner had to examine his statements and depositions before the trial could begin. The whole thing was just a waste of time as one could not alter any statements, or question any of the depositions. In my case, the NKVD examiner flashed a number of sheets of paper in front of my face, then asked me to sign a form to the effect that I had been shown the relevant papers. Since I could not really deny the fact, I signed.

I was still wondering what form the trial would take, when I was called out with my belongings some two weeks later. I was taken to the office of the prison Governor, who was sitting behind the desk as I entered. Behind him, hanging on the wall, was a big, kitchen-type circular clock. The guard left the office, the Governor looked at me, then picked up a piece of paper.

'*Kak vasha familiya*?'

I told him, still pondering what it was all about.

'You have been sentenced to seven years in the labour camp. Because of your youth, the sentence will be reduced to three years, but only if your behaviour is exemplary and you work hard to purge yourself from guilt. Until you come of age, you will serve the sentence in a Children's Working Colony.'

The day was 28 August 1940, precisely 3 p.m. Moscow time by the clock in the Governor's office. The sentence produced no emotion in me, but I had a very strong feeling that I would not serve anything like this term.

'Sign!' demanded the Governor.

I refused, so he signed it. Was there any difference? Who could ever tell that it was the Governor and not I who signed the form?

He told me that I had no right of appeal. The least I could do was to show my contempt by not signing.

In a few days' time I was called out, with things. I was loaded, with others, on to a prison van, which was so packed that the soldiers had to press hard against the door to shut it. I was lucky to have been first in the compartment, so I stood on the seat with my mouth towards the open slot which acted as a window, while the rest were packed behind me. Quite a number of men almost suffocated, and had to be revived on arrival at the station. We were loaded on the *stolypinki* and the next day, 3 September, we arrived in Kiev, the capital of the Ukraine.

The morning was beautiful, and I had a good look at the town from an open lorry. The streets were wide, with trees growing from the verges, intermingled with street pylons. There were also fairly wide pavements. After some twenty, most enjoyable minutes, we arrived at the jail. It was an enormous one, with no visible *yezhovki*. I learned later that it contained over 15,000 inmates, 5.8 per cent from Kiev. It was one of the two jails in town, the other, or inner prison, housing some 3,000 persons of unknown origin.

I sat down next to a man with a long, almost white beard, and a good head of hair of the same colour. His was a pathetic story. He was an odd-job man, and from the days of his youth he dreamt of owning a fur coat, the kind that had the fur on the inside, and reached almost to his ankles. He started saving hard, often at the expense of food, and at the age of seventy-two he had saved enough, and bought one. He was arrested the same day, and charged with speculation. The prosecution case was that on his wages, it was impossible to have saved enough, consequently the only other way possible to obtain the money was by speculation. He collected two years, and his coat was confiscated. He nearly broke down while telling me the story; there was nothing I could do, but sympathize.

One of the windows was facing the women's block, about twenty yards away. One afternoon a young thief climbed on to the window sill and shouted: 'Natasha! Natasha!'

In a minute or so, a young girl appeared on her window sill, lifted her skirt, and they both started masturbating in full view of everybody. After some twenty minutes of the long-distance love-making, the youngster in my cell shouted: 'Natasha, buzz off! I don't need you any more!'

Three days after my arrival, I was called out, with things. I was taken down to the basement, to a cell similar to the one in Chernigov, where I lost my watch. It was just as dark, but this time I was ready. As soon as the door closed behind me I braced for the attack, which came soon enough. I swore in the best tradition, kicking and punching in all directions. I did not lose a thing.

At about 8 p.m., the guards handed us five kilos of bread each, about eleven pounds. The more knowledgeable surmised that we should be on the train for five days. I had never had so much bread in one lot before. As I was starving, I thought I would just have a bit of it, leaving the rest for the journey. That, of course, was easier said than done, and by the time we were taken out very early the next morning, I had nibbled the lot.

As it turned out, I made on the deal. We were attached to a fast train, arriving at our destination about 10 a.m. We were loaded on a lorry, arriving soon after outside a wooden gate. Above the gate, in a semicircle, there was an inscription; *Detskaya Trud-Koloniya*.

I arrived at the Children's Working Colony in Zhitomir, not far from Kiev, on 6 September 1940 – a year, all but a day, after leaving home.

7

The gate opened, our heads were counted, and we passed through. We were divided into small groups by name, and met by a small man in civilian clothes with sharp features and piercing eyes. He was about thirty, with slightly greying hair. He was our tutor and he seemed to know all about me.

'You are a Pole, aren't you?' he asked politely as we were walking away from the gate. 'We have a number of your compatriots here, so you will not feel lonely. In fact you will be accommodated in the same block. I am sure you will like it here, provided you work hard and behave yourself. There is no room for slackers.'

In a few minutes we came to the dormitory, and climbed the stairs to the second floor. The room was big, containing some twenty beds. Beds! Not only that, but sheets and blankets as well! Each bed had a small cupboard by its side, with two shelves, the floor was cleanly swept, the windows large with no *yezhovki*. As far as I was concerned, it was palatial.

'This is your bed,' he told me, pointing at an empty cupboard, 'you can put your things there with safety, nothing is ever lost here, but keep it neat and tidy.'

That might have been his opinion, but I had been with the jackals before, so I took the last remark with a big pinch of salt. I was right too. Unless what was left in the cupboard had no value whatsoever, it would disappear before you could say 'Stalin'.

In a few minutes a young lad entered the room.

'Citizen Tutor,' he reported, 'I have inspected the block, and everything is in order.'

He was a trusty, or what was commonly called a *sooka* (bitch). They were the real kings of the manor. On arrival, a number of boys would try to show that they had finished with crime and would endeavour to become honest citizens. At least that was the theory. The fact was that only an infinitesimal proportion of the trusties would go straight on release. They in fact had nowhere to go straight to, as I was to discover when I met some of them after leaving the colony.

The main reason for becoming a trusty was to settle some old scores from prison days by obtaining a little power and authority over the others. Another reason was that they did not have to work such long hours as the rest of us. They had the responsibility of looking after the rooms which meant that they could spend a lot of time looking busy while doing nothing. They also got a little more food as the chaps in the kitchen doling out the grub wanted to keep their favours. Needless to say, every trusty was also a stool-pigeon.

'Thank you,' said the tutor to the trusty. 'Meet the new arrival, a Polish mister, Yurie Stanislavovich.'

'Hallo!' said the trusty. 'You will like it here. It's a great honour to work for the benefit of our Communist Fatherland.' He turned smartly and departed.

'For the next two days,' continued the tutor, 'take a good look round the colony, then tell me in which workshop you would like to work. I shall try to arrange that you are accepted in the one of your choice.'

'Thank you very much,' I replied.

'You must always address me as Citizen Tutor,' he reprimanded me. 'By the way, in the Soviet Union he who doesn't work, doesn't eat, but you are new here, so take those.' He gave me a few coupons, each one entitling me to a meal.

The Children's Working Colony was situated in the shadows of the red-bricked Zhitomir prison. It contained an area of some three-quarters of a square mile. One side of the rectangle bordered the jail, the other three being guarded by a wooden fence about ten feet high, with barbed wire on top. About a yard from the fence there was another barricade, and dogs ran between the two at night, chained to a length of wire. Next there was a belt of fine sand, presumably to indicate to the patrolling guards when somebody tried to make an escape. Finally another barrier, made of barbed wire, but only about four feet high. The whole thing was overlooked by guards, placed at intervals in small huts on top of the wall. At night the wall belt was illuminated by powerful lamps.

The entrance had a gate for vehicles and a separate doorway for the pedestrians, who could go in and out of the colony by showing a pass. All the two-storey buildings were either offices or dormitories, while the sheds were workshops. The first workshop I came to was an electro-mechanical shop with its name above the door and a big notice saying 'Keep Out'. It was operated by professional men doing short time for their misdemeanours, and I put it down as the one I would like to work in. Then I wandered along past the offices and kitchen, smelling a delicious aroma on the way. At the gate I turned left, along the wall, to a long shed, where some boys were cutting tree-trunks into planks. In the next shed the planks were trimmed and cut to size. Two boys standing by a big, circular saw rotating at high speed were singing while they worked. It was a popular song called *'Brodyaga'* (The Tramp), a song with a sad melody and the words, ironically, telling their own story.

> Oh tell me, tell me, *brodyaga*,
> Who had borne you, where are you from?
> I do not know that, oh I do not know that . . .

As it turned out, they lived in my block and I got to know them well. As the song said, they did not know who their parents were, where they were born, or when. They thought that one of them was thirteen and the other fifteen, but they were not sure. They were not even certain whether they were brothers or not, but they had been together for as long as they could remember. They had the same name and patronymic but they did not remember why, or who gave it to them. A few years back they were in a colony for the homeless, but discipline was so harsh – much more strict than in *Trud-Koloniya* – that they ran away.

They continually asked me to talk about my home life, which they had never had, how we played, learned and were punished when we were naughty. I shall never forget the remark the younger of the two made one evening:'Yurie, I wish I were you just for a year; wouldn't it be nice, eh? And I would never be naughty.'

I only wished that the architect of their misery could have heard that remark. The architect, one Vladimir Ilyich Ulyanov, who like a coward hid behind the pseudonym Lenin, so that in years to come, when history would be ready to pass judgement on his more eccentric follies, his family would not be the one to suffer. Because of him, those boys and girls had never known their family.

A siren interrupted their singing. The elder of the two switched the motor off and the sharp teeth of the saw slowly came to a halt. All the boys were lined up by their trusty and marched off for lunch, with me in hot pursuit. The dining room contained eight tables with two benches to each. When my turn came at the serving-window, I gave the man the coupon, receiving in return a bowl of *shchii* and a plate of *kasha*, a kind of porridge. The soup was of a much better quality than in prison, with lots of chopped cabbage and bits of fish. The rest of the hour allocated for lunch was spent either sitting outside the kitchen, or ambling back to the workshops. This was not really permitted as the journey to and from work had to be done in brigades. We were not allowed to enter our dormitories either, but this was done occasionally by carefully observing the movements of the trusty. If it rained, or it was winter, the brigades would return to their workshops immediately after lunch and sit inside.

I did not really want to sit and stare, I had been doing enough of that for the past eleven months, so I continued my walk round the colony. It was not long before I was stopped by a trusty who told me that he would report me to the authorities for breaking the rules. He was really obnoxious about it all.

'You can report me if you wish,' I told him in a slow, matter-of-fact voice, 'the fellow who told me to go and look around happened to be the tutor, so if you still don't like my walking about the colony, you had better find him and tell him that you don't agree with his wishes. I am certain he would be delighted to hear it, unless you prefer to go quietly away, like a good little trusty.'

There was little he could do, so he swore filthily.

I enjoyed my new freedom of movement, darting occasionally in all directions, just to prove to myself that I didn't have to ask for permission first. I slowly made my way to the next shed. Here the wooden planks were planed on machines, cut to finer limits, then stored to dry. In the following workshop they were made into crude furniture: beds, tables or sideboards. I didn't cherish the idea of working in any of the sheds I visited, as the atmosphere was full of dust and floating debris. All the boys were covered with it.

I had a pleasant surprise in the next shop. It was full of girls and women, who painted some of the furniture produced in the last workshop. I was politely told that I had no business there, so I departed. In fact, about half of them were free, and they went home each evening. The other half were accommodated in a barricaded compound, and we had very little to do with them, as the workshop was severely out of bounds.

The next shop had a painted notice above the door: 'Experimental Workshop'. I entered, not really knowing what to expect, or whether I was even allowed there.

Immediately past the entrance there was a small room with two benches, one on each side of the door. There was nobody in it. Hesitating for a moment, I carried on through a thin door into a large workshop full of furniture.

'What brings you here?' asked a thickset tallish man wearing a light brown working coat.

'I am a new boy in the colony, I've been told to look around.'

'Normally, you should get permission from the manager, but he is away. See his deputy, she might give you it,' he replied, pointing to the glass office on the far side of the room.

The furniture was of quite a good quality, some of it french polished, some still raw. On the left of the passage two men and two women were polishing, while on the right, a man and a boy were upholstering. They looked at me inquisitively. When I reached the office door, I knocked.

'Come in!' She was a short, rather stout woman of about thirty, with blonde hair and clear, honest, green eyes.

I told her my story.

'You are not Russian, are you?' she inquired, blushing slightly.

'No, Citizen Deputy, I am a Pole.'

'I speak Polish too,' she continued in Polish, 'yes, you may look around. There are three other Polish boys here, I shall introduce them to you; what is your name?'

'Yurie Stanislavovich.'

Her Polish was excellent, just a faint trace of accent. She walked ahead of me, swaying like a duck. We came to a tall fellow of about twenty, with short hair.

'Here is one of your contemporaries, Yurie Stanislavovich,' she told him in Russian, 'show him round, and introduce him to the others.'

The fellow put down a muslin-covered sponge with which he was polishing, and introduced himself.

'I am Edek, welcome to Zhitomir, what are you in for?'

'I am *bezhenyets*, what are you in for?'

'It's a long story,' he answered, picking up his sponge again. 'The snag with this job is that once you start, you must carry on, otherwise it takes twice as long. If I were you, I'd try and get into this workshop. We work with free people, so we do a ten-hour stint, while the rest do twelve. The work is not too hard, and most of the men are of Polish extraction. There is only one snag, can you french polish?'

'Well, I used to go and watch a carpenter in the village, and he did some of it; I never tried, but I think I could do it.'

'You see,' continued Edek, 'before you are accepted, the manager will give you a test. He is a Russian, but he is a very good fellow. If he thinks you will do, you are in, but if he says no, you have no hope in hell.'

'Well, Edek, in that case you had better start giving me the clues right away. I am all ears and eyes.'

'Hang on a second,' replied Edek, looking at the round clock above the opening to the second half of the workshop, past the office. 'I'll just give it a few more rubs and that will do for now. At three o'clock there will be smoking time, after which I'll start on a new piece and explain as we go along.'

Smoking time was a ten-minute break; two in the morning and two in the afternoon. Those who smoked could do so only during that period, regardless of whether they were heavy smokers or not, prisoners or free men. The break was ten minutes and ten minutes only, never a second more.

At three o'clock the men started converging towards the small room with two benches at the entrance to the shop. One of the first was a black-haired man of about thirty-five, wearing a work coat.

'Hey, Yitsek!' called Edek, 'don't run so fast, meet the new arrival from Poland.'

'Hello! What's your name?' he greeted me heartily, speaking Polish with a Jewish accent.

He was in fact a Jew from Poland. After my arrest, the Russians advertised the great opportunities awaiting those who would emigrate to work in the Soviet Union. Yitsek, a carpenter by trade, took the bait, emigrated, then applied to join the Communist Party since he leaned in that direction when in Poland. He received the Party card after some time, but in the meantime began to see daylight. When he got to know me a little better, he said to me quietly one day, 'You know, Yurie, I am looking forward to the day when once again I shall walk along the streets of Lvov in the evening, while the university students run alongside me shouting: "Let's fight the Jews!" '

In Poland, as in any other country in the world, there was a section of students who were of the opinion that they alone possessed sufficient intelligence to sort out all of the nation's problems. They decided that the only way to deal with the increasing population of Jews in Poland was to wage war against them. They would run along the streets of towns shouting, often smashing the windows of Jewish shops. Occasionally, they would molest people out walking, and sometimes, even beat up a chap or two. Idiotic, but true.

Poor Yitsek, sometimes he tried to convince himself, rather than anybody else, that what he had done was right, but he never really succeeded. I was genuinely sorry for him.

'Jakub, meet the new arrival,' called out Edek to a boy of about my stature who still wore Polish clothes. Before either of us could say a word, a third boy-prisoner entered the room. His name was Abbe, and he, too, wore ordinary clothes. I did not like his eyes, they looked treacherous to me. Jakub and Abbe were also Polish Jews. Their stories were identical, although they occurred in two entirely different places.

Like Yitsek, the parents of these two boys, together with other families, emigrated to the Soviet Union in search of the Promised Land. Many of them were Jewish, although some were Ukrainians. It was not long before most of them discovered the facts of life and applied for repatriation. The Soviet Union, however, is no ordinary country. In simple terms it can best be described as a gigantic prison with thousands of prisons inside it. No one ever leaves a prison simply by applying for a release, and that statement is also valid in the case of the USSR.

Thus, those who could stand the country no longer tried to

return to Poland without permission. They were picked up on the frontier between the Ukraine and the old Eastern Poland, charged under Article 16/80, and sent to jail. When the westerly traffic reached high numbers, the Communist Party responded, as always, with an instant solution to the problem. They announced on the radio and in the press that any family desirous of a return to Poland should report on a certain date with their belongings to a given railway station, where a train would be waiting to take them back.

Jakub's and Abbe's families, together with some 800 others, took this opportunity and reported to their respective stations. In due course the passenger train arrived and they went aboard: the train left and their spirits rose. In a few hours they hoped to be back home. But it was not to be: they did not travel for even half an hour. The train went only as far as the nearest siding, was surrounded by NKVD troops, and they were then off-loaded. They were told to board waiting lorries, taken to local prisons, charged under Article 16/80 with an attempted illegal exit from the Soviet Union and given the standard three years' sentence. That was how I met Jakub and Abbe!

More workers entered the smoking room, some of them on their way through to stand in the sunshine. Some did not bother to come in, but merely sat on their benches. At precisely ten past the hour they were all at work again.

Edek picked up a piece of furniture, placed it on his stand, so that one face leaned at an angle to the vertical, and began polishing, pointing out as he did so the essential movements, and stressing the more important tricks of the trade. It all sounded very simple: a touch of that, ease of this. On the other side of the passage, Abbe was making springs, while Jakub and another man, who was wearing a workcoat, were upholstering.

'Why don't you wear a coat?' I asked Edek.

'They are only worn by the free men, the only exception being the storeman who always wears one until he is pulled up by the tutor.'

'Is he a prisoner, then?'

'Oh, yes. He is doing two years for talking while drunk.'

'What the hell do you mean, Edek?'

'Well, one night he went for a drink and got plastered. When he woke up the following morning, he was in jail. When he complained, he was told that he ought to know the reason, and that in due course he would know the answer. It turned out that while he was drunk, he was overheard by an NKVD agent telling another fellow how he hated Stalin. He was arrested on the spot as an enemy of the people.'

'Would you believe it!' I exclaimed.

'Well,' snapped Edek, 'look in the store-room, he is there, all right, and if you don't believe me, ask him.'

One day I did; Edek was quite right.

'If those sods think,' the storeman told me, 'that by parking me here for two years they will stop me from hating *Oosatyi*, they have it all wrong.'

Oosatyi means moustachioed. There were about five people in the hierarchy of the Soviet Union with prominent moustaches, but the adjective was only used to describe one of them: King Communism himself. It was either used when someone wanted to say something derogatory about the despot, or mention him without attracting too much attention. The reason for the latter was, that on hearing the word 'Stalin', many ears would be cocked to hear what was being said, and amongst the ordinary people there were some planted there as spies.

At one stage during the polishing operation Edek handed me the muslin pad and asked me to have a try. I plucked up courage and lowered the sponge on to the wood. The drag on the pad was greater than I had anticipated, but the bloom left by the pad made it easy for me to see which part of the surface I had just been over. It transpired during conversation that the free men worked six days a week, while we worked seven, except the first Sunday of the month, 1 May and 7 November.

I decided to leave the workshop and look at the rest of the colony. I bid Edek goodbye, waved to Yitsek and the rest and left. The next workshop was a paint shop, and it smelt so strongly of acid, that I did not stay there long.

I went round the administrative blocks without entering, just in case some official took an interest in me, then walked along the far wall, keeping well away from it. At one stage, quite unintentionally, I strayed to within ten yards of it.

'Where are you going?' bellowed a guard from his box, pointing his rifle straight at me.

'I am new here, Citizen Guard,' I pleaded. 'I have been told to look around.'

'You go and look around somewhere else, not around the walls. Next time you will not have time to answer!'

One thing was clear, it was not going to be easy to escape from the colony. I retreated towards the dormitories while the guard kept me covered.

Nearing the side of the colony bordering the prison – the sight of it sent shivers down my spine – wooden *yezhovkie* looked at me from a great height. There was no sound coming from that quarter, unlike the others facing the open country.

I sauntered past a huge heap of slack, and a mound of sawdust. A stocky man and a slight woman were mixing the coal and the dust, adding some water to it. I stopped and watched; when they had mixed enough, they loaded it on to a wheelbarrow, the woman picked up the handles and wheeled it into the power house while the man watched. It did not seem right to me, so I spoke to him. He turned out to be one of the other Poles in the colony. He was about twenty and *bezhenyets*. He was picked up on his way to Romania a few days after the Red Army had 'liberated' Poland. He spent only two months in jail, was given three years, and now was working as a stoker.

'Isn't it a little ungentlemanly of you,' I asked, 'letting the girl do all the work?'

'Ungentlemanly, be damned!' he replied. 'Haven't you heard of the equality of sexes in the Soviet Union? She works here as a stoker, so she pushes one barrow, and I do the next. Besides, she gets paid for it and I don't; it's as simple as that.'

'Is she free, then?'

'Oh, yes. If she didn't like the job, she shouldn't have taken it.'

Of course, she might have had no choice; any job was better than no job at all. There was no social security in the Soviet Union, just the paragraph in the Constitution stating that he who doesn't work doesn't eat. She certainly was not built for that type of work. Those two were having a gentle affair. It was a little difficult, as there were others working in the power house, but they managed. She used to bring him goodies from time to time, perhaps to keep his spirits up!

A siren sounded signalling it was 6 p.m. Soon the men and women trickled out of their shops, converging on the gate. I came closer, just to be a little nearer to freedom, and had a nasty surprise. I expected them to laugh and joke as the workers in Poland did on their way home after work. It was not like that here. They filed past me singly or in pairs, looking like ghosts, particularly when they went through the gate, showing their passes. Out of some forty workers I saw, only one had a bicycle. That bicycle turned out to be the only one I would ever see in the Soviet Union.

I turned round and wandered back towards the dormitory. On the way I met the three boys from the Experimental Workshop. Having finished work for the day, they were permitted to return to their block before going for supper at seven. The evening meal usually consisted of a plate of *kasha* and a handful of tiny fish, the biggest no longer than two inches. The fish were salted and preserved in their own juices and eaten straight from the barrel – head, tail and the insides. On the whole the colony food was not bad, but only in comparison to prison rations.

At 9 p.m. the trusty lined us up in the free space between the two rows of beds, and we were counted by the tutor. This was also the time for him to pass his comments on the cleanliness of the block, discipline, or anything else that entered his head. Very often he would not turn up, and that was the time for the trusty to shine.

The room was lit by six very low wattage bulbs dangling from the ceiling. The light was not sufficient to read by. There was a small library in the colony, the usual propaganda books, but those could only be read in the common room, situated in one of the administrative blocks. That was the loneliest room in the colony, empty, except for the presence of a number of trusties.

One part of that room was taken by the Little Red Corner. Here, under the watchful eyes of Marx, Engels, Lenin and Stalin staring from the wall, the tutor and the trusties gathered round every Thursday evening for 'discussion'. I attended twice.

Where I came from, discussion meant a debate, or an examination by argument. So, when the speaker said something particularly stupid I tried to intervene, and correct his error. I was told to shut up and wait till he finished. When I tried to state my case then, I was told that the next speaker was ready with his lecture, and his train of thought would be disrupted if I were allowed to say what I wanted.

When his train of thought ran out of steam, again I put my hand up, only to be told that the lights out bell would toll in a minute, and we all had to go. Undaunted, I went again, but having listened to a lot of garbage, and not being allowed to pass any comment on the subject, I decided not to waste any more of my time.

That 'discussion' reminded me of a lyric poem we had in Poland. It describes what happened perfectly:

> A miracle happened one day,
> A faithful spoke to the Holy picture.
> The picture said nothing to him,
> Such was their conversation.

Before going to bed, I picked up my issue towel, a coarse piece of material the size of a large handkerchief, and had a good scrub in the ablutions room. There was no soap but the water was warm. What a pity I could not put on a nice, clean pair of pyjamas, but that would have been too bourgeois. I had no option but to revert to my cotton shirt and trousers. It was only then I realized how much they stank. I toyed with the idea of leaving them off for the night, but decided it would be too cold. Besides, it was prudent to have them on. I put my shoes under the pillow for safe keeping. At 10 p.m. the lights were turned off in the corridors, though not in the rooms, and the outside doors to the block were locked.

The sheets felt good and smelt clean. They were made of a kind of hemp, and were much coarser than they looked. I slept well.

I was woken next morning by a metallic sound. It was a guard hammering on a length of rail hanging outside the main door; the time was 5.30. I had a quick wash, made my bed up and swept the bedspace clean. By that time it was 6 a.m., and the first siren sounded, followed by other sirens and hooters in different factories in town. In Zhitomir, this first siren instructed 'the driven and hungry workers to rise', in accordance with the words of the International, in their united effort to get ready for work in time. The next ones were sounded at 7 a.m., then 7.30 and 7.45, ending with a very long blast at 8 a.m. The Communist bosses made sure that no one would have an excuse for being late for work. By 6 a.m. the bread was brought in by two duty boys and shared out. The ration was 800 grams of fairly good bread, together with a mug of something which resembled cocoa.

At about 7.15, we were lined up outside the blocks by the ever keen trusty to be counted by the guards. On the sound of the 7.30 siren we were off to work. It might seem silly to leave at such an early hour, in view of the fact that the furthest shed could be comfortably reached in ten minutes. However, in the USSR the work discipline was total. One could be early for work any day, but never, never, late! Anyone late for work was severely dealt with. This not only applied to us prisoners, but also to the free people.

I decided this first morning to get some more polishing practice, so I joined the Polish lads from the Experimental Workshop. When we reached the door, most of the free workers were already there, some of them spending the last few minutes outside the building. I had another practice in the afternoon, and was told by the Deputy to come for the test in the morning. The manager was a tall, well-built Russian of about forty-five. He had been educated in Berlin and spoke German well. I was called into the office. He asked me a few questions, such as what I did before the war, who my parents were, etc., then we went for a test.

'Do you speak German?' he suddenly asked me in German while I was preparing a piece of furniture.

'A little,' I replied in German, telling him about Max.

'Good,' he said. 'I shall have a chance to practise.'

Clearly, he had already made his mind up about me and that eased my tension. I picked up a sheet of glass paper in preparation for a rub down, but he stopped me and asked me to tell him what I was going to do. I related all I could remember. He then took me to the stand where Edek was polishing and asked me to do some. Very professionally I tapped it on my other hand, then went round and round as though I had been doing it all my life.

'You have another hand, Yitsek Shymonovich,' he said, turning his head towards Yitsek.

'Good,' he replied. 'I'll use him gladly, especially in view of the new project with which we are to complete the Five Year Plan.'

I started work under the watchful eye of Edek, who came to my rescue each time I messed things up. In the first week I messed them up more often than not. I learned the hard way the reason for going round in circles and figures of eight when polishing. I learned the hard way not to put my dirty, cellulose-stained paws on the newly polished piece of wood when changing ends. Above all, I learned that the only way to acquire a new skill is by hard slog, perseverance, and a little courage. There is no other way, regardless of what some of the more extreme of the revolutionaries might have preached.

There were two girls working as french polishers, and both were free. Natasha, a blue-eyed, slightly plump blonde was shy, naïve, twenty-one and pure. She blushed more often than not. Sonia, a dark-haired, petite Jewess, was the opposite. She had already been married and divorced three times, and she was not yet twenty-four. Fortunately, there were no children. She and Yitsek were the singers of the workshop. Often she would sing the popular songs with doctored words. Yitsek, however, being in charge of the polishing staff and therefore responsible for their behaviour, would try and drown her singing with his own version of '*Bei mir bist du schön*', then very popular, especially among Polish Jews. It was really comical to watch those two performing. Sonia knew that Yitsek was worried stiff in case someone unwelcome should overhear the words. The louder he sang, the louder Sonia would sing, laughing her head off. This might not sound funny to an ordinary mortal, but to us who had not laughed for months, in a country where few people laughed, it was hilarious.

It took about two months before I was completely accepted by the majority of the free workers. Very often I was a little late for the smoking time as I still had problems with timing the polishing. Being still an unknown quantity, I was conscious of the fact that the free men would often change the subject every time I appeared in the smoking room. I could not very well tell them that I was not a planted man, because that would only make things more difficult. I just had to sit it out in silence until they had made their minds up. It finally happened one morning.

As I entered the room, there was a momentary silence. Pavel, one of the free men working in the other half of the shop, came up with the verdict.

'Carry on, Vanka,' he declared. 'Yurie is as safe as a Soviet bank!'

I did not need any explanation. I wanted to thank them for trusting me, but decided it would only complicate things.

'What is this about the Soviet bank?' I asked him.

'Well, it's like this,' explained Pavel. 'In the Soviet Union it is easy to put the money in the bank but, brother, you try and take it out, it's almost impossible, hence the saying.'

The men were talking about the coming visit of the trade-union leader. They did not look forward to his meetings as they always ended up worse off than before. The discussion was about what they were going to lose this time: money, or time in the form of an increase in working hours. I decided to hide in the shop to witness the procedures. On the day I took a quick lunch and returned to the workshop unobserved. I quietly opened the door, hoping that as usual the workers would have their lunch in the other half of the shop. My luck held. I concealed myself amongst the furniture as close as I dared to the probable meeting place, so that not only would I be able to hear, but I would also see the meeting.

'Well, Comrades,' advised Kolia, the man who did the upholstering, and also operated a very modern woodworking machine. 'Anyone who wants a cigarette had better go and have one now. Comrade trade unionist will be here in ten minutes.'

Kolia was a kind of shop steward, Soviet style, whose responsibility consisted of clearing the space for the meeting and getting the men in position on time. He was the man who owned the only bicycle. He was not really disliked by the others, but was not really trusted either. He was about thirty, married, and I believe a Party member. Some of the men went to the smoking room, returning fairly quickly. As far as I could make out, they all sat in a circle, around a bench which acted as a table. On the dot, Comrade trade unionist arrived at the scene, having been met by Kolia at the door. He was about forty, tall, and was wearing army uniform. Judging by his hat, he was an officer.

My heart started throbbing hard and fast, since I had expected to see a civilian. It was one thing to listen uninvited to a gathering headed by a civilian, but it was entirely another when the head was wearing an army hat. For a moment, I wished that I had not thought about the idea at all. I was petrified. The reason for wearing the uniform, as given to me afterwards, was that the 'leader' was undergoing a voluntary army training in his spare time and came to the meeting on his way either to or from that training. However, I saw it as a purely psychological move. No one ever questioned a man wearing an army uniform in the Soviet Union; the NKVD wore that uniform too!

'Comrades!' began the trade unionist. 'I bring you the heartiest greetings from the Zhitomir cell of the woodworkers union of the Ukrainian Soviet Socialist Republic.'

He paused, while the workers clapped their hands with bored faces. Bored and apprehensive. Bored, because they had heard it all before, and apprehensive because they did not know in what way they were going to suffer. They clapped, because they were expected to, not for any other reason. Comrade trade unionist obviously did not intend to let them off the hook as easily as that. In flowery phrases, he told them how the working class of the Soviet Union, under the guidance of the never-tiring Central Committee of the Communist Party of the Soviet Union, ably led by their Great Leader, ever watchful in his pursuance of the policies of Marxism-Leninism, the Ray of Hope of all the workers of the world, the irreplaceable Yosip Vissarionovich Stalin, was winning its historic struggle against the capitalist and bourgeois degenerates, in accordance with the principles laid down by the immortal Lenin.

He paused, clearly out of breath, while the listeners clapped their hands. Then the crunch came. Starting yet again with the same sort of hyperbole, he told the assembly that the Central Committee of the Trade Unions had decided to ask the members to work an extra half an hour a day, without pay, to help that struggle. Then, in accordance with the 'democratic' eye-wash of the whole set-up, he asked: 'Comrades, is there anybody against the proposals of the Central Committee?'

The comrades knew better than to disagree.

'Thank you, Comrades,' said the trade unionist. 'I shall report your unanimous support of the proposals to the Central Committee.'

Having finished, he left the shop, escorted to the door by Kolia. The door to the smoking room had barely closed behind him when Sonia broke into her song: 'Stalin breathes over your head . . .'

'*Bei mir bist du schön* . . .' accompanied relentless Yitsek.

It was all rather pathetic, and it had lasted no more than ten minutes. No discussion, no arguments, and all in their spare time. Just a simple statement of fact. Well, perhaps not simple: he did wrap it up in the official propaganda jargon. I stayed hidden until the other boy-prisoners arrived. When work started, we were the only people who talked. The rest, the so-called free men of the Paradise of the Working Class, were deep in their thoughts.

At the first break, the men were talking about the new hours.

'Just think about it,' related Vanka, who had only been released from the Red Army a few months before, 'when we first started to work under the new bosses, we only worked four hours a day. At the sound of the siren we were obliged to drop everything, the cleaners moved in to put our tools away, and clean the mess we left behind. A few months later the hours were increased to six a day; then the cleaners were dropped; then the hours were increased to seven, then eight, then nine; now it's nine and a half. It won't be long before we have another meeting, and it will be ten hours a day!'

The extra half-hour which the workers had 'unanimously supported' was added that afternoon. We had to work extra too.

The whole *modus operandi* of the Soviet worker was entirely different from the one experienced in Poland. At the sound of the siren for 7.45 a.m. the workers would enter the shop, remove their coats, take their tools out and put them on the bench, and as the hooter sounded for 8 a.m., they would pick them up and start working. In the evening they would work until the hooter sounded for the end of work, then in their own time they would put the tools away and clean up. A worker was usually excused were he only a minute or two late. If he were five or more minutes late, he was automatically sentenced to three months in jail, unless he agreed to work on Sunday or lose one day's holiday.

The workers in the USSR had fourteen days' holiday a year. And a worker whose factory did not work on Sunday could only afford to be late fourteen times a year. In a country with no private transport of any significance, and no public transport except in big towns, it was not difficult to be late, especially in winter when a heavy fall of snow, two or three feet deep with drifts reaching ten feet or more, would make the going difficult. If the trams did not run because of heavy snowfall that was no concern of the management. With spies operating in all spheres of Soviet life, the manager would have to be very courageous not to report latecomers.

If the worker were ever late a second time after having done the three months, he was sentenced to a further six months in prison. On the third occasion, the automatic charge was the good old Article 58/14, anti-revolutionary sabotage, the standard dose for this being eight years.

In Zhitomir, the workers who were late took the rest of the day off and worked on Sunday instead. Most of them, just to show willingness and display penitence, worked for an hour or two before going home. Needless to say, they were not paid for those hours. In wintertime, out of some fifteen workers in my shop, three or four people worked on a Sunday. One morning, a worker came in ten minutes late, his inner clothing sodden with sweat. Seeing the snow falling heavily, he had decided to start at 5.30 a.m. to be at work on time. He lived two and a half miles away, and he did not make it. The prison manager was most apologetic but there was little he could do. He had to report him, or he would no longer be in charge. He was a good man, and a good boss, but the discipline was absolute. He had to do what he was told, like everybody else.

One morning as it started to get light, a trusty brought a message that all prisoners were to report near the main gate for clearing snow in the town. Without showing any emotion, I decided to try and escape if at all possible. By then I had been issued with a *fufayka,* a short coat filled with kapok, so at least I had some chance of survival if I did not stop too often. At the gate we were issued with big, wooden spades and were formed in groups of a dozen or so. Suddenly the tutor called me out of the ranks.

'You will have to stay behind,' he told me with a sickly smile.

Oh, well . . . I dawdled back to the workshop, a little down-hearted perhaps, but not unduly worried.

'What are you doing here?' asked Pavel, when I entered the smoking room.

'Citizen Tutor decided that I am much too valuable a french polisher to risk getting frozen, so he insisted that I stay behind.'

Kolia was doing some maintenance work on the special machine which only he could operate. To change some component he had to remove a plaque bolted to the body which was in the way. When he finally managed it, we discovered that it was there to hide the words 'Made in Sweden'!

Another morning when we reported for work I was told to help Jakub make springs, not a difficult job. The other polishers were sanding down big oak frames.

'What's going on?' I asked during the break.

'*Katsapskyi Reznik* requires a new bed, so we are making one for him.'

'Who the hell is *Katsapskyi Reznik*?' I inquired.

'They call him Khrushchiv, Nikita Sergeevich Khrushchiv, he's First Secretary of the Central Committee of the Ukrainian Communist Party. But,' continued the ex-Red Army man, 'his name is Khrushchov, and he is a *Katsap* [derogatory name given to a Russian by a Ukrainian]. When he first came to the Ukraine to do the dirty work of his boss, Kaganovich, his name was given as Khrushchiv, to make us think that it was one of us who did the filthy work. He did it well, too. Hundreds of thousands of Ukrainians have not been heard of since. So it doesn't matter whether he ends his name with "iv" or "ov", because we call him *Katsapskyi Reznik* [butcher]. He went back to Moscow to wash the blood off his hands, but he is back with us, this time as a tsar.'

Khrushchov's bed was enormous. The standard beds that we were making for ordinary mortals contained three rows of nine springs; his bed had seven rows of eleven springs. It was big enough for me to lie across it, with plenty to spare. Yes, everyone was equal in the Soviet Union, except that some were 'more equal than others'. I helped Jakub to sew the springs to the webbing, to speed up the process. Then we helped Kolia to put the hessian on top and nail it to the sides. A layer of kapok was packed above that, then cloth, and the top was finished with a specially supplied material. We all tried it for comfort; I must say, it was rather nice.

The grand bed was taken away, and we commenced the work on the final project with which we were to complete the Five Year Plan of our workshop. It was a massive, fifteen-metre-long table shaped like a letter U, the top made of black and white walnut squares. The five of us, Yitsek, Sonia, Natasha, Edek and I spent days sanding it down, then we started polishing it.

The table was for a conference room in the Kremlin, and had to be finished on time. We worked seven days a week, including the Christmas Day, which in that Godless state is just another day, but it was hard going. I found a big nail and scratched my name, and date on the bend of the 'U'. I hope it is still there.

On 31 December 1940 the table was still not completed, so we worked throughout the night until we finished it at 5 a.m. The only breaks we had were for lunch, supper, and seeing the New Year in. Our task complete, the manager thanked us all in simple words, words that came from his heart. He went to the guard's kitchen and brought us some delicious barley soup, half a bucket of it, thick and good-tasting. That was the last time I ever saw the manager. He was due for some holiday, but when he did not return I inquired as to his whereabouts. The reply I received was as follows: 'We in the Soviet Union,' explained one of the free workers, 'are very stupid people. We have an uncanny habit of falling under the trams, or off them. If there isn't a tram in our town, we go to one which has them. The manager went to Kiev for his holiday, fell off the tram and was run over by a car. Yes, we are very stupid.'

Poor fellow! He was a good man and an excellent boss. Unfortunately those qualities were not good enough for his Communist overlords. He was unsuitable because he was human, and that word did not appear in their vocabulary.

In the New Year I was transferred to the other side of the workshop, as a helper to one of the carpenters. Pavel spoke Polish very well and we used the language just as often as Russian. There was another prisoner working in the section, a man of fifty, small and frail. He had been a driver of a horse and cart before his arrest. His name was Pyetya.

In the Soviet Union each person was entitled to five square metres of space for his accommodation. If the family circumstances changed, they had to take in lodgers or move to another residence to adhere to the quota. In Pyetya's case his daughter married and left the house, while his sixteen-year-old son was going away to a school in another town. Their two-room accommodation was therefore too big for them, and so they were given the usual option of moving out or accepting two lodgers. They decided to move. By sheer chance, Pyetya's work route took him past his old and new abodes. So, coming back empty with his horse and cart, he stopped outside his old house, loaded his bed, the chest of drawers and a small bench – his only possessions – and off-loaded them outside his new room about 800 yards away. Since he did not deviate from the route, and was due for a break anyway, he saw nothing wrong with this manoeuvre. A day or two later Pyetya was arrested. His accuser and chief witness for the prosecution was his sixteen-year-old son, a member of the Komsomol, the Communist Youth Union.

'I will murder the brat when I come out,' vowed Pyetya, shaking with anger as he was telling us the story. 'He never gave me a chance, he never warned me.'

Pyetya was in fact charged with the misuse of State transport, convicted, and collected a two-year sentence. Long live the Soviet Union!

It was not, however, difficult to see why Pyetya's son behaved as he did. With the first Article of the Constitution, 'he who doesn't work doesn't eat' firmly enforced, both parents had to work while the State 'took care' of the children. It was the State that brought up the kids, not their parents. I, of course, had first-hand experience of what the upbringing was like.

Evening classes commenced in the colony for the illiterate and under-educated. The idea was that those who wanted to attend the classes were released from work an hour earlier, but had to stay in school an extra hour, making two in all. I went to see the tutor and told him that I should like to join in those classes. He was delighted at my eagerness and sent me for a short interview with the Education Authority. The woman I saw was aged about thirty, and there was something sinister about her face.

'Can you write?' she asked me.

'No, Citizen,' I replied.

'You will address me in future as Citizen Teacher! You are a good example of the capitalist exploitation of youth. In the Soviet Union you would have finished the *desyatiletka* [ten-year school] by now, like the rest of our mighty Communist family. Report to Form One tomorrow evening.'

'Yes, Citizen Teacher,' I replied. I did not think I was going to get along very well with the Citizen Teacher.

I had to report the fact to my manager. She was the Polish-speaking Deputy, promoted after the arrest of the old one.

'You, an illiterate?' she queried with raised eyebrows.

'Well,' I answered. 'Citizen Teacher did ask me whether I could read and write. Since the only writing in cyrillic I have ever done was with my index finger on the palm of my hand, I have never actually seen it.'

She wished me well in my new venture, giving me a knowing look as she spoke. The next evening I reported to the classroom, with another Polish lad, the one who worked in the power house. We were given a framed slate-board and a stone pencil each. The first lesson began; it had absolutely nothing to do with writing or learning to write, it was a 'history' lesson: a lesson about the Communist Party, how it was formed by the great Lenin, and why it was called *bolshevik* (of the majority). As far as I was concerned, Citizen Teacher was talking a lot of rubbish. Having listened to many discussions on the subject, in different cells and prisons, I had come to the conclusion that all those people could not be wrong and she right. True, when Lenin took the vote, he did get the overwhelming majority, but the circumstances were entirely different, to put it mildly.

Citizen Teacher, after about half an hour of non-stop talk, eventually ran out of steam and let us out for a break. Five minutes later we were back in the classroom again, being bombarded with yet more 'history', this time from a man. I could not help thinking that if this kind of education was for children attending the First Form, the Comrades certainly took pains with the development of young minds. Another break, and we started to learn the alphabet. The teacher wrote a large letter 'A', a small one, then one in long hand saying 'Aaaah'! We repeated it, then copied the letters on to our slates as best we could. He walked about, helping here and there, and after two more letters the lesson ended. I decided at this point to explain I had some knowledge of all the letters, and I would therefore like a transfer. He agreed and told me to report to Form Two the next day. I had hoped to get away from the 'history' lessons, but no such luck. After two more periods of it, we started to read. Each boy had to read a few lines of a story aloud. What a story!

'Misha aged eight, and his younger sister Katia, lived in a collective farm. They often played by a tree, not far from the

115

village. One day, clasping their hands while walking towards it, they noticed something unusual. High in the crown of the tree there was a black object. They did not go any closer, but turned about and hurried back to the collective farm to report the mystery to the militia.

'The soldier picked up his rifle, checked that it was loaded, and went to investigate, led by the two children. The black object turned out to be a bourgeois spy hiding in the tree. Through the vigilance of the two young pioneers, yet another enemy of the Soviet Union ended where he belonged, in jail! Misha and Katia were rewarded for their initiative with packets of sweets.'

I could not help thinking, that when I was a little boy of the age this kind of book was intended for, I read a story about Red Riding Hood. There was nothing about rifles, spies and enemies of the people. But that was Poland. Here in a Soviet primary school the comrades started to work on the minds of the young early in life. However, I read my lines as well as I possibly could because I had once more decided to ask for a move in a vain attempt to avoid the perpetual propaganda I was being fed. The teacher congratulated me for my effort, and agreed to my request. The lesson in Form Three began as in the others with two periods of 'history', and the next was geography. I hoped it would have nothing to do with propaganda but I was once more out of luck.

'England is an island in western Europe, separated from the mainland by *Canal la Manche*. It is ruled by lords wearing red robes with white collars. They own the workers who toil for them, paying them little money.'

That was not what I had heard, except for the first sentence, but I kept quiet. I did not keep quiet when the Fount of Wisdom, namely the Citizen Teacher with the nasty face, referred to my beloved Poland.

'Poland is a small state, situated to the west of the eastern border of the Soviet Union. It is a capitalist country and, like the other, a poor one. The workers are so poor that they boil their potatoes six times in the same water because they have not got enough money to pay for salt at each mealtime.'

I could not stomach that.

'Citizen Teacher,' I interrupted. 'I come from Poland and I lived close to one of the largest salt mines in Europe. There is so much salt in Poland that we feed it to the animals. Big slabs are thrown in the fields, so that the cows can lick them when they please. What you have just said is therefore not correct.'

Citizen Teacher went as red as a beetroot. She rose from her chair and drew herself up to her full height, looking for all the world like a wounded elephant.

'Are you calling me a liar? Are you saying that what we teach in the schools of the Soviet Union are lies?'

I wished that I had the guts to say 'yes', but I did not. It would have been foolish anyway, and I did not suppose the comrades would start rewriting their textbooks at my insistence.

'No, Citizen Teacher,' I replied. 'I didn't mention anything about lies. All I said was that what you told us about the boiling of potatoes six times in one amount of salted water was incorrect. The salt in Poland is as cheap as sand. The information you have might refer to another country, I don't know.'

She seemed pleased with this response, but she did not stop there. She told me that I would be reported to the tutor, and asked me to leave the room immediately, and wait in the corridor. When she left the classroom she went past without even looking at me. I waited for some time after everyone had gone but she still did not reappear. The male teacher came out of his room so I asked him yet again for a move to the next class! He told me to report to Form Four. By the sixth day I was in Form Six, the highest in the colony. My classmate was Edek, who had also joined the school for a lark.

In Form Six, after the usual two periods of propaganda, we began to study geometry, and my 'friend', Citizen Teacher, was expounding the Theorem of Pythagoras. Having played buttons for most of the 'history' lessons, Edek and I carried on, but with one ear cocked in case she should ask us a sudden question. She was almost at the end of the proof when she must have noticed our lack of interest in the proceedings. She had been trying to pin something on me since the fiasco of the salted water, and this was her chance.

'You are not paying attention! I am trying to instil some knowledge into your silly head, but you think you know it all! Get up when I speak to you, you Polish mister!'

'I am paying attention, Citizen Teacher. I like geometry, and I think it is a most interesting subject.'

A flash of genius appeared on her face, as though she was the one who discovered the theorem. She dropped the chalk in the box, put her hands on her hips, and half-smiling, half-jeering, she sternly demanded: 'In that case, Arrested One, repeat Pythagoras's Theorem for me!'

I knew very well that she had never mentioned anything about the square on the hypotenuse equalling the sum of squares of the adjacent sides. I had paid enough attention to be certain of the fact. She must have known too, and that was precisely why she asked me to repeat the theorem. This was her chance to humiliate me as I must have humiliated her only a few days before.

'Very well!' I replied and repeated it in Russian.

The blood drained from the face of Citizen Teacher. What the propaganda machine did not know was that some years before I had read a nineteenth-century story about a Polish boy living in a part of Poland occupied by the Russians. He had to know the theorem by heart and it was reproduced in the story in Russian, though not in the cyrillic alphabet. For some unknown reason I had learned it by heart, and I still remembered it! The classroom became very quiet and surprised faces turned to look at me. Citizen Teacher did not quite know what to do, and I must admit I enjoyed her misery. In the end she pointed her shaking finger at the door and I started marching.

'Get out!' she shouted. 'And never return to the school again!'

'Goodbye, Citizen Teacher,' I replied.

I met her several times while in the colony, and I always bid her the time of day, though she always ignored me. Perhaps she had not found out how to deal with the situation in any of her propaganda manuals! She did, however, report me to the tutor about the salted water affair. I told him what really happened and he let me off. He was not a bad stick, really, certainly not very officious, and quite helpful. There was a story circulating in the colony that he had done ten years inside himself. Maybe that was the reason.

In the morning I told the manageress that I was no longer attending the school. She was not altogether surprised. As a manger of the workshop, she was earning 500 roubles a month, or about half of what the workers on the shop floor were earning. This kind of disparity was due to an effort by the ruling clique to keep another myth going: namely in the Soviet Union only the workers were paid well, while the professional classes got the crumbs. The myth crumbled when one realized that they did not buy their goods in the same shops as the ordinary workers. Indeed the prices they paid were approximately one twelfth, or even less, of the prices charged in workers' shops. All the workers in my workshop knew about this particular deceit. They were upset about only one aspect of it, which was that the Party genuinely believed it could hoodwink the workers into believing anything. To me, too, it proved a point: the leadership of the USSR was hopelessly out of touch with reality. The people who held the power were totally oblivious of what was in the minds of the citizens, or even of what their wishes were. And the leadership was safe to assume that since no one had ever voted them to power, no one had a right to topple them from their self-appointed perch. Of course, the leaders of the Soviet Union did go through the motions of elections, and voting was compulsory. But the 'swindle', and every Ivan knew that it was nothing but a swindle, worked as follows. Ivan Ivanovich Ivanov reported to the polling station, where his name was checked against the register, and a piece of paper with the names of the candidates was handed to him. Ivan retreated to the privacy of the polling booth, marked with a tick or a cross the candidate of his choice, sealed the paper and placed it in a locked box. All very democratic, except that it really did not matter which candidate he chose. They were all nominated by the Communist Party.

Perhaps due to the cold, or perhaps because the food deteriorated a little over the months, I began to feel hungry again. One free Sunday, Edek and I rigged up a trap, dropped a few breadcrumbs round it, and caught a crow. We killed it, plucked it, cut it into pieces, put it in a tin can with a little water and boiled it in the power house. The exercise was not a success. The meat was almost black and tasted very strong. We ate it, but did not repeat the experiment.

Things were happening outside the fence. We could hear the army training for an assault, with their spine-chilling yells, echoing from all angles, and from the nearby aerodrome, we heard the airmen flying more often than before. One day an army officer appeared in the workshop looking for volunteers to join an army training unit. As the officer came close to our bench, Pavel asked me to speak only Polish so that with any luck, he might be thought a prisoner. The officer took a long look at him, then passed him by. Unfortunately, the officer asked someone about Pavel and he returned to sign the unfortunate man on. Others volunteered in the same way.

Gradually, the snow began to melt and we knew spring was coming. The first day of April duly came and marked my eighteenth birthday. Officially I was now of age, and with my sentence I was bound to be sent to one of the dreaded work camps I had heard so much about. Deep down I dreaded the idea of losing my new 'freedom', and wished dearly that I had been able to escape. I had tried once, at the end of January, when I noticed one wall lamp not working. Immediately after the count, before the doors were locked for the night, I made my way to the wood-cutter's shed which was in front of the defective lamp. To my horror, I saw the guards replacing it, and I managed to return to the dormitory in time for another check.

On 15 April 1941, after the morning count, I was told to stay behind. Soon I found myself back on the top shelf of a prison train.

I had said goodbye to Zhitomir Children's Working Colony where I left behind many friends, especially the 'free' men and women. From them I had learned many facts about the true state of affairs in that unhappy land, affairs which no visitor or a correspondent of any country from the Western world could ever discover. Those people opened their hearts and told me what they would never have told a stranger simply because they trusted me. They were conditioned to silence by years of life under the tyranny of a government they had never voted into power, and by the constant vigilance of their secret police.

8

I had no illusions that I would be taken back to Poland, so I was not surprised when I found the train was travelling in an easterly direction. The sun was shining brightly, and I saw many people working in the green fields of the Ukraine. I also saw huge convoys of troops moving westwards. We stopped in Kiev for a few days, arriving in Kharkov six days after leaving Zhitomir.

The jail at Kharkov was enormous, a dirty-white building with the notorious *yezhovki* in the windows. After careful scrutiny of the graffiti in the arrival cell, I discovered Adam's name and address, and added mine to it.

I was taken to a cell on the second floor, measuring about seven yards by eight, and it was full of people. There was only room in the vicinity of the overflowing *parasha,* so we had no option but to stand in the filth. After about an hour more people were brought in, and some of the prisoners complained there was no room for any more.

The authorities thought otherwise, and after another hour more people were pushed in, to the accompaniment of much shouting and swearing from the inmates. That last batch of prisoners made up the total in our cell to 154. In a cell of that size it meant twenty-one square inches per person!

Because of this we hoped before night came that some of us would be transferred to another cell, but it was not to be. So, we decided to divide our number in two: half would stand tightly packed while the other half tried to get some sleep, and the change-over was to come halfway through the night. I was in the first group to stand, and to say that it was hell would be a gross understatement. The temperature rose quickly and some of the

121

older people fainted. Their bodies could not fall on the floor because of tight packing. When our turn came to sleep, we collapsed in one mass. By morning everybody had collapsed, and I woke up under a pile of arms and legs. I stayed in that cell for eleven days!

On the afternoon of my tenth day in that horrible hole, I and a number of other prisoners were taken out for a medical examination. The medic was a Czech woman of about forty, with grey hair and wearing a white jacket. She was a prisoner too, we believed.

'How do you feel, generally speaking?' she asked me, shaking her head gently.

'I feel very weak and tired, almost spent. I get dizzy spells and often see black spots in front of my eyes,' I replied, realizing what she was getting at.

She poked me here and there, took my pulse, then strolled to the table behind which sat two NKVD officers, and murmured her verdict. One of them wrote something on a pad and that was the end of my examination. I am certain that she was my saviour. After the others had been seen by the medical team, we were taken back to the cell. The next day, on 3 May, a number of us were ordered to leave with our belongings. I was not sorry to go, but in a way I was glad to have been incarcerated in that cell. I was glad because I saw with my own eyes the conditions under which human beings were forced to live, ninety-five per cent of whom had done no wrong in the eyes of any civilized community. These were human beings who were shepherded by their Communist masters, thrown into an overcrowded cell to live and sleep in their own excreta. By being there I know it to be true; I slept in the filth myself.

By evening, I was back on the prison train, one of the twelve men sharing a compartment. Where to now? The train appeared to be travelling in a north-westerly direction. On the afternoon of the second or third day we stopped in the middle of nowhere among some pine trees. Compartment doors further up the corridor were opened and we thought that we had arrived at our destination. Some prisoners were being taken out, then suddenly there was an almighty shout:'You bastards! You can shoot me, but one of these days thousands like me, still outside, will rise and hang you, for the crimes of Babii Yar, Vinnitsa . . .'

And then the shouting stopped. On the grapevine we later discovered that the man who shouted was a twenty-seven-year-old Ukrainian. He and the others had been taken out to be shot.

Inside the train it was as quiet as a morgue. No one spoke, no one moved, not even the guard. He leaned on the window-bars, looking at the falling rain. The only noise came from the bogies as they thumped the rails. I woke up at about 4 a.m. and looked through the window. It was still raining, and in the dim light of the passing lamps I saw tiny flakes as well. Snow? In a few minutes I saw a sign in the distance. It read: 'Moskva'. I tried to see as much as possible of the town which so many Poles before me had seen on their way to Siberia. The place was not sufficiently illuminated to see anything except the closest buildings. Soon after we were parked on a siding with a dirty brown wall blocking the view. A day or two later the train rolled again. It did not take me long to establish the direction. Siberia, here I come!

I remember viewing the news with mixed feelings. On the one hand I thought it would be interesting to find out what the place really looked like; on the other, I knew from my fellow prisoners just how tough life in the Siberian camps was. A week later we crossed an astonishingly wide river which could only be the Volga. The train took twenty minutes to cross it, travelling at a walking pace. Below us, I saw ships steaming up and down and tugs pulling barges. One thing became abundantly clear: if I managed to escape from the labour camp, the way back would not be westward. There were guards on either side of the bridge, with patrols at intervals, and I knew I could never swim across that expanse of water.

In a few days the scenery changed. The steep, sloping mountains covered by pines, the little streams with fast-flowing, crystal clear water, reminded me of the Tatra mountains in Poland. Here and there was a house, or a building, then the buildings became more numerous as the train, now pulled by two locomotives, was laboriously making its way up and up. The sun was shining and I really enjoyed the scenery. In the afternoon we arrived in Sverdlovsk. I was no longer in Europe, but in Asia, on the outskirts of Siberia, on the other side of the Urals.

After a short stop, we rolled again and before sunset we found ourselves in a flat country, with pine trees on either side of the trace. So this was *taiga*, I thought, not really knowing whether we had reached that famous woodland or not. By morning I had no doubt at all. The trees were tall, much taller than I had expected, and very dense. I tried to visualize the picture as it would look in winter, with the familiar *troika*, a sledge drawn by three horses, making its way home across this endless plain.

On occasions, the *taiga* receded some distance from the railway line, which in those places was protected from winter snow by a fence some twenty or so yards away. The idea was that the currents produced by the fence would make the snow fall short of the track, keeping it clear. At other times scars would appear in the *taiga*, man-made scars stretching for miles on end. They were made by the countless prisoners who were ditched on the side of the track and made to cut trees until they died of exposure, overwork and hunger. Later on I was to meet one of the survivors of such an exercise. From late March to early December he had never been inside a building, however primitive. They slept on the branches of the trees they cut, with a branch or two on top of them as a protection against the rain, snow or frost. According to him, the death rate was forty per cent.

After a few days the novelty of the view wore off, but the woodland did not. It was still there, miles upon miles of it, stretching as far as the eye could see. We passed through Petropavlovsk, then stopped at Omsk, a sleepy-looking town, with the railway station made of brown-stained wood. There was a water tap in the wall, with a sign, 'boiling water', underneath it. In the old days, the tap did really produce boiling water for the travellers to enjoy, free of charge. Like many other services it dried up with the onset of the October Revolution, and had stayed dry ever since. We had no boiling water at Omsk, just engine water.

We were off again in a few hours. Where to? How many more days? We had been travelling for about three weeks now, and the immobilization of our bodies had begun to show. I was still in relatively good shape, but then I was much younger than the rest. The next stop was Novosibirsk, a big, dirty-looking town on the river Ob. The slow-running river was much wider than I expected, and when I saw guards on the bridge I again decided that if I did get away I should head south. By my reckoning, due south was

Sinkiang, with its notorious *Takla Makan* (Hungry Desert), and the dreaded Gobi was to the east of it. Further south was Tibet, India, and freedom. I was glad that I had been keen on geography for as long as I could remember. It was for that reason that I was given a big atlas of the world for my eighth birthday. Even so, I wished that I could have had a quick look at the map to refresh my memory!

Some of the prisoners were taken out of our compartment at Novosibirsk, including one from my shelf. It was nice to have a little more room, just three people instead of the usual four per platform. We set off again in a southerly direction. One thing was certain: we were not going to Kolyma, Sakhalin or Kamchatka. The names of the stations meant nothing to me; and we crossed another big river, most probably the Ob, then stopped at Semipalatinsk, wherever that was. No one was taken out as far as I could see, although more prisoners were taken on board. One of them was put in my compartment and became my neighbour on the top shelf.

He was a man of about thirty, small in stature, with a round, brown face, black hair and faintly Chinese eyes. He knew only a few words of Russian which did not help much. Slowly, by signs, then by an odd word here and there, I learned that he was a Kazakh. When he spoke to me, the language sounded guttural, vaguely Hungarian or Turkish. Most of the words had one or two syllables with an accent on the last one.

The first word of Kazakh I learned was *su* (water), then came *ata* (father), *ana* (mother), and *apa* (sister). In a week I was going great guns, I could even make up a sentence! I was never shy of learning anything, and I was glad I had that yearning. I did not know then that a slight knowledge of this seemingly obscure language was going to help me considerably in the future.

We now appeared to be travelling in a south-westerly direction (later I learned it was more southerly); it was becoming hotter and hotter, the steppe began to change to sand, and the names of the stations that appeared were in Kazakhi. The guards opened the windows, but this only brought in hot air smelling of rotten grass and oil.

I began to wonder what kind of a job I was going to get when we eventually reached the labour camp. I had never heard of a camp in a desert area; as far as I was concerned all of them were in the far north.

'*Dgamanchol!*' exclaimed the Kazakh, pointing at sands to the right of the train.

I knew by then that *chol* meant the desert. Obviously the man was referring to a desert called Dgaman, but I could not remember seeing it in my school atlas. To the south and east we made out a mountain range, 10,000 feet or more high. The train turned towards the range and puffed its way through the pass. Once through, the scenery changed dramatically; the desert was gone, and in the distance there were acres and acres of what looked like orchards. As we came closer my Kazakh friend became quite excited, pointing out the orchards to me.

'*Mevazar,*' said he, nodding his head knowingly.

The orchards comprised apricot and peach trees first, then apples and more apples, stretching for miles.

'*Alma mevazar,*' said the Kazakh. '*Alma yakhshi!*' rubbing his stomach with obvious pleasure.

I learned a number of things from that conversation: *yakhshi,* by the way he rubbed his tummy, could only mean good, *mevazar* was obviously an orchard, while *alma* meant apple.

By the early evening we approached a large, attractive-looking town, with white-painted houses and apple trees lining the streets. Here and there was a peach tree, with big, juicy, yellow-red fruits. We didn't stop there, but I spotted the sign in the distance: *Alma Ata*. I knew what the name meant: the Father of Apples.

As the train turned in the direction of the setting sun, I looked through the window and my mouth opened wide in utter disbelief. I had thought the mountains we had passed were high, but the ones I was now looking at were monsters! They must have been at least 15,000 feet high and they seemed to be only a mile or two away, glistening in the sunset. Gradually, they changed colour to amber, then purple, then violet, until they dissolved into darkness. It was a wonderful sight. I learned later it was called Ala Tau, beyond which was Issik Kul, or Feverish Lake, and beyond that was Tien Shan.

We stopped at a place called Chu, then carried on north. The mountains were long gone and neither were the orchards to be seen, just sand. Soon we smelt the rotten grass and oil again, and a lake appeared on the right. I knew it had to be the western edge of Lake Balkhash, it was too big to be anything else. The sand changed into steppe, and we were still travelling in that train. The long journey had begun to take its toll on everyone. On occasions, as I descended from my shelf and stood up to walk to the toilet, a twice-daily exercise, I could feel blood running away from my head and thought I would faint. I would promptly crouch for a second, getting up slowly, and that cured it.

Gradually, the slightly undulating steppe changed into a generally hilly country, with hardly any settlements. I began to lose all sense of distance, as quite often we were stationary when I woke up in the morning, having been on the move when I had fallen asleep, or vice versa. Five weeks after boarding the train at Kharkov in Europe, I was somewhere in the middle of Asia, having travelled some 5,000 miles. In the early afternoon that day, the train turned sharply right from the main, single-track line, with much screeching of the bogies. Half a mile further it stopped on a low embankment. There was no platform, but some 300 yards away I saw a group of mud huts with flat roofs on the side of a hill, surrounded by barbed wire. There was a reception committee waiting for us in the form of NKVD troops. The doors were opened and our marathon train journey had come to an end.

I had arrived in Karabas, Karlag NKVD. Karabas was a made-up word, standing for Karaganda Bassein (Karaganda Basin). Karlag, another made-up word, stood for Karaganda Lager (Karaganda Labour Camp). Karabas was a holding unit, the Clapham Junction of the enormous Karlag empire. From here prisoners, men and women, were sent away to various divisions, to while away their time toiling for the glory of Communism. Nobody was free in that gigantic camp. It was an open secret that even the guards were sent there as punishment for misdemeanours, the normal stretch being five years. Karabas itself was not very big, covering perhaps ten to fifteen acres, and housing about 2,000 prisoners.

It was nice to breathe fresh air again, but it felt as if the ground were moving under my feet, so unpractised was I in walking. Indeed, a number of men lost their balance and fell. When the guards were satisfied that all the numbers tallied, we were taken to our huts. They were made of bricks of straw and dried mud, and contained two tiers of shelves on either side of the long wall. These were to be our beds. There were two small stoves in the narrow passages between the shelves; their presence indicated that the winters were going to be hard. A few lamps dangled from the roof, and here and there was the odd window, merely an opening in the wall. However, the doors were not locked at any time so we were free to move within the enclosure. A barbed wire fence separated the two sexes, and conversation was discouraged by the guards who were strategically placed in their boxes along the perimeter of the compound.

About a mile away there were a few huts set in two rows, and the rumour was strong that in the old days they had housed workers belonging to a British company which was mining copper for the Tsar. In fact, the story went that one of the British fellows was still there, working as a 'free resettler'. We hoped to receive something hot to eat that first day, but we were definitely out of luck. All we had was water which was stored in a big barrel in the middle of the compound. A person requiring it simply lowered his head and drank straight from the barrel, like any other well-behaved animal. In the evening I watched the sun disappear beyond the horizon. It was a magnificent sight, and I waited till dark before making my way to the hut. Inside, I found my spot and fell asleep almost immediately. Obviously, after weeks of travel, I must have been more tired than I had imagined.

I had to get up during the night, to discharge the liquid supper I had consumed earlier in the evening. I crept out, stumbling occasionally, as there was no light that I could see by. The camp was in darkness except for the dim fence lights, so I decided not to try to find the latrines for fear of getting lost. I looked at the sky but could not see any stars. I thought it strange, but decided that it had probably clouded over. I returned to the hut quietly, touching the top shelf with my right hand, keeping my left out in front, feeling for the stove. My bedspace was only a couple of yards beyond that so it would act as a guide. As I crept along the passage I looked towards the ceiling and thought I could make out a grey hue in the blackness. I lifted myself towards it and to my surprise it was not only brighter but also felt warm. I inched closer still and discovered a thin red wire, looking uncannily like the wire in an electric bulb. I closed in until I could feel the heat burning my nose, and it was indeed an electric bulb, except that I could only see it at very close range. I realized I was blind.

I felt my way to my bedspace, put my head on the folded rucksack and reflected on my plight. It was clear that I was not totally blind because I could see during the day, at least I could until that evening. I remembered my mother telling me what would happen if I did not eat carrots: 'If you want to be a pilot, you must eat carrots whether you like them or not. All pilots eat them so that they can see at night like cats.' The diagnosis was accurate. My blindness was caused by the lack of vitamins, and all I had to do was to wait for daylight and obtain some. I put my mind into neutral and went to sleep. I woke up absolutely frozen, but I could see!

For breakfast we received 500 grams of bread and a mug of warm water, those who worked collected 800 grams. I went to reconnoitre the cookhouse and its surroundings. I soon realized it would not be very easy to steal anything as the area was a prohibited territory to all except those who worked there. Being small in stature and having some experience of dodging the trusty in the colony, I managed to get close enough to observe there were no carrots to be seen anywhere. Looking around I saw an old cabbage; that was better than nothing, so I stole it and returned to my hut to take the medicine. I then went to the barrel for a drink of water, only to find there was hardly any left. With the rise in temperature many had the same idea and they had drunk the lot. The reasoning behind this action was simple: the barrel was replenished twice a day, once in the morning and again in the evening. If you did not have a fill up when it was first put out, you suffered in the heat until the evening. After this, I always had a top-up after breakfast whether I wanted a drink or not, just like a camel.

I did not think that eating the cabbage would improve my sight immediately, but I hoped it would make some difference in a day or two. Thus, as the sun set once more, I sat on the stone outside my hut watching it disappear beyond the horizon, knowing that when it had gone I would be blind again. The steppe was undulating slightly, giving an appearance of sand dunes in the desert. I started to whistle 'The Caravan', a popular tune of the time. The lower limb of the sun touched the horizon, and hung there like a huge golden melon, before continuing its downward path. When about half of it had disappeared, I saw something crossing its face. It looked like Sancho Panza of *Don Quixote,* a man on a donkey, his legs almost touching the ground.

I continued whistling the song, watching the spectacle. When the man on the donkey was about halfway across the face of the sun, something else came into view. It was a camel! Then another, and another! A caravan! I rubbed my eyes in utter disbelief. It was exactly as the song said, and it was the first time in my life that I had seen a true caravan. There it was: a man on a donkey followed by his camels, silhouetted against the setting sun. There were ten camels in all and I followed their stately progress until they disappeared. What a magnificent sight! I rose and strolled to the hut. I looked up but there were no stars that I could see. I did not worry: I knew my sight was going to return.

9

My leisurely life in the heart of Asia came to an end the next day. At about 10 a.m. the Kazakh, myself and another man were rounded up and taken to the gate. Here we were given pickaxes and shovels, then escorted outside the camp. The whole party consisted of the three of us plus two other men, all wearing the standard black shirts and trousers of labour-camp inmates. The reason for the whole exercise was as follows.

One of the two men (a storeman) had been in charge of the oil tanks for the past five years, and was going to hand over to the other as his release was due. When they checked the quantity of oil in the tanks with the quantity he ought to have had there was a discrepancy, so he was accused of misappropriation. The man pleaded not guilty to the charge, asking the accusers how, and to whom, he could possibly have sold the oil.

The tanks were nothing more elaborate than huge underground holes lined with a one-inch thickness of mortar, and covered on top. He therefore maintained that the oil had seeped out over the years or that possibly there was a crack in the flimsy lining. This simple logic was clearly beyond the intelligence of whoever preferred the charges against the wretched man. Since in the Soviet Union nothing was ever done without a directive from the top, it therefore follows that it was also beyond the intelligence of the ruling clique. However, in their benevolence, they allowed him to try to prove his theory, hence the expedition with pickaxes and shovels.

The tanks were situated close to the railway spur. The storeman marked three spots, three, five and ten metres from the edge of the tank, and we went to work. I dug the hole closest to the tank and found the smell of oil overpowering. The top-soil was nothing but sand and underneath there was a layer of hard, but quite workable clay. Only occasionally did I have to use the pickaxe, which was a good thing since I had lost almost all the muscles I had developed in *Trud-Koloniya*. We had a half-hour break for lunch and we were at it again. It was mid-June and the intense heat was making the work much harder. I took my shirt off, exposing my white body to the sun, because I wanted to get tanned while I had a chance.

When we reached a depth of about five feet, not only was the stink unbearable but the clay started changing colour due to the oil in it. I brought some up and showed it to the guard, telling him that I had difficulty in breathing.

'All the same!' he shouted. 'Carry on digging. You won't die yet!'

I did not at this point inform the scoundrel that I had no intention of dying. Instead, I made a few steps in the wall of the hole so that I could get out in a hurry if I needed to. When I reached a depth of seven or eight feet the stink became over-powering and I climbed out quickly, telling the guard that if he wanted the hole any deeper he would have to do it himself. I even offered to hold his rifle while he dug, but he declined my offer. Then he kneeled, put his head down the hole and started to cough. The storeman lowered himself down into the hole and brought out a sample of soil in a mug. He covered it with paper, securing it with a piece of string.

While they were performing this rigmarole, a goods train arrived at the embankment. The doors were unlocked and opened by the 'reception committee', and for a while no one emerged. Then slowly, one by one, old women dressed in black, some of them wearing white headgear reminiscent of a nun's coif, began to lower themselves to the ground. In their efforts not to fall and break their frail bones, the women tried to grasp the side of the doors with one hand, searching for some anchorage with the other. Some of them managed it, some of them did not. Some of them caught their skirts on some projection or other, slipped, and displayed their bare backsides, to the great amusement of the waiting heroes of the Soviet Union, the thugs of the NKVD.

It transpired that the women who alighted from the train were the fit ones, and that inside there were many more too weak to move. No amount of encouragement, or shouting and swearing from the guards, could make those women leave. So the Leninist–

Stalinist storm troopers went into action. They boarded the waggons and began 'helping' the poor, wretched women to disembark. True, I did not see one being actually thrown out, but it was not far from that. The ill-fated women fell to the ground like bags of grain. Some of them shrieked in horror, some of them howled, and the ones who had left unaided began to pray aloud. I heard one of them call: 'Father forgive them, for they know not what they do.' I could have wept.

Their task completed, the guards tried to line up the doomed women for the statutory head count. Most of them could not get up so they were counted where they lay. Then the journey to the compound began. Those who could, walked; the others were literally dragged along by the NKVD.

I know how I felt walking up that incline. But I was forty, fifty or even sixty years younger than those women. I learned later that the women were nuns who had been in prisons and labour camps since around 1922. When I witnessed that macabre spectacle on the embankment it was mid-June 1941.

Back home, my father used to kill a pig once a year. I was always sent away when the slaughter took place because the act sickened me. Even when he was going to kill a chicken, he would always dispatch me on some errand or other, knowing how I was affected. But if, at the time I am describing, someone had told me that he had all that Communist rabble lined up on the ground and ordered me to smash in their heads with my pickaxe, I would have done it without regret, and without batting an eyelid. Alas, nobody did come to me with such a proposition. But there was something I could do: I could make sure that I remembered every detail of the grim spectacle, and one day tell the truth to the civilized community of the Free World.

'Don't stand there staring!' yelled the guard. 'Go and help the Kazakh!'

They decided to keep digging even deeper and the only way to get the soil up was with a rope and basket. When we finished, it was getting dark. The soil, even in the hole furthest away from the tank, stank of oil. The outcome of the investigation? The storeman was convicted and got three more years. My own opinion was that the whole exercise was just a pretext. Stalin and his mates had no intention of freeing him.

A few days later I was loaded on to an open lorry with twenty-four others and began another stage in my career as a prisoner of the Communists. There were five benches to a lorry, and two guards sat just behind the driver's cabin to make sure that no one fell off. The lorry itself was an old banger which used wood gas as fuel. This was produced in two large generators placed on either side of the cab.

The lorry convoy of five set off early in the morning, heading south. We crossed the railway line fairly soon afterwards and headed south-west. We travelled at no more than fifteen miles per hour along an unmade track, carefully avoiding the deeper pot-holes. We crossed a small mountain range, and then made our way over a high plateau, crossing a few charming little streams and a river. The two front lorries veered off westward, while the rest of us continued on in a south-westerly direction. There was something fascinating about that vast, empty space. The soil was sandy, covered by dried grass, and here and there were grey-green plants covered with thorns, standing about two feet high. My Kazakh friend called it *yantok*. I was doing quite well with the new language in return for teaching the Kazakh some Russian. We became good friends and slowly I pieced together his story.

He had been employed as a driver on a State farm, somewhere near Semipalatinsk. One night the previous spring, in pouring rain, he was driving the lorry along a track which in places was covered with water. The lorry went into a deep pothole and the front wheel broke off. He was charged with sabotage, and collected seven years!

At about midday we stopped outside a wooden gate similar to the one at Karabas. Our guards were relieved by others, and they returned about an hour later picking their teeth, while we did not even get a drink of water. After all, we were only people, and there were plenty of those in the USSR. We set off once more in a southerly direction. Darkness fell and we were still travelling, though making slow progress. I looked up at the sky and saw the stars. I could see! The cabbage must have done the trick. I soon found the familiar Great Bear, the Little Bear, and the Pole star marking the North. It seemed to be at the same angle as it was at home; this signified that I was more or less on the same latitude as my village and could therefore fix my position, give or take a few hundred miles. We had travelled approximately north from the western edge of the Lake Balkhash, so my longitude was about the same as the southern tip of India. The Pole star indicated the latitude of my village. I knew where I was in the vastness of Asia!

The sideways rocking of the slow-moving lorry, and the fact that we had spent the whole day in the open, lulled us to sleep. We all sat down on the floor and dozed off. When we awoke, the sky over the hill to the east looked a little lighter. We stopped, and were allowed to get down to stretch our legs and relieve ourselves.

The sun was just rising when we boarded the lorry. We were still travelling south, now between two hills about 2,000 feet high and ten miles apart. At about 10 a.m. we stopped outside the gate of a compound much smaller than Karabas and were told to get off.

I had arrived at the sixteenth Kizil Tau (it means Red Mountain in Kazakhi), courtesy of the Communist Party of the Soviet Union, at the ripe old age of eighteen years, two and a half months. It stood on the top of a hill and housed about 600 prisoners of both sexes in eight flat-roofed mud huts. To the north, say half a mile away, was a gorge across which the prisoners had erected a dam to supply water during the dry season. The reservoir was fed by a tiny stream, and to ensure an adequate supply of water in summer the prisoners pushed snow down the hillsides in winter to fill the gorge. This opened into a valley which ran for about two or three miles, becoming a plateau further west and south. About five miles to the north and north-west, there were two mountain peaks with a pass between them, and beyond that there was a mountain range called Ak Tau, which means White Mountain in Kazakhi. The immediate south and all to the east were hidden by the side of the hill.

We were counted, of course, shown to our huts and told to assemble outside the gate in fifteen minutes. The hut had four rows of double-tiered platforms (our beds) which contained a blanket or two folded up at intervals. There were two big stoves in the middle of the room, and that was that. My hut was nearest the gate, to the right of which was the guardroom, the guards' quarters, and the kitchen. Behind my hut was the second row of huts, beyond which was a barbed wire fence separating the sexes. We reported to the guardroom where the guard told us not to bother to attempt an escape as no one had ever succeeded.

Following another head count we walked down the hill towards the valley along a well-used trail. About 300 yards from the gate on the right-hand side, there was a precipice, and at the bottom men were quarrying stone. We walked past them and were split into groups, told to roll up our trousers and were attached to different brigades. Swinging our pickaxes, we began breaking up the parched, stone-hard earth marked out in a circle by our brigade leader. Each circle was about fifteen yards in diameter and the earth had to be crumbled to a depth of two feet. Having done this, we poured on soiled water, then started mixing the two ingredients with our bare feet. We went round and round in an anti-clockwise direction, our legs sinking deeper and deeper into the mud as the water penetrated the soil. From time to time a man would fall into the mud, having lost his balance and being unable to withdraw his leg in time from the gluey mess. My feet were cut in several places but there was little I could do about it.

The sun was beating down on our sweating bodies and some of the men put their shirts on their heads in an effort to provide some shelter from the sweltering inferno. The temperature must have been at least 65 degrees centigrade, and it was only late June. What was it going to be like in July and August?

As our legs sank deeper into the mud it became increasingly difficult to walk. I had to stop watching the golden eagles flying to and fro from the nearby mountain. They were huge, deep brown birds with white necks, their wingspan reaching about six feet. About an hour after we started, we saw a cart drawn by two bullocks descending from the direction of the camp. It was *staryk*, the 'old one', bringing a huge bucket of soup and porridge for our lunch. So we left the soggy mess of the circle, scraped most of the mud off our legs with shovels, and converged on him. He gave us a wooden bowl each, doled out a ladleful of *shchii* – thicker than at Karabas, with a trace of oil floating on top – and when we had eaten that, he added a dollop of porridge the size of a fist. I had no spoon, so I started sipping my soup straight from the bowl.

'Haven't you got a spoon, sonny?' inquired the brigade leader.

'No,' I replied, 'I have never been given one.'

A roar of laughter followed my statement. No one was ever issued with a spoon; the system was to 'acquire' one, either by stealing it from somebody in another hut or by taking one from a guard. The brigade leader picked up his jacket – he was the only one who had one – dipped into his inner pocket and gave me a spoon.

'Take good care of it,' he said. 'They are difficult to come by.'

Another man with a barrel on wheels arrived, bringing water from the reservoir. He removed the top from the vat and we ascended in a fairly orderly fashion and drank our fill straight from the barrel like the well-trained animals we had become.

I put my shirt on for fear of getting burned by the relentless sun. We all sat down on the scorching soil and rested. The mud on our legs dried up, cracking here and there, pulling the hair embedded in it. The trick was to try and crack the mud on one's legs into small pieces, thus causing less discomfort. The lunch-break lasted about an hour, or less. Then the brigade leader called a number of men forward, they went to a nearby heap of hay, picked up an armful each, and were instructed to drop it in the circle full of mud. The rest of us got up, stepped into the quagmire to spread the hay evenly on top, then started walking round yet again. My feet were cut once more, this time by the hay, and I complained to one of the prisoners walking beside me.

'Don't worry, sonny,' said he. 'Soon your skin will become as hard as a camel's.'

In the meantime there was nothing I could do except hope that the stickiness of the mud would prevent any blood-flow. I knew I had none to spare. About half an hour later the brigade leader judged that the mixture was of the desired quality, so we were split into two groups. One gang transported the mud in wheelbarrows, the other made the bricks. For me, loading and wheeling the barrow was hard work. My shirt was soaked with sweat, so I took it off and rolled up a sort of a turban for my head. And when we had finished the circle, we picked up pickaxes and shovels and started another which had been marked by the brigade leader. We hacked away, my aching muscles not really responding to the commands of my brain. I was extremely tired and thirsty. The water we used to make the mud with was totally undrinkable, and we had not had anything to drink since lunchtime.

'That will do!' shouted the brigade leader. 'Form up!'

At last! The sun was still above the horizon and I was fool enough to think they wanted us inside the camp before dark. I was disappointed. We came closer to it admittedly, but that was all. We were taken to the quarry and told to heave stones up the slope to the top. We formed a chain, passing the rocks one by one. The bigger ones, too heavy to carry, we rolled up the slope, some of them requiring four men to do it. Once at the top, the stones were formed into cuboids. The sun disappeared beyond the horizon, and we were still at it. Back home I had often been tired when working in the fields, but that was nothing in comparison to this. I had almost no energy left when the guards told us to form up. We struggled the few hundred yards to the compound, too tired to talk. The usual double count on both sides of the gate, and we were let loose.

'When do we eat?' I asked one of the inmates. I was more than ready to.

'Eat?' he replied sardonically. 'Sonny, you were not sent here to eat, but to work. Unless your brigade number, or your name, appears on the list of *stakhanovtsov,* your next meal will be your bread ration tomorrow morning. Take my advice and don't use any of your energy walking up to look at it, because your name won't be there!'

It all started with one Alexey Stakhanov, a miner in the Donbas coalfields, who during his nightshift, back in 1935, produced over 100 tonnes of coal. His achievement was hailed throughout the Soviet Union, and in that allegedly classless society a title was instituted, a title of *Stakhanovets.* Any worker achieving 130 per cent of his norm was given it, his name appeared in the papers and on the radio. He was wined and dined in the Kremlin, the sole reason being to make others work harder. A lesser title, that of *Udarnik,* a shock worker, was also instituted, and given to those who achieved 115 per cent. Thus, in Kizil Tau, those who achieved 130 per cent were given the appropriate title, their names appeared on a notice board, and they were the only ones to receive a meal in the evening. *Udarnikie* got nothing to eat, but their names appeared on the board beneath the *stakhanovtsy.* And the ordinary mortals, which accounted for almost everyone, received no mention and no food. Those who did not achieve 100 per cent, well, that was another story.

Roughly speaking, we worked anything between twelve and sixteen hours a day at Kizil Tau, seven days a week. The food never varied, and neither did the work for the first few weeks. At the end of the day, we either worked in the quarry or on the building-site nearby. On a number of occasions, those of us making up the cuboids of stones tried to 'increase' our output by rearranging the direction of the existing ones to make it look as though we had heaved more stones up the slope than we actually did. Sometimes we managed it, but even then our brigade did not appear on the list of the famous.

The whole purpose of our being in Kizil Tau was to build a labour camp. At least by the time I arrived on the scene there was somewhere to put our heads down for the night. Those who came before me did not have such luxury, they had to start from nothing.

One morning on the way to work, we passed a small group, of maybe fifteen, shambling towards the bottom of the hill. They appeared to be drunk and were staggering from side to side. One or two men lost their balance, only managing to save themselves from falling at the last moment.

'Who are those people?' I put the question to a man walking beside me.

'*Dokhodyagi,*' he replied.

I had never heard of such a word, but concluded that it must come from the verb *dokhodit,* meaning 'to reach the goal, to reach the end'.

'Lucky people,' said I naïvely, thinking that they were the ones who had reached the end of their sentence, and were perhaps under the influence of some illicit alcohol.

'Don't talk rot!' he said scornfully. 'I hope neither you nor I will ever become a *dokhodyaga!*'

The word was in fact a labour-camp concoction and it did come from the verb *dokhodit.* Those ill-fated souls had indeed reached the end, in this case the end of their tether. They were the prisoners who could not take it any more, the people who could not produce 100 per cent of the norm, the living dead of the labour camps, the ones dying of malnutrition, starvation, and overwork. They were sent to their ugly deaths by the humanoid monsters of the Kremlin, whose directive ruled that no prisoner was ill unless his body temperature was at least 38.5 degrees centigrade.

The beginning of their irreversible slide started when, for one reason or another, they did not accomplish their norm. Accordingly, their bread ration was cut to 500 grams, but they were still expected to do the same stint. The self-appointed Doctors of Medicine in the Kremlin said so. When they failed, the ration was further cut to 300 grams, and that was the end. No one, no one in this world could survive working as we did on such inadequate food. After my companion had explained to me who those doomed men were, I looked back and could still see them slouching and shuffling. That episode made me determined never to become a *dokhodyaga* myself, whether the medicine men of Moscow liked it or not.

Gradually, I started to develop muscles in the right places, the soles of my feet became as hard as the hide of a hippopotamus, and with the daily exposure I became as tanned as the rest. The sores that started appearing on my legs a few days after my arrival began to heal, and I did not feel as tired as I had during the first few days at the camp. One day a slim blonde woman of about thirty, wearing a white, civilian frock, came to see us. She stopped with our group for a while, then departed in the direction of the sheds further along the valley.

'Who is she?' I asked one of the men.

'*Normirovka,*' he replied. 'The woman in charge of the norms.'

She was the one who decided how many prisoners would be employed on a certain project to keep the plan going smoothly. She also kept the record of daily work and in some cases decided what the norm ought to be.

'Nice girl,' I commented.

'Forget it!' he advised.

At that time I was the only youth in Kizil Tau, and I estimated the rest were men of between forty and sixty-five. I was pushing a wheelbarrow full of mud when she arrived the next day. She stopped by the men making bricks. While I was standing, stripped to the waist, waiting for my barrow to be unloaded, she looked across at me and smiled. I smiled back.

'How are you?' she inquired.

'All right,' I replied, shrugging my shoulders. My barrow was empty so I went for more; by the time I returned she was gone. I was disappointed: I thought I might have got to know her and perhaps been able to scrounge extra food.

That evening, the head counting over, we sat outside the hut, enjoying the cool of the night. The full moon sending its silvery rays in the direction of Ak Tau made it look as though it was topped by a layer of snow. The visibility was so good, the 'White Range' appeared to be no more than a mile away. It was a peaceful and strangely beautiful night. A man entered our hut, emerging a few moments later with what was once a guitar. He sat on the step of the hut and tuned it. He was a fifty-four-year-old thief (he had been stealing since before the Revolution) and was currently doing seven years. When he was satisfied that his playing-box was producing passable notes, he started to sing. He sang the folk songs of the old Russia: 'Black Eyes', 'The Nightingale', a tune spanning three octaves. He had a deep baritone voice, and I could not help thinking how fine it must have been in his youth. Then he sang a song I had not heard before, it might have been his own composition. Some twenty-six years later, I was sitting under the starlit skies of Singapore, enjoying a long drink, when I heard a radio playing somewhere in the distance, and suddenly I recognized the tune. I started to whistle it, at the same time trying to remember where I had heard it before. In a few moments, my mind went back to Kizil Tau, and the evening I am describing. I am certain it was the same tune, it was called 'Evenings Near Moscow'.

Each time he stopped, the silent listeners sighed, then somebody would plead: 'Sing some more, pal, sing some more!' Usually he obliged. Here and there, a man would rub his eyes, surreptitiously drying an odd tear or two. The work-hardened slaves of the Communist empire could not help showing their emotions. Listening to those lovely tunes, their minds were thousands of miles away amongst their dear ones, whom they had not seen or heard of in years. I was humbly proud to be amongst those men. They were not criminals or wrongdoers. Most of them were ordinary, good people who by a strange chance happened to be selected to fill the prisons and labour camps as a reminder to others that if they did not toe the line precisely as required by the ruling clique, they would become part of the prison fraternity themselves.

At about 10 a.m. the next day, news spread that a man had escaped. No one doubted that he would be recaptured by the afternoon. He was. I thought about escape too, but before such an exercise I thought it would be wise to know more about the geography of the place. There were a number of Kazakhs and Uzbeks in the camp, and from them I learned much. I was not interested in the westerly direction; to the east, Asia stretched for thousands of miles, while to the north was Siberia – neither very exciting propositions. It had to be south, and that did not look very promising either.

Kizil Tau camp was somewhere on the northern edge of Bet Pak Dala, which meant 'the face of unstained fields' as far as I could make out. The Uzbeks called it Mirzachul which they translated into Russian as Golodnaya Step, the Hungry Steppe. It was a huge area of steppe, sand and dried-up salt lakes. To the south of that was Muyun Kum, the Oily Sands desert: sand, sand, and more sand. All the Kazakhs and the Uzbeks I talked to agreed that it was difficult enough to traverse this country with a well-prepared caravan, but to do it on foot bordered on insanity. I also learned that about three days' walk away to the east was the railway line I had travelled along on my way to Karabas. However, it was only used by the military, or to transport prisoners. This method of escape was definitely ruled out!

As for the climate, I had had personal experience of the summer. I had not seen a cloud for two months, and the current temperature must have been at least 50 degrees centigrade in the shade. What it was in the open, I did not dare imagine. The winter was just as bad, for the usual winter temperature was between −10 and −20 degrees centigrade. Providing there was no wind these conditions were bearable; normally, though, there was some wind and the temperature often dropped to as low as 45 degrees below zero! And that was not all. The greatest threat to survival was the Kara Booran, the Black Storm.

The Kara Booran usually arrived on an easterly wind. First, black clouds, laden with snow, appeared in the east, then the wind freshened, soon reaching gale force, driving snow with it. Visibility dropped to zero and it became very, very dark. Anybody caught outside was usually a goner. The wind was so strong that it was impossible to stand, never mind walk against it. The storm raged for anything from half a day to two days, sometimes longer. No human being, certainly no underclothed and underfed prisoner could survive such an ordeal. It was for this reason that a rope was stretched between each hut and the lavatory, so that a man could drag himself back into the hut. No, the Kara Booran was not an ordinary snow storm: it was a killer.

I had no shoes or headgear. All I had was a pair of thin cotton trousers, a shirt, and a *fufayka*, a kapok anorak, full of holes. With sand temperatures reaching 70 degrees, it would have been quite mad to attempt an escape in summer; I would have been burned alive, assuming I could get far enough away before the guards realized I was missing. And for reasons I have mentioned it would have been just as mad to attempt such an exercise in winter. So my plans had to be made for spring or autumn. I had no illusions about escape being easy. It was possible to disappear from the camp, but then what? I had to carry food and water. So even if I saved a quarter of my daily bread ration, it would take me a month to collect enough food. And I also had to acquire a suitable vessel to carry the water. I therefore removed from my head any idea of trying to escape that coming autumn. I had to learn more about the geography of the region, and about the possibility of encountering the local population or, heaven forbid, another labour camp. This was not as remote as it sounded. I had heard that there was a man in Kizil Tau who used to work in the 104th division of that gigantic slave empire known as Karlag. How many more divisions were there? Where were they situated? I had to find out these things.

We had just resumed the morning's work, following a short break, when the girl in charge of the norms arrived on a four-wheeled cart pulled by bullocks. She spoke to my brigade leader for a moment, then approached a guard, telling him something. He did not even get up, just nodded his head. The brigade leader came to the edge of the circle and called: 'Yurie Stanislavovich. Come here please!'

Anything was better than swinging my pickaxe; even a short respite was better than nothing.

'You have been transferred to another place of work,' he told me. '*Grazhdanka Normirovka* will take you to it. See you!'

'See you, Citizen,' I replied.

I took the shirt from my head, and walked towards the cart.

'Good day, *Grazhdanka Normirovka*!' I greeted her, throwing my shirt into the empty cart.

'Good day to you, Yurie Stanislavovich. Let's climb aboard!'

She placed one hand on the side of the cart, while offering me the other to help her up. She put her foot on the hub of the wheel, then the other on top of the rim, and sat down on the forward cross-plank. 'This is definitely much more pleasant than squeezing that confounded pickaxe handle,' I thought, as I climbed aboard myself, sitting to the right of her. She picked up a stick, touched one of the bullocks with it, and we were off.

'You look nicely tanned, Yurie,' she commented, using the familiar *ty* and my Christian name, instead of the formal *vy* and the patronymic as well.

'Well, *Grazhdanka Normirovka,* the sun hasn't stopped shining since I arrived . . .'

'Stop calling me *Grazhdanka Normirovka,* Yurie,' she interrupted. 'My name is Sonia, and I am a prisoner like you!'

Yes! Sonia, although wearing civilian clothes, was a prisoner. She was twenty-eight years old and married to a man with a doctorate in electrical engineering. One day those in authority had decided that a man of his calibre was required in one of their labour camps. He was arrested, charged with belonging to some fictitious anti-revolutionary group, was duly tried and collected ten years. According to Soviet 'law', Sonia, being his wife, was automatically guilty as well. She was arrested, tried and received five years.

We drove slowly in the direction of the sheds further down the valley. Sonia did not seem to be in any hurry, and each time a bullock stopped to pick up a blade of dried grass she let him, before encouraging him to move with the gentle touch of the stick. She seemed to enjoy the ride, and so did I! In front of the nearest shed there was a circular hole with a flat bottom, similar to the ones we had been making for the past few weeks, except that it was only about half the diameter. In the centre of it was a wooden post which acted as an axis for a pole attached to it with a steel band. In turn the pole acted as an axis for a number of drums with spokes sticking out of them at regular intervals, terminating at the edge of the circle. At the end of the pole, about three feet past the edge of the circle, there was a wheel which kept the pole a couple of feet above the ground. There did not seem to be anybody about. I jumped off first, offering Sonia my hand so that she could get down safely. She took it, stepped on the rim of the wheel with both feet and, with the most wonderful smile, jumped to the ground, her body coming fairly close to mine.

'Thank you, Yurie. You are very considerate,' she said, still smiling.

'Well,' I replied, 'we were taught manners in Poland, although you might not believe me.'

'I do believe you, Yurie, I was taught them, too. Nowadays they seem to be going out of fashion. What a pity, it made life so much nicer.'

The smile disappeared from her face and she let go of my hands.

'We had better go inside and I'll introduce you to your fellow workers. They will tell you precisely what to do. Your job will be to mix clay with this machine. Do you think you can do it?'

'Of course I can. It will be easier than mixing the mud with my feet!'

The shed was full of yellow-brown, dried bricks. In the open, beyond it, a number of women were busy carting bricks from one place to another.

'Ludmila Syergyeevna!' called Sonia to a plumpish woman of about thirty-five. 'Meet the new co-worker, Yurie Stanislavovich. He will mix clay for you.'

'Welcome to the brickworks, young man!' said Ludmila. 'You will like it here, I am sure.'

I noticed that the other women's ages ranged from twenty to fifty, and that there were many more working further away by the other outhouses. When we returned to the machine area, Ludmila explained the job to me and left me to it. Sonia sat down on some bricks in the shade of the shack while I went back to the cart to retrieve my shirt. I twisted it a few times and made myself a turban.

'I love seeing you in that turban,' said Sonia laughingly. 'You look like a real dervish.'

'Well, that is precisely what I am,' I replied. 'A dervish; a man of the desert.'

I put the shovel in the barrow and wheeled it to the nearby heap of clay. It was so easy to load the well-crumbled soil, without having to hack it to pieces first with a pick. It was so easy to wheel the loaded barrow on the even surface of the brickworks. A few more journeys and the mixer was filled to the required level.

'I must be away,' said Sonia, moving towards me. 'I have to work too, you know.'

We walked to the cart, and I helped her climb aboard.

'Take it a bit easier, Yurie, you are sweating already,' advised Sonia. 'There is no need for you to work as hard as you worked over there. See you!'

'See you!' I replied, waving my hand.

I watched her driving away, and after a while she turned her head and waved. I waved back and went to work. I filled the hole with the required amount of water, then pushed on the pole, just inboard of the supporting wheel. This rotated the drums with spokes, mixing clay with water. It was quite hard work, especially as my feet tended to slip on the bone-dry surface. I cut a number of cavities round the circumference to make the job easier. Ludmila came along later to check the texture of the mix, after which I wheeled it to the other side of the shed where the bricks were made. My old brigade leader came to tell me that I should return to the vicinity of the camp with the women, and report to the building-site. I worked there until dark.

A new load of prisoners arrived at our hut that evening. They were all young thieves, and from them we learned that Germany had invaded the USSR the previous month. They had also heard a rumour that all non-political prisoners were going to be released and made to join the Red Army.

'If that happens, I will immediately volunteer for the front,' declared one of them.

'So will I,' I commented.

'Yes,' said he. 'You would volunteer to fight the Germans, but I? I would throw the carbine on the ground, run as fast as I could to the other side, shouting "Heil Hitler" as I went!'

He was not alone with his suggestion. Almost every man in the hut agreed with him. This came as no surprise to me as I had discussed the subject with others in various jails. The verdict of the overwhelming majority was that the Germans would be greeted with open arms as the liberators of the people from the yoke of Communism. And it seemed that, provided the German Army conducted the operation in a humanitarian way, the whole population would rise and there would be a massacre: the massacre of Communist rulers.

I worked in the brickworks for about a week. Although pushing that clay-mixing machine was hard work, at least I had some time in between the mixes to relax a little. The brigade leader came on a number of occasions but only to talk to Ludmila. I thought perhaps they were having a little affair. Sonia came a few times as well. One afternoon she sat down on the bricks underneath the roof of the shed as she always did. As I was returning from the other side of the shed, pulling the wheelbarrow behind me, she gave me a little tap on my behind as I was passing by.

'Hey, *Grazhdanka Normirovka*!' I called jokingly. 'What was that for? Am I not working hard enough or something?'

'I didn't say anything at all, prisoner,' she replied. 'All I tried to do was to hurry you up a little, then *Grazhdanka Normirovka* can show you to your new place of work.'

'Where do I go from here?'

'Don't be inquisitive, just finish your job!'

I did not press the point; I knew that any job given to me by Sonia must be an improvement. When I had delivered the last barrow of clay I bade the women goodbye. They did not seem to be at all surprised about my move. I washed my legs and presented myself to Sonia.

'Do you think you can drive the bullocks, Yurie?'

'Of course I can, Sonia.'

I had been watching the *staryk* each time he arrived. I noticed that when he wanted to turn the bullocks to the left he said '*tsyp, tsyp*', and to the right, '*tsybeeh*'. To start up he smacked his lips twice, to stop he called 'hoaaah'! I had driven horses many times in Poland, and I did not think bullocks would be more difficult.

'Well, Yurie, you may as well show me the proper way to do it,' Sonia said, handing me the stick.

'Princess,' I replied, bowing almost down to the ground. 'Your coach is waiting. Where would you like to go?'

'I will show you as we go along,' she said, trying to look mysterious.

I helped her to climb up and we were off in the direction of the camp. The bullocks were responding to my commands as though I had been their driver for years. My old mates were knee-deep in mud, walking round and round, as the slaves of the Roman Empire must have done in the past. The sight looked even more ghastly from the perch of the cart.

'Where do we go now?'

'Along the valley, below the quarry, to the reservoir.'

'That will be nice, I have never been beyond the quarry. In fact I have never been to the bottom of the hill.'

'It's lovely there, Yurie. The trail runs along the edge of the water, under the crag of a hill, to the clump of trees. I hope you will like it, too.'

'It certainly sounds beautiful, Sonia. Did you say trees?'

'Yes, I did. They are a kind of a poplar, but not as tall and a little more bushy.'

Sonia used to carry a rectangular board with some papers pinned to it. The sun was still beating down on us, so she used that board as an umbrella.

'Now perhaps you will appreciate why I keep wearing that turban, which you dislike so much.'

'I never told you that I don't like it, Yurie. I only said that you look like a dervish. In fact, I love you in it.'

'What did you say?'

Sonia did not reply. She looked straight ahead with her lips slightly apart, her elbows resting on her knees. After a short pause, still looking ahead as though talking to herself, she said: 'The camp Commandant asked me why I visit the brickworks so often. He is a good man, so I told him.'

'Well, what did you tell him?'

She looked at me with her beautiful blue eyes, hesitated for a moment, then looked ahead again.

'I told him that there is a nice young fellow working there, and I love him.'

As far as I knew there was only one young fellow, as she put it, working at the brickworks, and at that precise moment he was sitting right next to her. I felt very honoured. In her position as *Normirovka,* perhaps number two in the camp hierarchy, she could have chosen anyone she wished, and she had chosen me. I felt like hugging her, after all she was a lovely girl. Unfortunately, we were just coming to the quarry and the time was most inopportune.

The prisoners were hammering away with sledge-hammers, chisels and jemmies; no drills, no dynamite. I drove past the guard lying on the ground. He looked up at us with some interest, but said nothing. We reached the dam, a thick wall made of rock and cement, then drove along the water's edge to the clump of trees. From the dam, the road veered to the right past the crag of a hill, hiding us from the quarry. We came to a flat space between the trees and the side of the hill, and Sonia told me to stop. She made a move as though she were going to descend, so I jumped off and gave her my hands. She squeezed them, then jumped off herself. As before, her body came close to mine, but this time I took her in my arms and kissed her. Not only did she not object, but she started kissing me passionately, then pushed me away suddenly, still holding my hands.

'*Lyubchik* [darling],' she said, pausing to regain her breath. 'This place is not as private as you think. There are lots of hidden eyes watching the surroundings of this camp. I would hate to get you into any trouble.'

She told me what my job was going to be. I was to load the cart with sand, then transport it to the building-site. While I was loading, she strolled to the quarry, having told me to pick her up there. In comparison to the clay or mud the loading was easy. However, I still had to stop from time to time to catch my breath. Each time I rested I had a good look for those hidden eyes, but I could see nothing suspicious. I was certain they were there, otherwise Sonia would not have told me about them. Besides, I did not think I would have been allowed there on my own. I picked Sonia up on the way back and we drove towards the camp and the building-site. She told me to off-load the sand near the four elderly women who were sitting on the ground, sieving it by hand. It transpired that all I had to do was to bring enough sand each day to keep them occupied! She also told me that at the end of each day the *staryk* would collect the cart and the bullocks, while I should report to the brigade leader on the site to end my day there. I was going to pick up the team (my bullocks and cart) each morning at the building-site. It all sounded great: no more mixing with my feet, no more wheelbarrows!

Next morning I went out with the site workers and kicked my heels for an hour before the *staryk* appeared with my team. The sun was well up when I went down to the sand-pit on my own. I wondered what the guard at the bottom of the quarry would have to say but he did not seem to be at all interested. I was really thrilled with my new 'freedom', and for the first time in ages my spirits were high. When I arrived back at the building-site, Sonia was already waiting there.

'Yurie Stanislavovich,' she commanded, giving the most wonderful smile. 'When you have unloaded the sand, I will go with you to bring the vegetables.'

'*Khorosho, Grazhdanka Normirovka.*'

The official familiarity was to be expected with all those people about, and I could detect her face was saying something entirely different. I slid up the tailboard of the cart, letting the sand fall, then shovelled out the rest in no time at all. While I was fixing the tailboard Sonia climbed up and sat down on the left edge of the cross-plank. I took the hint and sat down on the right edge, leaving a gap between us. I smacked my lips twice and we were off.

'Good morning, Princess,' I greeted her as soon as we were far enough away from the guards and the prisoners. I looked straight ahead as I spoke, pretending I did not really care.

'I love you,' she replied. Sonia also looked ahead.

This strange behaviour was simply to show any spying eyes that there was nothing between us. But as soon as it was possible Sonia moved her hand along the board in my direction. I took it and squeezed it gently.

Before reaching the circles where I used to work, we turned right and drove to the vegetable garden which was irrigated by a trough leading from the reservoir. I cut some cabbages with a shovel while Sonia loaded them. Our hands touched on several occasions and it was nice to feel her velvet skin. When we came to collect the beans, propped up with long sticks, we were well sheltered from the view of the men working in the circles, or anyone else for that matter. Sonia put her hands around my neck, kissing me passionately, pressing her body against mine. After a moment or two she lost her balance, and fell to the ground taking me with her. I broke our fall as best I could, and it was quite obvious what she wanted me to do.

Alas! My health was not of sufficient standard for such an exercise; I had been fed too long on the meagre rations of the slave labour camp of the Communist empire. I had been worked too hard, for too long on that minute, vitaminless and proteinless portion, to behave like a full-blooded man. My mind went back to prison, and I could almost hear the examiner shouting at me: 'You will live, but you will not be able to make love!' They certainly knew what they were talking about, the scoundrels!

We kissed and cuddled for some minutes, and I think Sonia was happy. For my part I was very ashamed. When she opened her eyes all I could do was to say to her:'I am sorry, Sonia. I really am.'

'Don't worry, my love. It's not your fault; you can't be responsible for something which is not of your own doing. Please, my darling, don't worry.'

It was nice of her to say those words, although it didn't prevent me from feeling only half a man. On the way back I dropped Sonia off near the circles. Before she left, she looked at me with her big, beautiful blue eyes and murmured: 'My love, don't forget to look at the list of *stakhanovtsov*. I think your name will be on it.'

If Sonia said so, there was no point in even looking; it was bound to be there! My spirits soared and I dismissed the failure from my mind, looking forward to the evening meal. The first evening meal for months! After I had off-loaded the greens in the kitchen, I went back to the sand-pit. I was almost there when I saw a snake curled up at the water's edge. I clubbed it with the spade, cut its head off, made a fire out of thin twigs and put the body in the middle. The snake was black in colour with a grey underbelly, and about three feet long. I kept the fire going with dried up *yantok,* or what the Russians called *kolyuchka,* the prickly thing. After loading the cart I covered the fire with a hot, top layer of sand, and left the snake to bake.

When I returned about an hour later, my oven was still very hot and the snake too hot to handle. When it had cooled, I skinned it with a twig and ate it. It tasted quite good, something like a burned octopus, and a great improvement on the crow which I had cooked at Zhitomir. That evening in camp I went to inspect the notice board. There was I on top of the list with 140 per cent against my name. Good old Sonia! I followed the rest of the lucky few to the kitchen and received a dollop of thick porridge containing a few lumps of meat here and there. It did not spoil my appetite when someone suggested that an old camel must have died, hence the meat!

I saw Sonia almost every day. Sometimes she would travel with me as far as the turning to the quarry, sometimes all the way to the sand-pit, where at least we could sneak a kiss and a cuddle. One day in the middle of August she came to the building-site, looking very excited.

'Yurie Stanislavovich,' she said formally. 'Take me to the brickworks as soon as possible.'

She was visibly shaking with excitement, and I did not know how to take it. Was it something good, or bad? Before I had even finished attending to the rear of the cart, she was already sitting in her usual place, eager to go. I hurried as much as I could, and when I thought we were out of hearing range, I asked her: 'Princess, you seem to be a bag of nerves. Is there anything wrong?'

'Wrong, *lyubchik*? Nothing wrong at all, I am so happy for you! I have just been told that you are going to be released. Isn't that marvellous!'

I felt as though I had been hit with a huge hammer. For a moment everything seemed to spin around me, even the majestic Ak Tau wobbled from side to side. When everything became normal again, I turned my head towards Sonia, as if in a dream.

'What did you say, Princess?'

'It is true, Yurie. You are going to be released. After the Germans invaded our country there was an agreement between England and our leaders, which meant that all the Polish political prisoners will be released to form the Polish Army and fight Hitlerite Germany.'

I could feel my stomach knot into a tight ball while my heart thumped madly. Having conditioned myself to the idea of spending at least the next six months in Kizil Tau before attempting to escape in the early spring, the news of my unexpected release had to come as an enormous shock.

'I am going to be free! I am going to be a human being again!' I kept saying to Sonia, who was both crying and smiling at the same time.

'Oh, Yurie, I am so happy for you. I am so happy.'

She burst into an almost hysterical howl. Poor, dear, Sonia! She did not want to go the brickworks at all. She only wanted to take me away from the others to give me the news, and to share the happy moment with me. However, I thought that I took the news calmly. Two years in Communist captivity, and the experiences of others whom I had met had taught me not to expect anything until it happened. Thus, I worked for the rest of the day as though nothing had changed, and I went back with the others. The next day when I had finished with my team, I was told to return to the compound. I expected to be told something officially, but no such luck. I was not particularly worried because I knew Sonia would not have told me something that she did not believe to be the truth. On the third day I was summoned to the camp Commandant.

He told me briefly he had orders to send me back to Karabas for release, and that I would be sent there in due course. Until the day came I was still a prisoner and I had to work to earn my keep. So I worked as before, except that I did not have to heave those rocks up the hillside in the evening. I ate what the prisoners ate, my head was counted innumerable times each day, and I was locked up in the compound for the night like the rest.

A week after Sonia had given me the news of my release, I was told to stay behind in the compound, while the rest of the prisoners went out to their labours. An old banger of a lorry, very similar to the one which had brought me there, backed up to the camp entrance. I and a handful of prisoners were rounded up, searched, and ordered to climb aboard. At the last moment, Sonia appeared only a few yards away, looking very sad. We never said goodbye. I wished I could have just said 'thank you', but it was too late. I gently raised my hand. She returned the wave in the same manner, and I watched as two large tears rolled down her cheeks.

The lorry started up and began to move. I waved again, and she responded. Poor Sonia, she still had three years to do in that labour camp. I often wondered what happened to her and how she got on. I fervently hope she survived.

While waiting for the train at a small railway halt, I saw a long column of prisoners escorted by Red Army soldiers and dogs. All of them were heavily bandaged, some with missing limbs hobbling as best they could. When they came close enough, I realized that

153

they were German prisoners of war. It was not a pretty sight. Quite a number of them, their heads so heavily bandaged that they could not see, were marching with their hands resting on the shoulders of the men in front. Judging by the amount of dust on their clothes, they must have marched for some distance. I felt genuinely sorry for them. In my view, it was cruelty of the first degree.

After many hours, a prison train arrived, we boarded, and after a short wait we set off in a northerly direction. In the morning I looked through the window and spotted the familiar hill in the distance, with a group of mud huts surrounded by barbed wire. I waited for the screeching of the bogeys, and by the late morning I was back in Karabas.

A few days later I was called by the governor, who told me that I was going to be released and asked me where in the Akmolinsk Region I would like to settle. I had never heard of Akmolinsk, but so long as I was going to wriggle out of the clutches of the NKVD I did not really care. I settled for the town itself. The brute did not tell me a thing about the Anglo–Soviet Agreement, or about joining the Polish Army. And I could not very well ask him as it would have amounted to a betrayal of Sonia. It was obvious that Akmolinsk was not a major town; no political prisoner was allowed to settle in a first or second category town, places like Moscow, Kiev or Kharkov. Not even if he and his family lived there! So, I tried to find out where Akmolinsk was from other prisoners, and from the guards, but I drew a blank. The next day, in the afternoon, I was called to the guardroom.

I entered and saw the guard Commander sorting out some envelopes. When he found what he was looking for he sat down, inviting me to do likewise.

'Sit yourself down, Yurie Stanislavovich,' he said quite politely. 'Your release has come through and I shall not keep you long. You will catch the train, don't worry.'

He showed me the brown envelope he was holding in his hand, asking me if the name on it was mine. I nodded. He opened it, turned the envelope upside down and a pair of laces fell out.

'That pair of shoelaces is all that you have to collect,' he said, looking uneasy about the whole business.

'I should have received a St George medallion and my school

badge which were taken from me in Gorodnia prison, my watch which was taken in Chernigov jail, and a french-polished black walnut cigarette case which was taken from me in the Zhitomir Children's Working Colony,' I commented.

'You can have a look yourself,' he answered, offering me the envelope. 'There is nothing in it.'

I shrugged my shoulders, there was no point in pursuing the matter further. The goods had been stolen from me while in the custody of the NKVD, an agency of the Government of the Soviet Union. The guard Commander then produced a piece of green paper, about three inches by five, and handed it to me. The heading read: 'Certificate'. Underneath, written in longhand, was my full name, followed by a printed statement which said I was released from the labour camp on that date. At the bottom was the stamp, a big, five-pointed star, surrounded by some unintelligible print. The paper itself was very coarse and of poor quality, a factor which was to prove vital in the not-too-distant future. I folded it twice and stowed it in my pocket. The guard Commander gave me a pair of crude worn 'shoes' made of old tyres, usually called *ChTZ* and fifteen roubles as payment for my labours. Fifteen roubles for slaving away every day for a year! In terms of the bread which I knew I could get on the black market it amounted to precisely three kilos.

The guard handed me a railway ticket to Akmolinsk, saying that the train ought to arrive at the nearby halt at around 6 p.m. He took a few steps to the door, opened it, bidding me goodbye.

'Until I see you again!'

'Not if I can help it!' I replied, smiling.

He grinned, and I was out in the open steppe.

I estimated from the sun's position that it was approximately 5 p.m. The date was 5 September 1941.

PART THREE

Flight from the Workers' Paradise

10

I took a few smart steps away from the gate, turned left, then right, and ran a short distance. I looked back: there was no one behind me! I was free, free at last!

Yes, I was indeed free, but Communist-style. I was free in the sense that I was out of one of many thousands of 'small' prisons, but I was still inside a gigantic prison popularly known as the Soviet Union. And I was thousands of miles away from a truly free world, uncertain of my whereabouts.

I marched briskly to the junction where the spur of the railway leading to Karabas joined the main line. There was no platform, no building, just a well-trampled belt in the steppe by the side of the track. I paced up and down it a few times just to prove to myself that I could do so without having to ask permission. I took stock of the situation. There was I, in the middle of nowhere, waiting to go north. Akmolinsk had to lie south of the Trans-Siberian Railway, somewhere between Sverdlovsk and Novosibirsk. It could not be connected to that famous railroad, or the Comrades would have transferred me and others who ended up in Karabas, to a train going south from that point. I had no wish to stay in Akmolinsk until I died. If it had no rail link with the Trans-Siberian Railway, the only way out would be south, passing the same spot I was standing on, or walking hundreds of miles north. How many, I had not the slightest idea. Would it not be logical to start south now? No, I had to go to Akmolinsk wherever it was; try to find out where *I* was; fatten myself up a little; then disappear when I was prepared.

The sun was on the horizon when the train finally appeared in the distance. It was travelling very fast and for a moment I thought it would not stop. As it approached the halt it gave a long, multi-tone blast on its siren. I climbed aboard with some difficulty, since the step was rather high above the level of the ground. In a minute we were off. I had one last look at Karabas as it disappeared into the distance. I felt a little scared and insecure. Nearly two years in Communist captivity, and the knowledge of how easy it was to be arrested without really knowing why, must have weighed heavily on my mind.

We arrived in Akmolinsk just after one in the morning. By comparison to Karaganda, it was a small station. After I had handed over my ticket to a man at the door, I entered a large hall with a counter on the right but there was no one behind it. There were, however, a number of people sleeping on the floor, and since I could not think of anything else to do at that hour I found a spot by a wall, took my shoes off, spread my coat on the floor and went to sleep. When I woke up at about 5 a.m., one of my shoes was missing. There was no point in worrying, it was still early September and the chances of frost slight. I stowed the remaining one in my rucksack and strolled to the counter, now manned by a hefty-looking woman.

'Have you any bread for sale, Citizen?' I inquired.

'Bread, *molodchik*? You know we never sell bread at the station!'

Well, I did not know. I was aware that bread was rationed, but had thought the station restaurant might just possibly provide some for travellers. There seemed no harm in asking further.

'Do you sell anything to eat at all?'

'Yes, we shall have *kasha* [barley] after 6 a.m. Say! Where did you come from? You don't seem to know much!'

I just shrugged my shoulders and walked away. I was not sure whether to tell her that I had never lived in the USSR, that I had been released from the labour camp only the previous day. Her face was honest enough, but I knew how long it had taken me to gain the confidence of the free workers in Zhitomir, and I did not want a brush-off on my first day as a 'free' citizen.

Next I went round looking for a lavatory, hoping to have a wash. I found one all right, it stank of some pungent disinfectant and creosote. There was a tap, too, but the handle had been removed. I kicked my bare heels until 6 a.m. then asked the woman for a plate of *kasha*. It turned out to be semolina, no more than five teaspoonfuls, with a half-teaspoonful of very liquid red jam on top. It cost me sixty-five kopecks (100 to a rouble), but I could have eaten ten of those portions without making any impression on my hunger. I ate the food slowly, chewing each spoonful carefully, handed back the plate, and walked off in the direction of the town.

I must have criss-crossed the town of Akmolinsk many times north to south and west to east that day in search of work. But I had no luck. I asked several people but all I received was a shrug of the shoulders, or a simple 'don't know'. My stomach was empty so I returned to the station for a few plates of semolina. The woman behind the counter was the same one who had served me in the morning.

'Do you know where I could get a job, Citizen?' I asked, handing back my empty plates.

'Oh, I couldn't tell you. I thought you were a thief, and they never look for work.'

'No, I am not a thief, but I have just been released from Karabas Lager, and all I have is about eleven roubles in my pocket. That is not going to last very long.'

Suddenly, the woman lost interest in the conversation, retiring to the other end of the counter to clean some plates and cups. I could not really blame her. Since I had come out of a labour camp, and I was not a thief, I had to be some sort of 'enemy of the people' and she was not going to be seen talking to me. She had a job and she was not going to lose it on my account. I picked up my rucksack and wandered off in the direction of the town.

It was not long before I spotted a man painting a roof with red paint. I watched him for a while until his paint ran out and he had to come down for more. He was well over sixty, with sunken eyes. The can he was using to carry the paint up held no more than a gallon; it seemed such a waste of time and energy. He refilled the can, looked up the rickety old ladder, his eyes saying: I hate going up that thing! I offered to go up and do some while he had a smoke and a rest, but he would have none of it. I asked him if he knew of a job.

'You can try the place where I finally got mine, but don't be too hopeful. The place is open, although there isn't usually anyone around till late afternoon, if they come.'

'Many thanks. How much do you get for painting the roof?'

'Two roubles a day for a start. And if I prove I can do the job it will go up a little.'

Two roubles a day! By my calculations it amounted to three plates of semolina at the station, with five kopecks to spare! I went to the address he gave me. From the outside there was nothing to suggest that it was an office where one could get, or inquire about, work. As the old man had said, it was open; there was nobody about. The room was small, perhaps eight feet by twelve, divided in two by a counter. The walls were covered by the usual propaganda posters: a well-built youth carrying the infernal red flag in one hand, and a hammer, fork and spade, or something similar, in the other. Behind him was a smiling, buxom young girl carrying a sickle in one hand, and a bunch of corn, vegetables, or even flowers in the other. Underneath, in big letters, a slogan: Death to the enemy of the people and the capitalist bourgeoisie! Help build our Socialist Fatherland! Join this, that, or the other! I thought it all rather naïve, juvenile and silly. I walked out in disgust and continued my fruitless search for work, returning to the office from time to time in case someone did turn up. When it became dark I returned to the station, had a plate of semolina and went to sleep on the floor.

When I returned the next day for my lunch, the woman behind the counter gave me a bigger portion than normal, put a slice of bread in front of me and urged me to put it in my pocket. At about 3 p.m. a train arrived from the north. Hundreds of people emerged from it, all of them carrying their belongings in suitcases, pillow-cases, or bags. Listening to their conversations it transpired that the train was a special transport from Leningrad. One thing became very clear: there was a link between Akmolinsk and the Trans-Siberian Railway!

When the crowd in the waiting room had thinned down a little, I noticed a very high-ranking officer of the Red Army, together with a woman and two children, standing in the corner, surrounded by suitcases. I closed in, keeping my ears cocked. They, too, were refugees from Leningrad, and the officer was on leave of absence to help his family settle down. Their problem was that they could not all go to their house at the same time, since they could not possibly carry all the luggage. On the other hand, they did not want to leave any behind for fear of losing if. After a discussion, he decided to take the children and some of the luggage to the house while the woman agreed to stay behind.

'Citizen Commander,' I butted in, not really knowing how to address him, 'I am not doing anything, I will help you carry the luggage.'

'I am most grateful to you,' replied the officer. 'Unfortunately, the station staff cannot leave the building, otherwise I would have no such problems.'

I picked up two suitcases; it was not long before I discovered that I had bitten off almost more than I could chew. Those suitcases weighed a ton! Stopping a number of times, we finally reached a nice, big cottage. He had obviously been there before as he knew the route and had the keys. Halfway back to the station, I noticed a boot lying in the scrub; I made a mental note of it, hoping to retrieve it later. There was hardly anyone in the waiting room and it occurred to me that there was no point in the officer and his wife wasting any more time with their luggage, they had enough to do settling in after a long journey. I suggested to him that I would ask the woman behind the counter to keep an eye on the rest of the suitcases while we all went together, and I would return and collect the remainder myself.

He looked at me as though he had seen a ghost, but before he even uttered a word I asked the woman, and she agreed. The officer looked even more puzzled, not knowing what to do.

'It will be all right, Citizen Commander,' I assured him. 'I am not a thief, although I look like one.'

'He is all right,' interrupted the woman, smiling at the baffled officer.

'Do you know him, then?' he inquired.

'Well, yes,' she replied, with some hesitation.

We picked up most of the luggage and we were off. On the way back I retrieved the boot. It was an army boot, a left one, with the heel and the top in perfect condition, but the sole was missing. I thought if I could find a piece of old tyre and a length of wire, I could make it serviceable. I was approaching the house with the last piece of luggage when the officer's wife emerged with some rubbish which she threw into a large box standing at the side of a wall. I looked with interest, in case there was something of use there; there certainly was! Three pieces of bread, looking a little dry and old, but bread just the same.

'Citizen, would you mind if I took the bread that you don't want?' I asked.

'It's very old and full of mildew, but if you want it you most certainly can have it.'

So I took the bread. It was bone-dry and covered with mildew, but for me it was food and the mildew added to the flavour. I deposited the suitcase in the hall, bade the woman goodbye, and was just going through the door when I was called by the officer. He put his hand in his pocket and gave me thirty roubles. I was rich! I would have no financial problems for the next week at least. I could eat twice the amount I had eaten to date.

'Hey, Citizen!' I called to the woman behind the counter, beaming as though I owned the place, waving the money in front of her. 'He gave me thirty roubles! May I please have five portions of *kasha* on one plate?'

'I am very sorry, sonny, this is not allowed, but you most certainly can have five portions of *kasha*, one plate after another!'

I licked each plate clean before starting on another, to make sure I had my money's worth.

'Where are you from, laddie?' asked the woman, looking at me with interest.

'You tell me,' I suggested, licking the plate.

'Well, you are not a Ukrainian or Byelorussian, we have them here, but they speak their own language. You speak Russian, yet now, I don't think you are a Russian either. Are you a foreigner?'

'Yes, I am. I come from Poland.'

'Well, well, you did fool me. I would never have guessed. You have no accent at all.'

I was pleased to hear that, not out of conceit, but because it meant that I could pass myself off as a Russian, should it ever be necessary.

I went yet again to that confounded office, although it was dark, but it was a waste of time. I tried the bread, but it was very hard. I sprinkled it with water and left it for the night. It was quite edible by the morning, and I did not bother with semolina.

Every time I went anywhere, I kept my eyes open for anything with which I could repair my boot. One day I found a piece of thick wire, and decided to make a knife out of it. I made a loop at one end – that was the handle – then I hammered the other end with stones to make it flat. I spent a lot of time sharpening it, then I tried it on a piece of bread. It was the best knife I had ever possessed!

Four days after my arrival at Akmolinsk, on 10 September 1941 I noticed a lorry with a flat tyre. The driver was inspecting the damage when I got there and I gave him a hand changing the wheel. Needless to say, I asked him if he knew where I could get a job. To my astonishment he suggested that I go with him to the Soviet farm where he worked. He was sure I could get some form of employment there. We agreed to meet in a couple of hours. Since I did not know when I was going to eat next, I had three plates of semolina and bade the woman goodbye. When we met as agreed, the driver had another man in his cabin so I travelled on the back of the lorry. It was no hardship; I was well used to it!

We drove along a track which appeared as a thin scar on the steppe. The scenery was dull, an undulating expanse of country with only an occasional bushy-topped tree, about six feet tall, which relieved the monotony of it. Late in the afternoon, about fifty miles north of Akmolinsk, we arrived at a hamlet lying in a slight hollow. It comprised several mud huts and a number of sheds, and nearby was a wood.

The driver dropped me off outside a building, suggesting that I should go and speak to the farm manager whose office was there. I did go in but there was nobody about. The settlement was divided in two by a wide track running roughly east–west through the centre. The living quarters were on the south side, while the offices and the sheds were on the north. To the west, by the side of the track, there was another building, emitting smoke from the chimney. It was, in fact, a canteen, but there was no food for another hour.

I returned to the manager's office and found a woman there who told me that my chances of getting work were excellent. I was to return the following afternoon. On my way back to the canteen, several people gave me a second and third look as I passed. My head was shaven so perhaps they were wondering what an ex-prisoner was doing amongst them. They were shabbily dressed, the women wearing headscarves tied under their chins, and, all but a handful, bare-footed. There were a number of men in the canteen when I entered. The room was small and lit by a very low wattage electric bulb; it was so dark that it would have been impossible to read. When the hatch opened, the men got up and asked for soup or *kasha*, or both. They paid one and a half, or two and a half roubles, then sat at the table and ate using their spoons. The food smelt good, the soup was thick and the *kasha* had a spoonful of golden oil poured over it. I plucked up courage, then walked nonchalantly to the hatch and asked for both.

'I haven't seen you before, laddie,' said the chef. 'Where do you work?'

'I came to the farm only this afternoon.'

'Do you know where you are going to work?'

'No, I haven't the faintest idea. I went to see the manager, but he is away and won't be back till tomorrow.'

'I am sorry, laddie, this is the workers' canteen. When you are accepted, and the arrangements are completed for you to eat here, you will get a card. Only then will you be able to get food.'

So, there was to be no feast. All I could do was to watch others enjoying their food and smell the aroma. When the men had finished their meal, they chatted for a while, then left the room in ones and twos. After they had gone, I asked the chef if I could stay in for the night. I was not surprised when he refused. I went out, found a spot in the lee of the canteen, cuddled up to the wall and fell asleep.

As the sky to the east began to show signs of dawn, I woke up, frozen, even though I wore my *fufayka*. The canteen was still closed so I went to the centre of the settlement to have a drink of water. It was too cold to wash.

When the men started arriving, they collected a kilo of bread and a mug of tea, paid ninety kopecks, and sat down at the table to eat. When they left, I went round the tables picking up crumbs; the chap behind the counter saw me doing it, called me over, and gave me a small wedge of bread and half a mug of tea. He would take no money.

That kind of thing was to happen to me many times in the future. I had no option but to conclude that the ordinary people of that vast Communist empire, regardless of their nationality, were a good, honest, kind, and warm-hearted bunch, unlike their tormentors who were domineering, ruthless, brutal and unbending to the point of imbecility in their pursuit of the policies directed from the top.

Late in the day I saw the manager. He was a small man, about my height, with light blue eyes, wearing an army uniform. The standard belt he was wearing on top of his olive green shirt seemed out of proportion to his stature, and the narrow cross-belt was about six inches too long. He asked me for an identity card, and I showed him my release certificate. He examined it carefully, asked me what I was doing in the labour camp and whether I had any experience of working in the fields. He seemed quite pleased with my answer, turned the certificate on the obverse side, and wrote something on the top left corner of it. He picked up a file and perused it, flicking the pages backwards and forwards.

'Very well, you are registered,' he muttered. 'You will be accommodated with Citizen Prosniewska, a countrywoman of yours.'

He told me how to find the hut and where to report in the morning. I looked with interest at the release certificate, wondering what the official had written. It stated: 'Registered in the Soviet farm named after Kaztsik, Akmolinsk Province.' That was all, but it meant that when the time was ripe for me to leave, unofficially of course, anyone who saw the certificate would know I was on the run. In other words, I had no means of identification away from the Province of Akmolinsk, a major disadvantage in a country where the citizens were obliged to have an internal passport if they wanted to travel from one place to another.

Citizen Prosniewska was a woman in her forties, living in a small, two-roomed dwelling, part of a long, white-painted mud hut. One room was about nine feet by twelve, and the other slightly larger. With her lived her son, Jurek, and another woman, who I thought was her sister or possibly sister-in-law. They had come to the farm, like the rest of the community in the settlement bar a few Kazakhs, under a scheme of 'free settlement'. Like many other such schemes in that Communist empire, the meaning was much more sinister. For Madame Prosniewska, like millions upon millions of other people living east of the Urals, had been woken up one night by a knock at her door. When she opened it, two NKVD men had invited themselves in, telling her to pack her

167

things up. She was not told why or where she was going, except that she had an hour to get ready and the order was also valid for her son and the other woman. They were loaded on to the usual freight train and in due course off-loaded at a small station near the farm. Once at the farm, they were informed that they were free to move within Akmolinsk Province but not any further. They were 'resettled', although they did not want to be resettled. They were not under lock and key so technically they were free, hence 'free resettlement'. What a misnomer!

When I found Madame Prosniewska and told her who I was, she greeted me with open arms. She immediately put a kerosene-burning stove on a table and prepared a meal for me. It tasted fabulous. I had almost forgotten it was possible to eat without having to block one's nose! I spent most of the evening telling them my story, and at about midnight we went to bed. I slept in the same room as Jurek, on a bag filled with straw. I felt like a king! We got up at six, and after a meal of *kasha* Jurek and I went to work.

There was room for about forty animals in the stables, although there were only a few bullocks inside, tethered to their troughs. A large man appeared, pointed to a wheelbarrow and told me to muck out the stable. I put my back into it, and by ten o'clock the place was spotless. All that was required now was some straw, but there was no sign of the man and I had no idea where to find him. I spent the next couple of hours doing nothing.

'Sorry about that,' said the brigade leader when he returned. 'The man who should have brought the straw has not come back from Alexeevka. He must be lost, or something.'

'Well, there is a cart,' I replied, pointing to a waggon. 'The bullocks are in the stable. I'll rig them up and fetch it, if you tell me where from.'

'Can you handle the beasts?'

'Of course I can. I was doing that in the *lager*.'

'I'm glad to hear that as we're short of drivers. So, after you've spread the straw, hook up the cavalry to the milk waggon and bring the milk from the farm to the piggery. You've got yourself a job, Yurie Stanislavovich!'

I knew I was going to enjoy being a driver, going from one place to another instead of being tied to one spot. The bullocks were docile and gave me no trouble. Having spread the straw, I harnessed them to the milk waggon, a huge vat on wheels, and we were off in the direction of the wood. Once there, I could not resist stopping the cart to run about for a time, as though I were a little boy. I felt wonderful. The wood was not very large, about half a mile in diameter, and when I emerged from it the farm was not far away. Later, when I reported to the office, I was surprised to find the manageress was a Pole and not yet nineteen. She seemed to be full of self-importance but otherwise quite pleasant. She offered me a pint of milk which tasted absolutely splendid. I was under the impression that I was drinking pure cream. She told me that the milk I was taking to the piggery came from a herd infected with tuberculosis. That took the smile off my face as I had planned to help myself to a litre or so. I filled the vat, covered the top with a lid and we were off. By the time we entered the wood again, I came to the conclusion that the odd litre ought not to affect me in any way, and my stomach was rumbling in full agreement. I stopped the team, took the lid off, lowered my head into the vat, and drank till I could drink no more. I left the cart in the piggery and brought the bullocks back through a short cut to the stables.

I finished work about seven and went to the canteen, hoping that arrangements had been made for my messing there. I was disappointed. I returned to my lodgings and the untiring Madame Prosniewska produced yet another excellent meal. After the dishes had been cleared away I was asked to continue with my story, some of which they could not begin to comprehend. And I was ashamed when I realized that I could express myself in Russian more easily than I could in Polish.

As the days progressed, I was sent to different parts of that gigantic farm. I met more and more people: Poles, Russians, Ukrainians – all of them 'free resettlers' – and a few Kazakhs. The latter were very surprised when I spoke to them in their own tongue, however imperfect it was. They gave me much encouragement since most of them did not speak Russian, or knew only just a few words appropriate to their work.

Most of the interpreters were, in fact, the children, who, playing together, soon picked up the language. It was fascinating to watch an eight- or nine-year-old Polish child talking Polish to its father, Russian to a Russian, at the request of a Kazakh who could not speak the other two languages, and the child translating as though all three of them were his native tongue!

One day the brigade leader saw me passing through the settlement and waved me to a stop.

'Yurie Stanislavovich,' he called. 'Do you think you could handle a team?'

The team was a convoy of three bullock carts tied one behind the other, each cart being pulled by its own pair of bulls.

'I think so,' I replied. 'I have never done it before but I'll try.'

'Good. As you know, we are short of drivers. The harvest has to be gathered and the wheat transported to Alexeevka. If you think you can do it, have a bite to eat, and you can take the first load this afternoon.'

I was quite thrilled. I knew Alexeevka was about twenty miles to the west and, most importantly, there was a railway line going through it all the way to Petropavlovsk! When I returned to the stables, my team was ready. The lead bulls were the experienced ones I had been driving up till then, followed by four young ones, yoked together in pairs. The brigade leader told me where to go and what to do for the next few days, and I was off.

The team behaved quite well, and once I grasped the feel of the whole length of the convoy the driving was fairly simple. I found the wheat in a huge heap on the ground, growing bigger as more grain arrived from the combines. Leaving the field behind me I reached the trail and turned the team towards the west. Like the other tracks in that region it was just a well-trodden scar in the steppe. When potholes began to appear, a driver would make a detour to one side or the other and the oncoming teams would follow suit. In time, the whole length of the trail would be shifted away by as much as a mile from the original.

It had been dark for some time when I finally arrived at Alexeevka. I deposited the wheat in the store as directed, then went to the canteen for a meal. Since I had no ration card, the cook would not sell me any food. This time though, I was no longer a greenhorn; I argued with him until he was convinced that I was telling him the truth, then ate my fill. Passing the railway station out of the village, I decided it would be a good idea to find out how the trains ran. The station was poorly lit and it was too dark to read the timetable so I had to ask the ticket-seller for details. I also weighed myself on an ancient weighing-machine. I balanced at fifty-four kilos, or just under eight and a half stone. The weight included the *fufayka* I was wearing, which must have weighed at least a kilo, and the meal which I had consumed only minutes earlier must have accounted for a further half a kilo. I weighed myself on the same machine two weeks later. I had gained seven kilos, or fifteen pounds. I never did regain my normal weight, namely sixty-five kilos, until I departed from that land of milk and honey.

Later, I drove my bulls perhaps half a mile into the steppe, released them from their yokes, tied their legs and let them graze. I found a level spot under the cart and went to sleep. I woke up as it was getting light. With some apprehension I looked round for my bulls, but they were all there. I rounded them up and soon we were on our way. It was in this fashion that I spent the next week, transporting grain from different parts of the farm to the main store in Alexeevka, without staying indoors even one night. It did not worry me unduly; I loved the freedom of movement and being more or less my own boss.

Gradually the nights became colder and it rained occasionally, although the days were still fairly warm. I was now registered at the canteen, but I was still without a ration card. The money I had expected at the end of the week did not materialize either, so after a big argument I was given food on account. I did not think it fair that I should pay for the privilege of working on the farm.

One very dark night, just after a shower of rain, I was sitting on the cross-plank with my bare feet on the steering-pole getting progressively colder. I was driving more by instinct than anything else, looking forward to some hot soup in Alexeevka. Suddenly the bulls stopped. I yelled, shouted, and swore at them, but they would not budge, so I lowered myself to the ground to see what was the matter. My heart stood still; the middle left bull was lying on the ground! My immediate thought was that he had broken a leg, and my mind went back to the Kazakh lorry driver who had told me he received seven years for breaking a wheel in similar circumstances.

I crouched over the animal, stroking his legs with my hands, feeling for something unusual. All the legs were there and the bones seemed to be connected in the normal fashion. I sighed with relief. His hide was wet, but so were the hides of the others. I could not see any froth, a sure sign of sweating. It now became clear to me that the bull had decided he had had enough, and had called it a day by lying on the ground. I tried to raise him by a gentle tap of my stick, then a not-so-gentle one, but he did not respond. I gave him a sharp wallop on his hind-quarters without success. I scratched my head, trying to think what could possibly be the matter with the animal. Nothing like it had ever happened in my short and distinguished career as a bull driver. I put my hand in my pocket, fished out a box of matches, crouched over the bull and struck a light. There he was lying in the mud with his eyes open, looking nowhere in particular. His mouth was open, too, and his tongue was hanging out.

'Oh my God!' I thought. 'He is dead! What do I do now?' My first thought was to run. I could walk to Alexeevka, have a meal in the canteen, then catch a train to Petropavlovsk. 'Yes,' I thought. 'But then what? Where do I go? What do I use for money? What do I use for identification?'

I had left my rucksack and my release certificate in my lodgings, and I only had a few roubles left. I still did not know enough about travelling on the trains and the difficulties connected with them. No, I decided to wait and see; maybe the bull was just very tired, or had collapsed due to some illness. I knelt in front of his head, and lowered my ear to his nostrils, listening for any sign of breathing. He was breathing! He was alive!

I could hear the noises of a team approaching from the east. I strolled towards it to warn the driver that I was stuck ahead, in case he did not see in time.

'Woah!' I called, as the first pair of the bulls were about to pass me. 'Good evening, pal,' I greeted him in Russian.

'Greetings, my friend!' replied a voice in Kazakh.

I corrected myself hastily. I told him about my problem. He lowered himself to the ground, put his hand round my shoulders and assured me everything was all right. He would get the animal up in no time at all. He crouched over the beast putting the first and third finger of his right hand in his mouth and lowered his head until his mouth was inside the bull's ear. He then blew, producing an ear-piercing whistle. To my utter amazement, the animal jumped up and pawed the ground, obviously eager to go! I was dumbfounded; I stood there with my mouth wide open unable to speak. I shook my head as if I had just woken up from a bad dream only to see a miracle. By then the Kazakh was standing beside me, smiling. I patted his back with my hand.

'Good man, good man!'

'It is nothing!' he replied in a matter-of-fact voice, shrugging his shoulders.

I escorted him to his cart and we continued our journey together. I had plenty of time for reflection before we reached Alexeevka. I was glad that I had learned the Kazakh language when I'd had the opportunity, unlike others who did not bother. At least I could explain to the Kazakh in his own tongue what my predicament was. Not only that, had I spoken to him in Russian, he might not have come to my aid. The reason was simple. To all but a handful of Kazakhs, or for that matter any other indigenous people east of the Urals and south of the Trans-Siberian Railway down to the border, anyone speaking Russian was automatically taken for a Communist, and therefore an enemy of the tribe.

When we off-loaded our respective carts, we went to the canteen for a meal. I tried to pay for his supper but we would not let me. We chatted for a while, then drove our teams into the steppe for the night. We parted company a couple of miles from the farm. He was going to pick up another load, while I was returning to the farm. On arrival, I led my team into the stables, fed them with a mixture of chopped straw and oats, then spent the rest of the day greasing the carts and the milk waggon. I was glad to be back. It suddenly became very cold and snow began to fall. The shower did not last very long but it was a sign that winter was not far off. As always, Madame Prosniewska greeted me with open arms. She did not know what had happened to me, and frankly thought I had already departed to pastures new. I told her it would not be long before I did, but I wanted to gain a little more strength, learn more about the problems of travel, and earn more money. She asked me if I would take her son with me when I decided to leave. I agreed readily.

From the bits of information I had received here and there, it became apparent that the Polish Army was being formed somewhere south of the Urals. On one occasion I even heard the name of the alleged place, Buzuluk, but nobody had any idea where it could be. My plan therefore was to travel to Petropavlovsk and pick up a train going as far as the Urals. Then I would start looking for Buzuluk. However, this scheme was not as simple as it sounded. To travel anywhere out of the immediate area one had to have a permit, and before a person could obtain one he needed to have a very good and valid reason for doing so. To leave the Province an individual required a passport, and nobody in a Soviet farm ever possessed one. I decided to worry about these problems when the time came to leave, and for the moment I needed to make as much money as I could.

As far as I knew *Sovkhoz Imenia Kastsika* comprised 18,000 hectares (45,000 acres) of wheat, of which 4,000 hectares had been gathered before the snows came, leaving the rest to rot. It also had two hectares of potatoes, but I had never seen the field, nor eaten a potato. There were also some oats and turnips. I wondered how much of that failure was due to the management and how much to Communist dogma. I had been to the office on a number of occasions. I had seen the face of the manager when he walked in to ask one of the staff if this or that had arrived, only to be answered in the negative. I had seen operations in the fields in accordance with the Communist dogma, the dogma which belonged to the nineteenth century. I also wondered how many of those 14,000 ungathered hectares would have been harvested if people like Mischa and his fellow Kulaks, Red or Plain, had been given the task instead of doing time in the Communist labour camps. I had my own answer.

One day I was sent to fetch wheat from the most easterly part of the farm, a place called Ivanovskoe. When I arrived in the field there was no heap of grain. The combine was stationary and the attendant workers were lying on the ground doing nothing. It transpired that a split pin had sheared, allowing a bolt to work loose. I could have made it serviceable in less than a minute by securing it with a piece of wire, but that would mean initiative.

'I'm paid to drive the combine, not to repair it,' said the driver. So, a brigade of some thirty workers spent most of a long day doing nothing.

On the way back to the farm it started to snow. The shower did not last long, but long enough to leave a good sprinkling of snow over the steppe and the still unharvested cornfields. As I entered the wood it became quite dark. After some minutes, I thought I saw a small, greenish light floating low amongst the trees. It looked similar to the light produced by glow-worms in May. But it was not May, it was the end of September. I thought perhaps I was imagining things.

A few more minutes passed and I saw the light moving again. I looked over to the other side of the road and spotted the same phenomenon. Fascinating! The bullocks cocked their ears and were breathing heavily through their nostrils. I did not like the look of that. I had crossed the wood many times before and could not recall any such spectacle. There were a few dogs in the farm, but they never strayed this far. Suddenly, my blood froze in my veins: wolves! A pack of wolves!

I smacked my lips several times, tapping the bulls on their hind-quarters to make them go a little faster. There was no real need for me to do so, they had already increased the pace themselves. They were as scared as I was, and they did not like the idea of staying in that company for longer than was necessary. My heart, no longer in its usual position but stuck in my throat, was thumping hard. My brain was working fast, trying to find a solution. Now and then, I could see the vague outlines of the beasts, snaking through the wood parallel to the cart, closing to within a couple of yards of us, jockeying for position in preparation for an attack.

My mind went back to my classroom in Poland, and a story I had read about a family riding home on a sledge drawn by a pair of horses. They, too, were about to be attacked by a pack of wolves while travelling through a wood. They saved themselves, and their horses, by shouting their way out of danger. Thus, I took a deep breath and yelled as I had never yelled before. In comparison, Tarzan's call of the bull elephant would have sounded like the buzz of a mosquito suffering from a chest complaint! My throat hurt, but I kept on yelling. It produced a double effect: it made the bulls break into a trot, something I had never achieved before, and the shadows of the wolves began to merge with the darkness of the trees, as they moved away from the edge of the road.

We shot past the last of the trees at a steady ten miles an hour, or maybe less, but it seemed to me as though we were travelling at some supercosmic speed, and I were sitting on a rocket rather than a rickety old cart. I looked back towards the open space between the wood and us to see if we were being followed. The moonlight was bright enough for me to see clearly, and with enormous relief I realized we were alone. I slowed down, then brought the bulls to a halt. They were still shaking, and so was I. I looked back once more towards the wood and there, about two or three yards from the edge, was a row of dog-like animals sitting on their tails. I smacked my lips and we were off to the safety of the piggery to deliver some milk.

By this time I had been working for nearly three weeks and still had received no payment for my toil. Madame Prosniewska offered to her son and me sufficient money to buy a ticket to Mamlyutka, a village just to the west of Petropavlovsk. However, I wanted to wait and collect what was legitimately mine.

So, on pay day I went to the office to collect my wages. They were not there: the money had still not come, it would perhaps come tomorrow. I waited until 'tomorrow', but no money arrived. As far as I was concerned, it was not going to come for a long time and I was not prepared to wait any more. I decided to leave that night.

Coming out of the office, I ran into my brigade leader. He instructed me to bring in a bull which had been left in the piggery to the stables. As always, I took the short cut across the still-standing wheat, and it started snowing again, really hard. By the time I reached the sheds, the ground was white. It was still snowing when I left the piggery with the bull, the big, white flakes cutting visibility to about five yards. I was glad of the short cut: I did not have to worry about direction, all I had to do was to keep to the path.

Somewhere along that path – just to the left of it – I saw an animal standing in the corn. I thought it was a calf that had strayed and lost its way in the snowstorm. I stopped the bull and went to retrieve it.

'Come on, you little fool,' I said lovingly to it. 'Time to go home, or you'll freeze to death out here.'

When I came to within a yard of it, the blood rushed from my head, my knees wobbled and I froze in my tracks: it was no calf, it

176

was a fully grown wolf! I wanted to scream, but my throat refused to oblige. I was petrified.

It was one thing to look at the beasts from the comparative safety of the cart, but it was an entirely different matter to stand in front of one without even a twig in my hand. How long that impasse lasted, I had no idea. When I did get my wind back, I noticed that the wolf was standing by the remains of some animal, most probably a young calf, and only then did it occur to me that it must have had its fill, or it would have attacked me before. I took a deep breath and yelled. I yelled so hard that I thought my temples would burst under the strain. The wolf jerked its body backwards, its feet still in their original position, lifted its top lip, baring its yellow fangs. I thought it was going to leap at me, so I yelled again, now more from terror than conviction. The wolf almost sat on its tail, turned slowly about, pivoting on its hind legs, its front ones moving through the air as though it were a thick glue, and ran away in big, slow leaps.

I must have stayed there for a full minute before venturing back to my bull, which was just as terror-stricken as I felt. I smacked my lips, and in a few minutes we were back at the farm. As if by magic it stopped snowing, everything returned to normal except for a thick covering of snow.

As soon as I arrived back at my lodgings, I told Madame Prosniewska of my decision to leave. She put a few things in a bag for her son, gave him the little money she had, then prepared a good meal. At about eleven o'clock in the evening I bade my friend goodbye, and left the room to let her say her farewells to Jurek. I waited about five minutes before he emerged, alone. She could not very well stand at the door waving her hand.

It was starting to snow again.

11

It had just stopped snowing, when, half an hour after leaving the farm, we heard the creaking of the carts catching up with us. Jurek wanted to dive for cover but I stopped him before he had a chance.

'Look, Jurek,' I told him. 'Let me deal with this. Like you, I don't want to be caught either, but I see no reason why we should walk if there is a possibility of a ride to Alexeevka. I have worked here for three weeks, without a break and without pay. I'm going to get some of that money back by being taken to the station on a farm transport.'

He had no option but to agree. He was a good fellow, though a little slow in dealing with various unexpected situations.

'Woah!' I called, when the first pair of bulls was about to pass me. 'Good evening, mate!' I greeted the driver. 'We are going to Alexeevka, may we cadge a ride?'

'Yes, of course,' replied the driver. 'Where do you work? I don't remember ever seeing you before.'

'I don't remember seeing you, either,' I replied. 'Like you, I am a team driver.'

'Well, that explains it. Hop in!'

I buried myself in the grain, and asked Jurek to let me know when he saw the lights of the village. We bought the tickets without any problem and by cadging the lift we had time to spare. We went to the canteen. I tried to persuade Jurek to eat while he had the chance, but he refused. Maybe his stomach was still feeling queasy, having left his mother only a short time before. I did not have such problems.

We arrived in Petropavlovsk without any difficulty. The main part of the railway station was the booking-office, a large hall with a high ceiling and tiled floor. It was here that I saw myself in the mirror for the first time. I nearly burst out laughing: I did look a mess! On my head, I had a Red Army hat without a badge and ear flaps down. The hat was too big, so its peak was permanently covering my eyes. On my body, I wore a very torn *fufayka* without buttons, so I had a length of string tied round the middle to secure the front. My legs were covered with black cotton trousers, a little too short, showing my bare ankles. On my right foot I wore a grey *ChTZ* which was too big so that I had to drag my foot on the ground to stop it from falling off. On my left foot I had the black boot with its steel rim round the heel which produced a loud 'clonk' each time I put that foot down, followed by the 'shshsh' of the *ChTZ* as it slid along the ground.

Once in the booking-hall, I looked round for the timetable to see when the next train would be going westward. Our luck held: there was a train going that night all the way to Moscow. I decided to board it and get off at Sverdlovsk, dodging the conductor on the way if at all possible. If caught, I was going to plead that we had boarded the wrong train.

There was a queue stretching from one of the booking-office windows, through the door and into the open. After some tactful inquiries, I discovered to my horror that before we could get on to the platform we had to change our tickets for new ones. In Poland, if I wanted to travel from A to B via C and D, the ticket was valid all the way, no matter how many changes there were on the journey. In the Soviet Union, at least while I was there, that was not so. Each time one had to change trains, one had to change tickets, and if necessary show the permit and the passport. This system prevented people like Jurek and myself going very far unnoticed. We had no option but to join the queue. When we finally reached the window, the ticket-seller wanted to know why we wanted to go to Mamlyutka, whom we were going to see, and how long we were going to stay. I gave him a well-prepared story, and after careful examination of Jurek's identity card and my release certificate, he gave us the tickets.

We waited until the bell rang twice before boarding the express, keeping a wary eye out for the conductor. The train was quite crowded, a good thing from our point of view, and the ride much smoother than the previous one. All the benches were made of varnished wood, a little uncomfortable for someone travelling all the way from Vladivostok to Moscow, a mere six thousand miles! After a few hours we arrived at Kurgan. I had never heard of the place, but my stomach told me it was time to eat. I left Jurek on the train, the safest place I thought, and followed my nose to the restaurant. It was a large room, with several tables occupied by people obviously enjoying their meals. With just over three roubles in my pocket, I did not plan on buying anything; I hoped I might pick up enough leftovers for both of us. What I had not realized however, was that I was not the only person with such ideas. There were a number of *bezprizornye* jockeying for the best positions, swooping down on tables recently vacated by some satisfied person or other.

A few moments after I entered the room a man, who had just brought his meal from the counter at the far end of the room, asked me if the train to Sverdlovsk had arrived.

'Yes! It has just rung twice!' I replied, with as much urgency as I could muster. 'Yes, you had better hurry!'

He did! To my great and welcome surprise, he leapt off the stool he had just sat down on, and darted for the door! In a flash, I sat down in front of the meal he left behind, claiming it as mine. I drank the soup, a thick, green pea soup, straight from the plate; I picked up the small roasted chicken leg from the second plate, and concealed it in the front fold of my *fufayka*. Then I scooped up what looked like soggy boiled potatoes, licked the plate clean, departed with my spoils, and caught the same train as my benefactor! The vegetable was not boiled potato, but chopped, boiled turnip. Jurek and I ate it with our fingers straight from my hand. Then I broke the chicken leg in half, put both pieces behind my back, and invited Jurek to choose. I thought it was the fairest way. That was the first solid chunk of meat I had eaten since arriving in the USSR.

We arrived in Sverdlovsk before midday, having successfully dodged the conductor several times. My plan was to catch a train going to Orenburg, the only town that I remembered from my atlas which lay to the south. I scanned the timetable several times, but there was no mention of such a place. To make our position more difficult, the booking-hall and the restaurant had become emptier. I was worried that it would not be long before someone asked us what we were doing there. Jurek was all right, he looked like a Russian, but in my rig-out I looked like a *bezprizornyi*. We therefore retired to the toilet until another train arrived. I decided to pluck up courage and ask someone if there was a train going south. I looked at several faces, trying to spot one intelligent enough to know what I was talking about, but at the same time unlikely to be inquisitive. I noticed a man in his sixties, with a beard. He sat alone, drinking tea.

'Excuse me, Citizen. I am trying to get to Orenburg. Do you know how I could do so?'

'Orenburg?' he replied, raising his eyebrows. 'Where do you come from, laddie?'

Obviously I had said something silly and I had to think fast. His face seemed honest enough; I had to tell him who I was.

'I am a Pole. I have been released from a *lager* to join the army. I was told that it was being formed near Orenburg.' I put my hand in my pocket and took out my release certificate, opening it slowly. 'Here is my release certificate, if you want to see it.'

'I don't want to see it, laddie,' he replied. 'Orenburg is not called that any more. It is called Chkalov, and if you take a train to Cheliabinsk and change there, you will find it!'

'I am most grateful, Citizen. No wonder I couldn't find it on the timetable!'

There was a train going in that direction, so while Jurek went to get some *kasha*, it being his turn to provide a meal, I sat down on the floor, meditating. All I knew about Cheliabinsk was that tractors were made there. I did not know how far south of Sverdlovsk it was situated. If it turned out to be a fair distance south, my decision was to get off there and start looking for the Polish Army. It was dark when the train arrived. To my horror, the waggons were small and the train almost empty. The conductors were standing outside the doors, and they would have spotted us entering even had they been half blind. I grabbed Jurek's hand, leading him to the dark part of the station towards the end of the train.

'Do you fancy riding on buffers, Jurek?' I asked.

'What? Don't you think it would be a bit dangerous?'

'I don't know about that,' I replied. 'I have never tried it before, but we must not miss this train!'

I told him to make a dash for it as soon as I gave him a push, and to sit on the collar not the shaft, keeping his hands well away from the latter and the buffer-plates. When the bell rang twice, a number of people dashed out of the restaurant and in the confusion I thought we would not be seen getting on to the buffers. I gave Jurek a push, jumping on the buffers myself a few moments later, and we were off.

I was riding the buffer facing the wind with my feet on the circular plate. The draught was becoming vicious, and the ride became rough as the train gathered its full speed. We were both frozen and a short respite we had while the train stopped at some station half an hour later was not sufficient to thaw us. There was nothing else we could do except to get off at the first opportunity. Fairly soon afterwards the train slowed down to walking pace, so I told Jurek to jump. We decided to wait until daylight, and then, if possible, pick up a goods train. The reasoning behind this move was obvious. I had seen several freight trains in Alexeevka, and they all included a long, platform-type waggon, with low side walls or none at all. And, without exception, they all had a board at the front and rear, about four feet tall, which would make an excellent wind-break.

It was one of these waggons that we boarded early in the morning. Poor Jurek, never an energetic fellow at the best of times, did not seem to know much about the mechanics of such an exercise and nearly kicked me to death in the process. Once he was on board, I grabbed the side-board with both my hands and kicked the ground as hard as I could, at the same time pulling myself up. I was sitting next to him before he had fully recovered from his ordeal. We slid along the platform towards the forward board, only to discover that we were not alone, that there were three other bodies already there. It was clear they were travellers like us, rather than railway guards; no one in his right mind would voluntarily stay in the open if he had a perfectly cosy box in which to pass the night hours.

A string of swear words greeted us as we sat down with our backs to the board. I knew then that we were in good company, the company of the *bezprizornye*. I warned Jurek to keep a tight hold on his bag or else he would never see it again. I knew the rules! It was quite light when we woke up to see three white, young, miserable faces eyeing us with suspicion. I knew I must put their minds at rest and also obtain some information. I swore juicily in the best tradition of the *bezprizornye*, and told them that we were not ghosts.

'Where are you from?' inquired the eldest of the three, a lad of about sixteen.

'I have just come out of Karabas. Where are you from?'

'We have been operating round here, but it's getting cold, time to go south.'

'We are making for Cheliabinsk. Any idea when we are likely to get there?'

'We shouldn't be far now, but what the hell do you want to go there for? It's not what it used to be you know. The grub's difficult, and there are too many troops and refugees.'

'Not to worry, we shall give it the once-over. Let me know when to get off.'

'All right, but I think you're fools!'

I toyed with the idea of telling him why we wanted to go to Cheliabinsk, but that would be admitting I wanted to go straight. There were three of them and two of us, and Jurek was not much use. He was too gentle, too naïve. They would have worked us over, taking the few things we had. No, it was not worth it.

We were in the middle of the town before the train slowed down sufficiently for us to jump off. We ran across a maze of tracks, ending up on a street paved with cobblestones. The town was obviously well-established and some of the buildings were quite impressive, although drab-looking. There was also a modern part of large industrial structures. I saw a small, red object lying on the other side of the street. I crossed over and picked it up. It was a Red Army hat badge, a red, five-pointed star edged with brass, and a brass hammer and sickle in the centre. At first, I was going to throw it away, but changed my mind and kept it as a souvenir.

Rounding a corner, I saw a mass of people standing in a queue, about three deep, with a militiaman at the end of it. I wondered what they were queueing for, but did not think it prudent to ask the uniformed man. We continued along the wide, unevenly cobblestoned street, keeping the queue on our left, until perhaps half a mile further on we came to a massive building. It was a railway station, and the people were queueing either to buy a ticket, or exchange the one they had for another. The reason for the militiaman being there was not to keep the queue in order. It was for another, most unusual, purpose.

Queueing for tickets in Cheliabinsk at that time was a very lengthy business. To enable people to break the queue in search of food without losing their places, the militiaman would write their place numbers in indelible pencil on the backs of their hands. They could then leave, come back several hours later, and return to their original place in the queue. The booking-hall turned out to be larger than the one in Petropavlovsk. It had several booking-windows but only one was in operation, the one with the queue. Next to this window diagonally opposite the entrance, there was a door with a notice on it: Commander of the Station.

There was no sign of a restaurant, so I parked Jurek in a corner, leaving my rucksack with him while I went looking for a place where I could 'obtain' some food. I did find the restaurant in the end; there was apparently nothing to be had. However, there were a number of *bezprizornye* in the room, a clear enough indication that it was worth waiting there. When some of them closed in towards the counter, I joined them, and when the *kasha* appeared I was one of the first to be served. By the time we had finished eating our portions there was no more for sale.

Afterwards Jurek and I walked for hours round the town, asking people if they knew anything about the Polish Army, only to receive a shrug of the shoulders. The message was clear: the army was not there. We spent the night at the station, and in the morning I asked Jurek if he had any money left. He gave me a banknote, popularly known as 'the Red one', and I went to join the queue to buy a ticket to the nearest station past Cheliabinsk, just to gain an entrance to the platform. When I reached the end of the queue the militiaman licked his middle finger, spread saliva all over the back of my left hand, picked up the pencil and scribbled a number on my skin: 10,115!

I left the queue and decided to see the Station Commander. I planned on spinning him a yarn about trying to join the Red Army and not being able to get a ticket, to see if he might be able to help. I did see him several hours later, only to be told that it had nothing to do with him, that I should get a chit from the Town Commander. I thanked him for this advice but did not feel like following it. What if he suggested I should join here, in Cheliabinsk? What if he asked me for my identity papers? However, on my way back to join the queue, I turned the proposition over and over in my mind. When I reached the end, it had barely moved a hundred yards since I left, so I asked the militiaman where the office of the Town Commander was. He gave me the appropriate directions and a puzzled look!

I walked along the street, trying to find the solution to my problem. Suddenly my mind was made up: I would go and see the man. When I reached the building, I grew scared. It looked too much like the Investigation Centre at Chernigov, except that the walls were yellow instead of white. I turned to walk away, then stopped and took out the release certificate from my pocket. It was now in four pieces, having split along the folded edges due to the very poor quality of the paper. I looked at my registration on the other side, wishing that I could erase it, but knew it was impossible. The ink had penetrated the paper and the only way to get rid of it was to cut the incriminating part off. That would have damaged the face side.

I started back towards the building, trying to convince myself that perhaps the Commander would not look at the registration side, and if he did the chances were three-to-one against picking the incriminating corner. As I approached the offices of the Town Commander, I hesitated again. I felt like a dwarf about to enter the mouth of a lion. One side of my brain was telling me that I was mad, that I should turn about and run, the other that I must go in. I plucked up courage and entered. A soldier sitting at the head of the corridor asked me who I wanted to see. When I told him, he became very polite and gave me the directions. I had a suspicion that he took me for some sort of spy reporting to his master. I marched briskly along the wide and long tiled corridor, found the door and knocked.

'Come in!' ordered a voice from within.

The Town Commander was a tall, well-built man with a kindly face.

'Citizen Commander,' I began, trying to sound very convincing and very truthful. 'I have been released from the Karabas labour camp to join the Polish Army which is being formed in the Soviet Union to fight the common enemy, the same enemy, the same Hitlerite hordes who crossed the borders of the peace-loving peoples of the USSR in the same treacherous manner as they did when they crossed the borders of Poland. As they did in my country, the fascist bandits are mercilessly killing innocent women and children of the USSR during their temporary advance. I know that the invincible, courageous and victorious Red Army, under the wise leadership of *batyushka* Stalin, will soon change that. It will be aided in this historic struggle by the brotherly Polish Army now being formed in Buzuluk, and I want to be at the side of that magnificent fighting machine not during the victory parade, but now, when I could help them most.

'My friend and I have come as far as Cheliabinsk, only to find that we can go no further. Could you please give me the necessary certificate to enable us to buy the tickets to Buzuluk?'

Citizen Commander lapped it all up, thought for a while, then asked me for my release certificate! My blood froze, my leg bones felt rather more than soft, and I wished that I were standing in the queue and not in front of the Town Commander. Trying to look very composed and without a care in the world, I produced the certificate, carefully placing it in front of him the right way up. He read it thoroughly, then picked up the bottom right-hand corner and looked at the other side. There was nothing there, of course. I did not give him another chance to look at any other piece.

'I shall put it together, Citizen Commander,' I butted in, offering my services. 'This is the only identity paper I have until I join the Polish Army. I must take great care of it.'

He let me do so, and I folded it neatly, making sure that he had no chance of seeing the offending quarter. He picked up a piece of paper and started writing. When he finished he stamped it, signed it and gave it to me, instructing me to hand it to the Station Commander.

'Thank you very much, Citizen Commander,' I said. 'Death to the enemy!'

He wished me luck, and I was off. I marched resolutely along the corridor, I bade the soldier goodbye, and I was out in the open. Out in the open, on my own, and still free! Not only that, I also had a piece of paper in my hand enabling me to buy a ticket. I did not dare to look at the contents until I was far enough away not to be recalled. I rounded a corner and stopped to examine it: the Station Commander was instructed to give me two tickets to Buzuluk!

The weight I had been carrying on my shoulders from the moment of entering the office of the Town Commander had disappeared, and I felt as light as a feather. I wished I could fly to let Jurek know of our good fortune. When I found him, I returned his forty-rouble note, suggesting that he went to get some *kasha* while I paid the Station Commander a visit with a view to obtaining a couple of tickets. He looked a little dumbfounded, obviously thinking that I had gone soft in the head. He picked up our bags and disappeared in the direction of the restaurant.

We arrived in Chkalov late the following night, tired and extremely hungry. We had to leave the train at this point because it did not go any further. The booking-office was jammed with people sitting or lying on the floor, as was the restaurant. Dejectedly, we joined the rest on the floor and went to sleep. When morning came I left Jurek sitting with the bags, while I scouted for food and information. The restaurant had, it seemed, been out of food for months. I saw a queue for bread not far from the station. I walked along for about half a mile but still could not see the end of it. I carried on, admiring the magnificent old buildings, some of which were badly in need of repair.

When I finally reached the end of the queue, I nearly wept. All those waiting people either had a ration card or a note given to them by the military authorities, together with their call-up papers. I had neither so there was little point in joining them. Despondent, I returned to the station, watching the queue as I went. They were a mixed lot, quite a large proportion being Kazakhs or Uzbeks, with their round hats and colourful wrapovers with wide sleeves which they put their hands into when it got cold. Some wore a type of moccasin on their feet, others nothing at all.

Squeezing through the mass of people at the station, I met a group of Poles in their twenties. Like me, they had been released from the labour camps in Siberia and what they told me was not very encouraging. They had managed to reach Buzuluk, a town halfway between Chkalov and Kuibyshev. There was a Polish Army unit there, but only qualified pilots were being accepted with the intention of sending them on to Great Britain via Arkhangelsk. The others were turned away after being told that the main Polish Army would form somewhere in the Tashkent-Samarkand area, although the exact place was not yet known.

They were advised to make their way there as best they could, since the Polish authorities were unable to help them in any way.

I found Jurek just to tell him the sad news, then continued my hunt for something to eat. There were no trains going anywhere, and the platform doors were open and unguarded. I went through them and turned right and when I reached the end of the platform, I saw an enclosure surrounded by barbed wire, with a sentry at the gate. I watched with interest the Red Army soldiers walking about the compound, especially the ones entering a particular hut and emerging from it with loaves of bread in their arms. My spirits rose.

Intending to steal some bread, I went right round the camp as far as it was possible, but I could see no opening. I examined every plank on the way back, but no luck. I returned to Jurek, rather tired; it was well past midday, and we had had nothing to eat since about six o'clock the previous morning.

I started a conversation with some Uzbeks sitting near us, hoping to buy some food from them. It was an uphill struggle. My Kazakh was barely good enough to make myself understood to a Kazakh, and Uzbek was a different dialect.

The Uzbeks did not sell me any food, but when they heard that I had not eaten since the previous day, they gave me a piece of their *non*, a kind of thick pancake about three inches in diameter. I shared it with Jurek; it tasted delicious.

While we were chewing, a Red Army officer with a white arm band on his sleeve entered the booking-hall. Several men went up to speak to him so, being inquisitive, I rose and listened to the proceedings. It transpired that any leader of a group of twenty-five men, en route to join the Red Army as call-up men or conscripts, who could prove that he had such a group in the room, would be given a chit to buy a kilo of bread per man by the captain. I saw no reason at all why I should not collect that voucher. I could be a leader of twenty-five men in a moment.

Not to arouse any suspicion, I strolled towards Jurek, 'enlisting' my men on the way, including the Uzbeks. I gave them a full briefing lasting a few seconds, then returned to face the officer.

'Comrade Captain,' I addressed him politely yet firmly, 'I am in charge of twenty-five men en route to join the Red Army in Kuibyshev. As you know there are delays, and we are running short of food. Is there any chance of some bread?'

He sized me up, while my heart missed several beats.

'Where are your men?' he asked.

'Over there, Comrade Captain!' I replied, pointing my finger in Jurek's direction, as twenty-five hands shot up towards the ceiling.

'Very well,' said the officer, 'there you are.' He handed me a piece of paper stamped with the usual five-pointed star.

'Thank you, Comrade Captain. Could you tell me where I can collect the bread?'

'Yes,' he replied, 'go outside the station, and you will see the queue on your right. That is it.'

I knew all about that one. I had hoped that there might be another, like the one in the Red Army camp at the end of the platform. I told them that we would wait half an hour each in the queue, picked one man and went with him to join the queue. It was as long as ever. I left my stranger in it, without a ticket, of course; I had been with *bezprizornye* too long!

On the way back to the station I formulated my plan of action. I decided not to go to Buzuluk but to make straight for Tashkent on the first available train. I told Jurek of my decision and he seemed unhappy with the idea. His reasoning was that since he had a ticket to Buzuluk he was going to take a chance on things having changed. I tried to argue my point but he was evidently tired of running. We decided to part and go our different ways. So, I went to examine the timetable to discover the way to Tashkent, which I knew from memory to be south-east of Chkalov. Unfortunately, there was no mention of the place, just Sverdlovsk, Kuibyshev, Kurgan and Aktiubinsk. The first three were of no use to me, and the fourth I had never heard of. However, it was reasonable to assume that Aktiubinsk was in a different direction to the others.

According to the table there was a train going to Aktiubinsk in a couple of hours, as if that meant anything, but I still had no bread, and I was not going to forfeit that for anything. The queue had moved about a hundred yards in half an hour, so it would take us between eight and ten hours to reach the head of it, no hope of catching that train south. I had a brainwave, a little insane, but worth trying. If the plan misfired, I was going to plead that I had made a mistake, or run for it.

I neatly folded the flap of my hat in position, pinning it in the proper place with two pieces of wire. I fished out the Red Army badge from my rucksack and pinned it just above the peak. Now my hat looked like the proper Red Army hat ought to. I marched resolutely to the end of the platform and headed straight for the Red Army camp. I called out to the sentry at the gate: 'Greetings, Comrade! I have been ordered to pick up twenty-five kilos of bread for my squad before the train going to Aktiubinsk arrives. Will you direct me to the store?'

I showed him the voucher from the captain. He looked at it, and no doubt seeing the five-pointed star at the bottom of the paper, decided that it was in order. He pointed to the hut which I had seen before.

As I approached it, I smelt a delicious aroma coming from the hut next door. I could see no reason why I should not partake of a good meal, so I entered. If I was thrown out, I would claim that I was looking for the bread store.

The canteen was not lit, although it was getting dark. I saw soldiers eating *kasha*, so I went up to the counter and asked for some. It cost me sixty kopecks, but the portion was at least four times as big as the station buffet one, had bits of meat in it, and glistened with some kind of oil. Having bought the portion, I was now the proud owner of a solitary rouble. I had to be more careful how I spent my money now!

I had no problem collecting the bread. The soldier on duty counted twenty-five loaves as he placed them on my outstretched arms, and I was off. When I deposited the load on Jurek's lap, pandemonium broke out. Hands appeared from all sides. I cut twelve loaves in half using my wire knife. I handed a piece to each one in the group except Jurek, then I cut the last half loaf in two and gave them to the two men who had contributed to the effort by standing in the queue. I was a little concerned that my 'troops' would not like the way I shared the spoils, but there were no complaints. I gave one loaf to Jurek, left one for myself, and packed the rest in my rucksack. The aroma of freshly baked bread spread throughout the booking-office.

I tried once more to talk Jurek into continuing our journey together, but without success. So, when the clock in the booking-hall approached the hour of my departure, I gave him three loaves, leaving the rest for myself. He had at least forty roubles, I only had one. Had he continued the journey with me we would have shared the bread equally until it ran out. He decided to press on to Buzuluk, a short journey; I had a thousand miles ahead of me. I shook hands with him, wishing him the best of luck.

'I will look out for you in the Polish Army!' I promised as we parted.

'So will I!' he replied.

I never heard of him again.

By now it was very dark and as usual the platform was poorly lit. There were a number of people milling around so I mixed with them, strolling in the direction opposite to that of the Red Army camp. At the end of the platform I saw a couple sitting on the bench, thin as rakes, with two crying children.

'Mummy, Mummy,' they pleaded through their tears. 'I'm hungry! I'm hungry!'

'I am sorry my little golden ones,' she replied, pressing them both to her breast. 'There is nothing to eat. Daddy's tried all day, maybe he will get something soon.'

The man was sitting half bent, with his elbows on his knees, his head in his hands. I knew only too well what it felt like to be hungry. I also knew what it was like searching for food and not finding any. I opened my rucksack.

'Here!' I said to the man. 'Take it!' I handed him the first loaf. In a daze he raised his head from his hands while I placed the loaf in his lap. Before he knew what was happening, I gave him another. This time he grabbed my hand and started kissing it.

'May God bless you!' he kept repeating. I snatched my hand and briskly walked away, or I would have broken down.

Perhaps a couple of hours or so later a train approached from the direction of Sverdlovsk. I decided to board it, and if it were going to Kuibyshev I would get off at Buzuluk. When it stopped and the doors were opened, the battle began. People trying to leave were prevented from doing so by the people trying to enter. I had very little control over my movements, I only followed the pressure. In the end, without knowing too much about it, I was bundled into a compartment and found myself sitting on a wooden bench. Any idea I might have had about travelling in the corridor and dodging the conductor disappeared swiftly. No human being could possibly have found a spot there, and if we had a conductor he would be obliged to stay wherever he was, whether he liked it or not! After several attempts, the driver of that sardine can managed to get it moving. The two youths sitting next to me unwrapped a large piece of *salo*, cut a piece off, and began to eat it. It was clear that they had no bread so I offered an exchange. After vigorous bargaining, I parted with two of my loaves for a good piece of *salo*.

It was obvious that I was sitting next to a couple of thieves who had struck it rich by robbing a store of some sort. No ordinary citizen of the Soviet Union could ever have hoped to possess such a large piece of *salo*, even if he saved his ration for a hundred years. Quietly, therefore, I explained to them that I had once been boss of a cell full of *bezprizornye*, so if either of them attempted to take a thing from me I would gouge out his eyes with my fingers. I then shut my eyes and went to sleep. I was awoken by one of the youths digging me in the ribs with his elbow.

'Hey! Wake up!' he said quietly. 'It looks as though the train is not going any further, we had better push off!'

'Right, lead on!' I agreed, carefully picking up my rucksack.

It was still dark and we found ourselves at some small station. While the rest of the passengers crowded near the exit, we jumped down on to the rails, ducked under the train and were off into the darkness. When we cleared the immediate vicinity of the station, and the tracks converged into an ordinary two-way system, we stopped and planned our next move. We shared a cigarette and soon agreed to jump on the next train going our way. The two lads were also going to Tashkent, but having done the journey before had decided to stop at Aktiubinsk to replenish their supplies. Dawn was breaking when we boarded the train, settled behind the forward board and went to sleep. I could not help thinking that although there was no honour amongst the *bezprizornye* there was great loyalty. They could have left me asleep in the passenger train, but they did not. They knew that I was one of them and it would be against their code of behaviour to leave me, perhaps to be picked up by a guard or a militiaman. I slept for a short while, and awoke to discover that we were not the only 'passengers'. Some of them jumped from one waggon to the next in search of their pals, or just to pass the time. They did this without a hint of worry about being discovered; they did it as though the train belonged to them.

We were travelling in a shallow valley, in a south-easterly direction. After crossing a wide, slow-running river, the town of Aktiubinsk appeared in the distance. My two companions prepared for a smart getaway, bade me a safe journey and slipped off, along with many others.

I opened my rucksack and had some bread with *salo*. I felt on top of the world. I had nothing to store water in, so I decided to do what I used to do in Kizil Tau: drink as much as I could every time I had the opportunity. It had worked there, it had to work in the present circumstances.

Early next morning the train struggled its way through a pass just as the sun rose from below the horizon. Ahead, there was a distinctly different type of terrain: more like the familiar country around Akmolinsk, gently undulating steppe with no trees that I could see. The train stopped in the middle of nowhere and the locomotive was disconnected, leaving us stranded. Moments after it went out of sight, hundreds of 'passengers' jumped down and made off in the direction of a stream. I decided to join them. The water did not taste very nice, but then I did not know when I was going to have a chance to drink again. The locomotive returned in the afternoon and soon the scenery changed to sand and dried-up salt lakes. We were now back in Asia, in territory that I had mapped out at school two years previously. I was looking forward to seeing with my own eyes what I could only imagine when I drew the map. I knew that a lake ought to appear on our right, the Aral Sea, so called because of its size. As it happened, I never saw the lake because it was night-time when we passed by. When I awoke there were miles of yellow sand. To the east, as far as I could see, was another desert, the notorious Bet Pak Dala, the Hungry Steppe. After passing Novokazalinsk, a river appeared on the right. Seeing its muddy water I was greatly disappointed, for it was named Syr Daria, which in Kazakhi means the River of Mystery. As we travelled along its bank for miles on end I wondered what sort of mystery it held for me. I had a good drink of water in Tyuratam, a small settlement on the left bank of the Syr Daria. We were soon in the heart of the desert, Bet Pak Dala to the east and the Kizil Kum to the south-west. With the exception of a narrow belt of arable land here and there, there was nothing but sand. About an hour after leaving Tyuratam, the Syr Daria, hitherto a wide and noble river, split into several small streams and almost disappeared beneath a tall grass- and reed-covered marsh. It was hidden until we reached Kizil Orda, when it reappeared in all its muddy mystery.

As we approached the town, mostly consisting of mud huts, I saw a sign in black letters painted on one of the few two-storeyed buildings. It read Ak Metchet, or the White Palace. When we stopped at the station, the sign in black, but not very big letters read Kizil Orda, the Red Capital. However, on the same board, but covered by white paint, I saw the old name: Ak Metchet. I smiled. It was clear that the comrades preferred a more revolutionary-sounding title for the settlement!

Kizil Orda was in the Kazakh Republic, and though mostly populated by Kazakhs there were also a number of Uzbeks who had probably settled there following the Revolution. I spent a few hours in the town looking for food but there was nothing I could easily steal. I also saw a group of five Red Army soldiers strolling about; I gave them a wide berth in case they wanted to ask me any questions. I thought they might have been on patrol, as on previous occasions, in Cheliabinsk or Chkalov, I had seen them walking singly or in pairs.

We left Kizil Orda during the night and by morning the faithful Syr Daria was no longer visible, although the railway track was running through arable land. The locomotive was making heavy weather going up the hill with all those waggons behind, and in the end gave up the struggle. It stopped only long enough to be disconnected, then chugged away. As soon as the engine disappeared round a left-hand bend, swarms of *bezprizornye* descended on a tomato plantation just below the track. I was not far behind. I settled myself on the edge of the track and made a meal of tomatoes with the rest of my bread. I had a few more tomatoes in the afternoon, on the way to a small river where I had a drink and a good scrub. By morning, those nice, red and juicy fruit did not look so appetizing, but since there was nothing else to eat I had a few for my breakfast. I ate some more for lunch, and when I heard the locomotive approaching from the south I picked as many as I could to carry to the waggon.

A range of mountains appeared to the east, and I knew we did not have to travel much further. I was a little sick at heart that the journey was coming to an end; I was enjoying my relative comfort and freedom, looking forward to being in a beautiful town.

I had my first disappointment when we arrived in Tashkent (it means Stone City in Kazakhi) in the very early hours of the morning. It was in fact called *Tosh*kent, and the white paint on the board was peeling off, making it look very drab. When the train stopped on the sidings, I made a bee-line for the fence accompanied by four other youths, jumping off it on to a dimly lit, paved street. We bedded down for the rest of the night on the nearest waste ground, huddled together as on previous nights, and went to sleep.

When we woke up, I had my second disappointment. I had expected to see lots of minarets but all I saw were the ordinary buildings of an industrial town. We had the rest of my tomatoes for breakfast and went in search of a market. When we found it there were lots of tomatoes to be had, but somehow they did not appeal to us any more! We stole a melon, then converged on an Uzbek grilling *shashlik*, pieces of mutton on a skewer, over a charcoal fire. I produced my solitary rouble, hoping to draw sufficient interest while one of my pals could steal one of the skewers. The Uzbek was no fool. He waved his hands, removing the delicious-smelling breakfast from our reach.

After we had eaten the melon, I told the boys I would see them later that day, and then went to look for the Polish Army. I walked for miles and asked hundreds of people, but without success. I saw some beautiful old buildings in the process, and even a minaret or two which made my day. I ambled towards the station, more from habit than anything else, and boarded a train going to Samarkand. It was a fast train, and I was unceremoniously kicked out twice during the journey. I finished the journey sitting on the buffers of the last waggon, and arrived in the town three hours after leaving Tashkent.

Samarkand was entirely different from Tashkent. It had mystique, class and some very fine buildings. In the middle there was a large square, surrounded by Islamic schools. The buildings were made of biscuit-yellow bricks, with fine portals. Nearby was a huge open market, which at the time was of much more interest to me than anything else. The market, also called a field market, was an area of some 500 by 300 yards, surrounded by high walls. It was in this market that Marco Polo must have stopped to buy supplies on his way to China.

I could not find much to eat since there was no one about. I did find an over-ripe melon and a squashed boiled beetroot, and that had to do for supper. I also found a good spot by the wall to bed down for the night. For breakfast next morning I managed to steal some tomatoes, which I shared with an old Uzbek whom I found by my side in the morning. He was out of work but there was little he did not know about the town. Our stomachs a little less empty, we went to explore the mysteries of Samarkand at the suggestion of the old man.

He showed me the mausoleum of Timur i Leng, also known as Tamarlane, a large fortress-like structure surrounded by an open brick wall in Arab style. It was called Gur i Amir, and made of the same coloured bricks as most of the town, with green bricks providing the patterns. On top of the octagonal block there was a tower which looked like a huge biscuit-yellow drum, with blue and black patterns spelling out a message from the Koran. This was covered by a sharp-pointed cupola comprising some fifty thick, vertical ribs made of light blue tiles with patterns in green and yellow. I tried to enter Gur i Amir, but the door was locked, so I looked through the partly broken window. In the middle of the tiled floor, I saw a tomb covered by a slab of what looked like jade, seven or eight feet long, about three feet wide and a foot thick!

On a hill towards the north of the town, there were several turquoise-coloured, domed tombs and narrow alleys. This was called Shah i Zindah, which means 'the King lives'. It had several gates built by the grandson of Tamarlane, Ulug Beg, or Beg the Great, embellished with stars and scrolls in rich blue and white, with here and there a touch of gold and green. Unfortunately, we could not explore it any further as entry was forbidden.

Yes, Samarkand was indeed a beautiful town, and quite clean, too. However, there was no Polish Army in evidence, and I was starving. My Uzbek friend and I returned to the market to see if I could steal anything. I found an old newspaper printed in Arabic script. I cut it up in pieces exactly the size of a rouble note, wrapped the package with my rouble and went to get some food.

Showing my bundle of 'money', I managed to get a vendor sufficiently interested to let me try one small piece of meat. I chewed it slowly, smacking my lips, the sign of approval. He watched me with some satisfaction, then turned to one side, and that gave me a chance to snatch one of the skewers. Alas! I was still clumsy then and he saw me doing it.

'Take your hands away!' he shouted.

I did not want to concede to his wishes. The small piece of meat he had given me to try was really delicious, and I was certain that the one I grabbed would proved to be just as tasty. I ran.

'Help! Thief!' he screamed.

I ran like a gazelle and mixed with the crowd before returning to my Uzbek friend. We shared the spoils, five pieces of meat each. The mutton was very tender with hardly any gristle in it. Maybe what I had done was dishonest, maybe I had robbed him of a rouble which he couldn't afford to lose. But I was hungry, and I had to live.

I strolled in a leisurely manner to the station and found a train waiting at the platform. I did not know where it was going to, but as soon as it moved I jumped aboard, only to be shown out in the standard fashion at the next station. It was a small place and I could see no sign of tents or a camp, so I boarded another waggon when the train moved. Besides, I did not like the name of the station: it was called Djuma, and that means 'leprosy' in Polish! I weathered the storm between Djuma and the next station, and was escorted off the train once more at the following stop. It had gone before I even had a chance to return to the platform, so I decided to stop there for the night. The name of the place, Kattakurgan, was not very inviting either, for translated in Uzbeki it means 'Big Burial Ground'. The village was situated on the shores of a big lake. I walked round, asking the locals about the Polish Army. No one could help me. I found a spot by the railway station and went to sleep.

Very early in the morning I was awakened by a locomotive pulling a heavy load. It was a freight train going in my direction so I jumped aboard. I knew that we were going west and the next big town as far as I could remember was Bukhara. Just as the sun was about to rise, we came to a halt at a small settlement. Judging by the hooting from the front end, we must have been held up by red

197

lights. I thought the name of the tiny station – Kermine – rather funny, it sounded almost like 'lipstick' in Polish. I climbed on to the roof of the next waggon to survey the small place, but I did not see anything of interest. The train gathered speed again and did not stop until we arrived at a modern-looking town called Kagan. I learnt here that no one had heard, or seen, anything of the Polish Army. I decided to try Bukhara, some nine miles away. But the only way to get there was on foot.

At first the unmade road passed through fine, yellow sands, but after some two miles the scenery suddenly changed. Ahead of me I saw what looked like a huge oasis. There were orchards and vineyards, rose bushes and melons. Unfotunately, most of the latter had been gathered, and my findings did not appear very appetizing. However, it was definitely better than nothing, and after eating I marched forward to inspect a long row of mud huts on the right-hand side of the road. The dark brown-coloured huts were made entirely of mud mixed with straw. There was no wood used at all in their construction, yet the roofs were as flat as pancakes, stretching fifteen to twenty feet from wall to wall. Those mud huts, all joined together, were the famous covered market of Bukhara.

One could buy anything at the market: magnificent carpets of all sizes and colours; felt, cotton and silk materials; caftans and wrapovers made of karakul wool; copper-ware and cutlery, including some fine daggers; all sorts of trinkets and stones; fruits of every description and size, both fresh and cooked; milk from different animals, fresh and fermented; tobaccos and snuffs. This was the slave market of past centuries, where the caravans replenished their supplies on the silk route to China. It looked absolutely out of this world, and I had a feeling that I was no longer in the Soviet Union but in Shangri-La, far away from the so-called Paradise of the Working Classes.

I stole some fruit, and sufficient locally grown tobacco to last me a day or two.

The market, stretching for about six miles, ended where the town of Bukhara began. It was a walled city, the walls in ruins in many places. They were made of unbaked, sun-dried bricks, sloping inwards towards the town, and were strengthened by semicircular towers, projecting slightly above the level of the wall.

Outside the walls, there were closely built, single-storeyed, flat-roofed mud huts with tiny windows. They were dwarfed by the massive-looking buildings inside the city walls, with large, blue domes and towers. I entered the town through a fairly large and impressive-looking gate, which constituted a pointed archway, surrounded by thick, almost vertical walls sloping towards the town, and topped by equally thick horizontal beams.

I walked along a narrow alley which opened into a square, looking for a spot to put my head down for the night. It was becoming dark, and the wind grew fresh. By the side of an imposing, fortress-like building I found a big, square hole, about ten yards square and five yards deep, part of it covered with timber. There was a log by the side of one of the walls, sloping all the way to the bottom. In view of the wind it was an ideal spot: I took off my makeshift shoes and walked down to the bottom. It felt quite warm there but the air smelt foul. I found a level spot under the covered part of the hole and went to sleep. Feeling so cosy, I slept well, too well. I woke up in the morning to discover someone had stolen my footwear.

Later, I went to the market, filched a melon and returned to the square for my breakfast. I sat down on the ground with my back to the solitary, circular tower, a couple of hundred feet high, which looked like a mighty skittle-pin. An old Uzbek, wearing a turban and a decrepit *khalat*, a wrapover, appeared from nowhere and sat down near me. As I cut the green skin of the melon, revealing the juicy flesh, I could see him eating it with his eyes, so I offered him a piece.

'Glory be!' he exclaimed, taking the dripping piece eagerly. He ate it quickly with much smacking of his lips, so I gave him another piece. He had an honest, intelligent face.

'What are you doing here?' he asked me.

I told him that I was looking for the Polish Army. He shook his head. I sighed with disappointment but decided to stay for a few days to fatten myself up. The Uzbek turned out to be a *mullah*, and was a very well-educated and intelligent person indeed. From him I learned a lot about the town of Bukhara and the surrounding region. He spoke a little Russian which was a great help.

He had been a teacher in one of the many Islamic schools, or *maktab*, in Bukhara until 1922, when the final revolt against the

Communist regime had officially ended. He had been unable to get any work since, and had become a beggar. After our breakfast together, he took me round the town which he knew so well. The tower where we had met was Minora Kalyan, or the Tower of the Hookah, which in the years gone by was used to send condemned criminals to their deaths by throwing them out of the topmost windows. The fortress-like structure on a small rise, and reached by the steps guarded at the top by two towers, was the palace of the Amir of Bukhara until 1922. The maidens of his harem used to bathe in the swimming-pool by the side of it. Nearby, stood a magnificent mosque with a huge, pointed cupola. It was named the Blue Domed Mosque. Indeed, it was one of many mosques in the town and my guide knew them all. Sadly, not one of them was open for worship.

And what of the hole where I had spent the night? I discovered it was the snake pit where the Amir used to torment his prisoners! Many years later I learned that I might have been the first European in a hundred years to occupy that snake pit. In 1842, Queen Victoria had sent a couple of emissaries to Bukhara to cultivate the favours of its Amir. Not knowing the ritual, they had entered the courtyard without invitation, and on horseback. They were thrown into the same snake pit and put to death at a later date.

Bukhara was a very old town. It had stood there from time immemorial, and its original name might have been *Vyavahara*, which means merchant. It was conquered by Alexander the Great, the Turks, the Persians, and by the Kara Kitais, the Black Chinese. It was sacked by Genghis Khan as his hordes swarmed across Asia into Europe. In 1920 the Amir fled to Afghanistan, but soon afterwards a revolt started against the Communist rulers. The leader of the revolt, Basmachi, sent an ultimatum to Moscow, demanding secession from the Soviet Union in accordance with the rule propagated widely by the Communists, which said that any state could secede it it so wished.

In reply, the comrades sent the Red Army to sort things out 'peacefully'. Basmachi was killed in that peaceful battle, and the Red Army became victorious yet again, but only on paper. True, many Uzbeks, Tadjiks and Turkmens had fled to Afghanistan, but many more stayed behind to fight for what they believed in. The final shots were fired in 1935, or thereabouts, although the fight had not ended. It was still going on when I was there.

I stayed in Bukhara for a couple of days. I walked about with the *mullah*, listening to his wisdom. I saw the Red Army men strolling about, admiring the views in groups of five. They were the only Russians in town as far as I could make out, and were obviously on leave, the rest were Uzbeks, Tadjiks, Afghans, and a number of Jews. I spent three nights in the snake pit, but the *mullah* would not come down. He must have seen what it really looked like some years before, unless the simple reason was that he was too old to walk down that log of wood.

I asked him about the geography of the region. To the west was a desert, the Kizil Kum, separated from another desert, the Kara Kum by the River Amu Daria. What he told me about that river was fascinating. It started in the Pamirs as five separate rivers, the main one being the Ok Su, the White Water in Uzbeki, so called because of the ice flowing in it. To the south, was the continuation of the Kizil Kum, the Amu Daria and the Kara Kum until the Afghanistan border. The Amu Daria separated the two countries for hundreds of miles, and the nearest point from Bukhara along the caravan route to the south-east was about two hundred miles. I decided that if I could not find any trace of the Polish Army, I would try to join a caravan going in that direction. I asked the *mullah* about my chances of putting this plan into practice; he was quite hopeful.

Since 1922, when many locals had fled the country rather than suffer under the Communist regime, those who stayed behind had unofficially visited them from time to time, by joining a caravan going in the direction of the border, then sneaking across at a suitable place. He suggested that when one of those 'excursions' was forming, he would try to persuade them to take me along. I was overwhelmed by the idea because the prospect of travelling across the desert with the nomads was certainly an attractive one.

The Amu Daria was only about sixty miles away and to satisfy boyish curiosity before I left the region for good I decided to go and see it. Before I departed, I thought I would have a quick dip in the swimming-pool by the Amir's palace, so that I could claim to have swum in the pool of the harem of the Amir of Bukhara! Perhaps it was childish of me, but I had already lost more than two years of my boyhood and I was not going to forgo such an opportunity now.

The *mullah* and I strolled to the pool; the wise old man was just as excited about the prank as I was. I sat down on the verge of the pool, pretending to admire the large, tropical plants growing in capacious stone pots round the water. I then undressed and took to the water. Later, satisfied, I bade my friend goodbye, promising to see him soon.

As it was to turn out, sooner proved to be much later!

12

When I passed by the last of the mud huts of the covered market of Bukhara, I left dreamland behind me and I was back in the Soviet Union. I kicked my heels at the station for a while, then jumped on a freight train going westwards. It followed a river with cultivated land on both sides, but a short distance past that green belt there was only sand. Soon after a station called Karakul, there was nothing but yellow sand as far as the eye could see.

I saw the Amu Daria when we were almost there. The train slowed down, and a dirty white settlement appeared on our right. It was called Farab. I saw the bridge before I saw the river, and it was because of it that the train had to slow down. It was an old, rusty iron bridge, and I jumped off before my waggon reached it.

The Amu was a great disappointment. Although it was about a couple of hundred yards wide, the water was muddy-yellow with not a palm tree to be seen on either bank. The Amu Daria just flowed through the sands and there was not a blade of grass in the vicinity. Walking back to Farab I saw a local driving an *arava*, a two-wheeled camel-drawn cart. Dangling from the rear was something I had been looking for for many days: a metal can in which black grease for lubricating the cart's wheels was stored. I appropriated it. It was a rusty old can, but it served the purpose. I cooked many meals in it before all the grease had completely disappeared from the inside. It did not worry me; it added to the flavour.

Farab was a very small settlement, perhaps twenty mud huts with flat roofs. There was no market, but I spotted some chickens running about the unmade alleys, so I thought I would knock one off. Looking for a suitable implement, I found a partition made of wooden sticks, between two huts. Scrutinizing each one in turn, I found one admirably suited to the purpose. It had a curved head at one end, like a golf club. I waited until dark before acquiring it, then retired for the night by a local wash-place. I woke up frozen. That snake pit in Bukhara had certainly been cosy.

Using a small pebble as a target, I practised with my stick for about an hour before successfully attempting the real thing. I plucked the cockerel straight away, cleaned it, cut it up in pieces, then spent hours boiling it, piece by piece, in my newly obtained can. I stole enough salt to last me a month, and each time a piece was cooked I drank the soup, and was ready to face the future in a much better frame of mind.

I then met a group of Poles looking for the Polish Army. They had heard a rumour it was being formed further down the river, and that a barge convoy was going in that direction in the afternoon. I wandered down to the river and decided to join it. The convoy consisted of five, long, flat-bottomed iron barges, tied one behind the other and pulled by a paddle-driven tug. Each barge had an open front half, then a wheelhouse with a covered hold in the stern. At the very end of a barge there were a couple of rudders, mounted on a thick, square-shaped wooden log fixed across the stern, and about three feet below the top frame. That was also our toilet.

There seemed to be hundreds of people of different nationalities on board. The Poles were either ex-prisoners, or free resettlers, and some of them were suffering from severe malnutrition. The locals were Uzbeks, Turkmenistans or Karakalpaks returning to their settlements down river. These barges were the only mode of transport in the area except for the caravans which took longer to cover the distance.

I pottered round the barge hoping to find Adam, or anyone I knew, but it was not to be. I was quite excited about the voyage: firstly because I hoped to find the army fairly soon, and secondly, because I was going to travel through an area that even the geography books knew little about. The captain of the tug worked very hard to establish some form of control over the convoy. We travelled sideways for some time before the tug gained sufficient speed to pull its unwieldy burden roughly parallel to the direction of the river banks. And just in time, too. The river, which had hitherto been flowing in one bed, had split into several little streams, and the ripples ahead indicated that the waterway was not only shallow but that the current was running faster as well. Indeed, the captain's job was made even more difficult by the fact that the river was continuously changing its course from day to day. The deep water on one voyage would become a sand bank on the next, and vice versa; the rapids going in one direction would go in another a day later. It was for this reason that the Amu Daria was often called by the tugmen the 'Wandering River'.

The little tug did not always manage to negotiate the shoals and the rapids. We got stuck on several occasions, especially at night. The river flowed towards the Aral Sea, with myriads of little sand banks and islands widening it from a few hundred yards to four or five miles. On either side of the river was a desert, the Kizil Kum on the right and the Kara Kum on the left. In the morning it seemed that these sand dunes, with their sharply defined edges, rose to twenty feet. Later, they appeared to be rising to even greater heights. They looked like great truncated cones, their sides rising almost vertically from the surrounding terrain, and reaching to about 300 feet. Generally speaking, they were all about the same height, but some had an overhang. They seemed to merge to form a solid range, only to split into individual mounds, as the movement of the convoy changed my viewpoint. It was an extraordinary sight; I could not help thinking that I was on the moon or some other planet.

I had a surprise that first morning out from Farab. We were told to form a queue and each one of us received about 800 grams of bread. I could not believe my eyes. I was a little apprehensive in case I was asked to pay for it, but I received the ration free. Whether I should have bought a ticket in the first instance, I could not say: I did not think it prudent to inquire. I enjoyed the voyage tremendously: the bread received free each morning, plus the boiled chicken made my life easy and carefree. I was glad to have the tin can as well. I used the string which I normally tied round my waist, together with my stick, to scoop up water from the river using the can. Not many aboard had such a marvellous apparatus so there were always eager fellow travellers ready to help me drink the water.

When I awoke early on the third day of our journey, a mountain range came into view on the right. About a couple of hours later we passed by its left extremity and noted the top was about a thousand feet high, rising rapidly from the river bank. By midday, the little tug had pulled up to the right bank of the Amu Daria and we were told that the convoy would go no further, at least not for a few days. We all disembarked, and, walking up a steep bank I saw a white-painted building which looked like a garage. Nearby were a number of brown mud huts with flat roofs. The 'garage' was a repair place for the tugs and barges, and the small settlement was Nukus, the capital of the Karakalpak Autonomous Soviet Socialist Republic, normally called by the locals *Karakalpagistan*, which means the Country of Black-hatted People.

At Nukus we were met by a number of NKVD men and led to an empty space. I did not like the situation and looked around for a means of escape. Luckily, I saw a man in a blue *khalat*, wearing a black hat reminiscent of the type normally worn by orthodox Jews on the Sabbath. He was riding a camel, followed by another which was tied to the front one's tail. Accompanying him were four young women, wearing long, colourful dresses. When they came close enough, I quickly attached myself to the caravan, walking alongside the rear camel as though I had been with them all the time. After some minutes we had left the last hut of the capital behind, and were walking along a raised path between a paddy-field and what looked like maize, except that the cobs were silvery grey in colour.

One thing was very clear to me. There was no Polish Army in the settlement, or we would have been met by the Polish representative, rather than by the NKVD. What happened to those who stayed I do not know.

As we travelled the women turned their heads towards me and smiled; I smiled back. They moved to one side, inviting me to pass forward. I obliged. *Babai*, the elder, looked at me from the top of his camel several times but did not say a word. I was not quite sure what to do: I thought I would walk along until we were far enough from Nukus, then part company. Somehow I had to make my way back to Bukhara, four hundred miles away.

'Do you understand Uzbek?' inquired Babai after some ten minutes of silence.

'Yes!' I replied, knowing that I was not really telling him the truth.

He rattled away like a machine-gun for a couple of minutes, but when he looked down expecting a reply I had to own up and tell him that I only spoke a little of the language. He stopped the camels and made them kneel. Pointing to the rear animal, he invited me to mount it. I had never ridden a camel in my life. I could not follow the Babai's example because his camel had only one hump and a kind of saddle on top. Mine had two humps and his back was bare. I sat on the animal between the humps, as one would on a horse. They all burst into laughter, giving me a clue that I was doing something wrong. I retrieved my right leg, and sat on the beast sideways. That was not right either! There was only one more thing I could try, and if that was not right I was going to get off and stay off. I sat on the camel side-saddle my bent right knee spanning the front hump. That was it! They liked that!

Babai smacked his lips several times, the camels rose, and we were on our way.

After I got into the swing of it, both metaphorically and literally, I took stock of the situation. There was I, in a very strange country sitting on top of a camel, going somewhere. What was I going to do when we arrived there?

I had attached myself to a strange caravan, but instead of being told to leave, I was invited to board the ship of the desert, while the four women travelling with it were walking. Why?

Once we arrived where we were going, how would I find my way back to Bukhara?

The simple answer to all three questions was that I did not have a clue. I decided not to worry about it, and to enjoy the adventure.

The terrain was almost as flat as a pancake, and from my perch atop the camel, I could see people working in the fields. Judging by the colourful dresses they were wearing, they were all women. By then, the paddy-fields were replaced by a crop I had never seen before. It looked like vines, with white flowers on them which the women were picking. Some of the flowers were two inches in diameter, while others only a quarter of that. Very intriguing, but what was it? I plucked up courage and divulged my ignorance to one of the women.

'*Pakhta*!' she explained, '*pakhta*!'

I was now much wiser, the only remaining mystery was what *pakhta* meant.

I did see a group of men, six in all, in their unmistakable blue *khalats*, digging a dyke. Those were the only men I had seen during my three- or four-hour journey, with the exception of an odd one, here and there, riding a donkey.

After about an hour on the camel, I started developing colic. It seemed the perpetual motion I was being subjected to was straining my stomach muscles. The simple cure was to get off the animal, so I had to admit defeat in the end and start walking, to the great amusement of the women. Just before dark we arrived at a small hamlet consisting of a few white-painted, circular mud huts with thatched roofs and no chimneys. They were set among palm trees and a patch or two of maize plants, with an odd banana tree here and there. The women entered one of the huts, while the elder took the seat off his camel, tied both of its front legs together, then let them loose. I helped him with this chore, and prepared to leave.

'Where are you going?' he asked me.

'I don't know,' I replied, shrugging my shoulders.

He took me by the hand and led me to his hut. As we entered the narrow door, I saw an open fire on the right-hand edge of the circular room. It was burning between two low fences made of stone about eighteen inches tall, on top of which rested a cauldron. A small, elderly woman was stirring rice which she was cooking in it with a big wooden ladle. There was no furniture of any kind, just a straw mat on the floor, on which sat the four women who had accompanied us from Nukus. Another tall woman, aged about thirty, was placing small clay bowls in the middle of the room. There was also a man present, much older than Babai, sitting by the fire nursing his foot. His big toe was swollen and oozing yellow matter.

The hut was spotlessly clean. Judging by the welcome I had received, the young women must have told the others about my arrival. I shook hands with all of them in turn, while the tall woman introduced me. I could not understand her at all well; she chattered away too loudly and too fast. *Ona*, the mother, was the woman cooking the rice, the girls on the mat were either *Singil*, younger sister, or *Singlim*, little younger sister. The man with the

208

bad toe was an uncle, a visitor from the neighbouring settlement.

I was invited to sit down, and the elder sister, *Opa*, gave me a bowl of rice soup full of fish pieces. It was the best meal I had eaten since Madame Prosniewska's.

As soon as I had finished eating, she gave me more, although I tried to be modest and pleaded not to be given any more. After a third helping I did not have to be modest, I had had enough, but no, she would not hear of it. I tried to explain that my stomach would burst if I had any more, but they all chatted away like geese. I did not understand a word. There was little I could do. I ate a few spoonfuls, leaving the rest, hoping that it would have the desired effect. All it produced was even more chatter. After another spoonful, I burped and that did it! They were all happy and my bowl was taken away. I was happy too; that was the first time I had been full since the time I got the bread in Chkalov.

Having washed the bowls, Opa announced that she was going to fetch water from the river. The least I could do was to go with her to help carry it. She picked up two buckets made of dried gourds, a shoulder yoke with two hooks at each end to carry them, and a length of rope. I offered to shoulder the burden, but she would have none of it, rattling away as always.

It was dark, and I had to walk fairly close for fear of losing her. What I could not understand though was, that we seemed to be walking up a shallow incline. After five minutes I had no doubt at all, we were definitely ascending. It did not make sense to me, the river ought to be at the bottom of the valley, however shallow, not at the top, unless Opa was deliberately leading me astray.

She was, but not just yet!

Some twenty minutes after we had left the hut, I heard flowing water. We came to some bushes, and below them, down a short steep bank, there was a river!

Opa tied one end of the rope to the bucket, and threw it down the bank. I tried to help her, but she would not let me, jabbering to herself. When she filled the other bucket, she coiled up the rope and threw it near the buckets. I put the yoke on my shoulders and had just begun to hook one of the buckets on, when she came to me, took the yoke away and started rubbing my nose with her finger, chattering what sounded to me like sweet nothings.

It was quite clear to me what she was after, but I had been in that strange country only a few hours, and had had no chance at all to discover their customs and rituals. Although the Karakalpaks did not carry their daggers tied to their belts, like the Uzbeks, it did not mean that they did not have them. I knew that the discipline in Uzbekistan was very strict as far as women were concerned, and it did not mean that it was necessarily different in Karakalpagistan. I was not prepared to have my throat slit simply because I did not obey the rules.

Opa, however, was of a different opinion. She was travelling along a one-way street, besides, she was at least four inches taller, and almost twice as broad as I was! We returned to the hut about an hour after we had left. Opa carried the water, while I carried the rope.

I was invited to sit down. Nearest the fire was Babai, followed by the uncle, then I followed Opa and the rest of the girls (there were three more by this time) forming a circle round the fire, ending with Ona, the mother, on the far side.

The uncle's foot began to bother me, first of all because it was looking really ugly, secondly because it stank to high heaven. He had cut it somehow or other, and it had gone septic. I was no doctor, but I thought something ought to be done about it.

I asked Opa for a piece of clean cloth, a bowl and some boiling water. She raked the fire to boil the water already in the *kozon*, handed me a bowl and started looking for a cloth. I put the bowl and my wire knife in the cauldron to sterilize them, then had a look at my patient's toe. It looked awful! It had a split right across its lower side, oozing yellow pus, and was about twice its normal size. My original idea was to wash the wound, removing as much as possible of the rotten matter, then dress the wound. Once I started, however, I thought the only way to do the job properly was to get rid of all the infected part, by carefully scraping it off with my knife. I did not cherish the idea, and wished that I had not started the job in the first place, but it had to be done. How much that fellow suffered, I could only imagine. I did it as carefully as I possibly could, washing the wound from time to time with warm water to which I added a few crystals of salt, which I thought might serve as an antiseptic. I wrapped the toe in a clean cotton dressing, hoping it would do some good.

We chatted for a while, then the time came to go to sleep. A felt mat was spread on the floor, and I thought it was time to bid them good night, and find a spot under a palm tree for the night. They would have none of it. I was shown my place, and Babai started the ball rolling by lying on the floor next to the fire, followed by his wife. Next to her were four of their daughters, then myself, Opa, three more daughters, ending the circle with the uncle by the other side of the fire.

'Have a peaceful night, little son,' said Babai, blowing the flame of the lamp out. Considering the circumstances, I did!

We all woke up more or less at the same time, when Ona, the mother, also called Aya, started the fire. Babai was already out, and I felt a little guilty for over-sleeping. One by one, the girls went out to wash, and when they returned, *chai*, a kind of herb tea, was already on the boil. The little sister who slept next to me offered me a piece of *obinon*, – a kind of thick pancake, and a bowl of tea. Aya looked on approvingly, while Opa and five of her sisters left the hut to go to work.

When I had finished my breakfast, Singlim and her sister went to work, leaving me behind with the mother. I did not know what to do. I wanted to do something to repay their kindness, but Aya would not let me do a thing. When she began cleaning the now almost extinct fire, I gently pushed her away and did the job for her, but she would not let me carry the ashes outside. Jokingly, she waved her hands indicating that I should go away, and stop bothering her.

The sun was shining, and the little settlement looked charming. The white walls of the huts looked really clean, contrasting sharply with the vivid green of the background. All the huts were the same shape and size, and just as neat and tidy as the one belonging to my Babai.

Except for a few sheep, some hens and an odd goat or two, the settlement seemed to be deserted. Leaving it behind me, I came to the open fields where women were picking those white flowers I had seen the day before. There were about twenty of them, Opa and the other sisters among them. Seeing me, they waved their hands, shouting and laughing. I had a good look at the 'flowers', only to discover that they were not like ordinary ones. Instead of petals, woolly material protruded from the brown shells at the tip of the plant, with black seeds embedded in it. I pulled one off, and

211

the entire contents of the shell came out, forming a ball twice the size of the shell, and slightly damp.

'*Pakhta! Pakhta!*' shouted the women, seeing me examining the fluffy material.

Of course it was *pakhta*, even I could see it now. I did not know that there were two words for cotton, the stuff I had in my hand. Cotton growing in the fields was *pakhta*, but the cotton material from which the garments were made was *chapak*. The mystery solved, I bade the girls good day and wandered off. I thought I would try and find the river, first to have a good scrub, and secondly to see whether it flowed on top of a small ridge.

I walked along a narrow path, away from the hamlet and up the gentle slope, admiring the scenery. I saw more women picking cotton, using both hands in quick succession, storing the fluffy material in long, narrow bags tied to their bodies.

'Lots of women, yes,' I mused, 'but where are all the men?' Since my arrival in Karakalpagistan I must have seen upwards of one hundred women, but only a handful of men, excluding the NKVD variety. Indeed, by the time I left Kolkhoz Voroshilova – that was the name of the hamlet – I had seen about a dozen men, including a lad of eighteen, but about seventy or more women. Even among the children the ratio seemed out of proportion.

I found the river without difficulty. Like the rest of the Amu Daria, it was muddy in colour, and at the spot where I bathed it was so deep that I could not reach the bottom. And it did flow at the top of a small ridge.

I spent some time killing lice, then strolled back to the field where Opa and the other girls were picking cotton. I thought I would help them gather it, to do something to repay their hospitality. To my great astonishment, they told me that it was a woman's job, and that I had to go away.

Before the day came to a close, Babai returned with his *arava*. I was really glad to see him and asked if I could help him in any way, but he just shrugged his shoulders. We went round the fields, picking up the bags full of cotton and deposited them in a store. He then took me to a hut which was only partly painted inside, and looked new. He suggested that I could finish painting it, if I really wanted to do something. I was only too delighted to oblige. I began there and then, only to be called out about an hour later by

Singlim, who told me that the meal was ready.

We sat in the circle as we had the previous day, a big bowl of rice was put in the centre of it, and they all started to eat with their hands. The rice was fairly loose, yet they managed to make little balls out of it, using only three fingers and a thumb, then throw them into their mouths. It looked very easy, but not when I attempted it. First of all, I could not even make a lump, let alone a neat little ball out of the rice. When I tried to throw it into my mouth, the lump either disintegrated, spraying my face with the individual grains, or trickled down my palm and into the sleeve of my *fufayka*. They were all in stitches of laughter, but I was not going to be beaten. Again and again I tried, with disastrous results. They showed me the method, but how they could possibly do it remained a mystery to me. In the end I pulled out my wooden spoon, and ate the stuff without dropping a grain on the floor, but much to the disappointment of my fellow diners!

After the meal I inspected the uncle's toe. To my great satisfaction, the swelling had diminished a little, most of the smell had gone too, and there was only a trace of yellow matter in the wound. I washed it with boiled salted water then dressed it in clean cotton. The uncle must have liked the look of his toe, too, because he shook my hand and grinned, showing me all his toothless gums.

Karakalpaks, like their cousins, Kazakhs, are small in stature, but their faces look more like the Uzbeks, that is, oval with sharp, pointed curved noses. All the men I saw had thin, goat-like beards, and sparse, black moustaches dangling at the side of their mouths, often to below jaw level. They wore blue or mustard-yellow *khalats*, and black hats. Their shoes were invariably a home-made type of moccasin of thick cotton material, but soled with soft leather or rubber.

The women were either hefty-looking amazons like Opa, or petite and rather pretty black-haired maidens. They all wore long, colourful dresses, and scarves tied either under their chins, or at the back of their heads.

When two or more Karakalpaks met and stopped for a chat, they would never stand, but crouch, sitting on the backs of their heels, their forearms resting on their knees. The posture was very comfortable really, and for many years afterwards I would adopt the same stance when talking to friends in the open!

Before the October Revolution, like the rest of the indigenous people of Southern Asia, the Karakalpaks led a nomadic life, moving their flocks of sheep according to the seasons. They lived well, and they were happy, but the new regime forced them to settle, and to grow rice and cotton. To them, as to the Uzbeks, Kazakhs, Tadjiks, Turkmenistanis, this was tantamount to a life of imprisonment. They hated it, as they hated their oppressors. It was for that reason that the troops of the Red Army never ventured too far outside their barracks in groups of less than five. They tended to disappear rather mysteriously if any of them were seen alone or in twos.

While we were chatting, Opa left the hut and Singlim took her place beside me. Babai and Aya looked very pleased, but it never occurred to me what their plans were. I told them that I was looking for the Polish Army, and that I would have to leave them soon in search of it. They tried to discourage me from leaving, but when I asked, Babai told me that there was a big settlement about forty miles away, and if the army was not there, it was not in Karakapagistan. The name of the settlement was Chimbai.

I thought I would finish painting the hut, then go and have a look at the place. I was up early, eager to start work, and when Singlim brought me some *obinon* at midday, I was wheeling the barrel of whitewash out of the hut. I spent the afternoon picking cotton, much to the disgust of the women, but I did try and earn my keep. I helped Babai with the bags, then we went to inspect the newly painted hut.

'Who is going to live in this hut?' I inquired.

'You and Singlim,' replied Babai. 'I don't think you will find your army in Chimbai!'

I was deeply honoured, though shattered, by that simple statement, but I had not left my home to marry a rather pretty black-haired eighteen-year-old, south of the Aral Sea, but to help restore freedom to my country.

When we returned to his hut, Babai made certain that I sat next to Singlim. The uncle had returned to his settlement, and I took his place by the fire for the night, Singlim sleeping next to me, with many speculative suggestions from Opa. I rose with Babai, had a piece of *obinon*, shook hands with all the family and departed.

'Don't go!' called Aya when we were a short distance away.

I could have stayed, had I so wished, and they would have made me one of their family, but I had other things to do. I felt as sad as I did when I left my own home.

I drove with Babai for a short while, until we came to the path I had to follow. He and the other men in the *kolkhoz* were digging a dyke some distance away. I shook hands with him, then followed a fairly well defined track roughly in an easterly direction. It twisted and turned, avoiding cotton fields and rice paddies. Before the evening came I picked some of the rice heads, separated the grain and started cooking it in the can. I scouted round for twigs and dung to keep the fire going, then left to have a wash in a nearby dyke. I tried the rice after an hour, but it was as hard as stone. I stoked up the fire before going to sleep, in the hope that it would be edible by morning, but because it was unhusked it would not soften.

Next morning the sun was well up by the time I came to a small dyke. A man was busy clearing a stoppage which prevented the water from flowing freely. I asked him whether I was on the right track for Chimbai. He looked me over, his eyes stopping at my bare feet.

'You aren't going all that way without shoes, are you?'

'Well,' I replied. 'I don't have any shoes, but I am quite used to walking without them.'

'Ahead of you,' continued the man, 'there is only desert, with many sharp stones. Try these.'

He untied the strings of his moccasins, and handed them to me. They were much too small. I thanked him for his most unexpected offer and carried on in the direction he indicated. This was only one of many such gestures. The people of the Soviet Union had hearts of gold, regardless of their nationality or the colour of their skin. Only their rulers were inhuman. The iron fist of those tyrants kept the unfortunate inhabitants in shackles in the desperate attempt to prove that Communism was the only way to live.

I emptied the remaining rice into my rucksack and filled the can with water, before veering away from the dyke and into the desert. As far as the eye could see, there was nothing but sand. The trail was quite distinct, except in places where the wind had blown off

215

the thin layer of sand lying on solid stone. The surface had many jagged edges, as though the softer parts of the stone had been eroded and blown off by the wind.

The sun was low on the horizon when I saw a big, rectangular building looming ahead. Increasing my pace, I marched directly towards it along the now fairly flat and soft sand, hoping to have a good look at the settlement before finding a suitable place for the night. When I came close enough to see that huge, dark grey block clearly, I stopped, my heart sinking. Instead of windows, all I could see were wooden planks, the same notorious *yezhovki* behind which I had spent so many, too many, months of my youth. Yes, the only brick building in Chimbai, the biggest settlement in Karakalpak Autonomous Soviet Socialist Republic was naturally the prison, symbol of the Communist empire.

It would have been madness to go any further. Where there was a prison, there was the NKVD. I sighed, turned about and followed my tracks in the soft sand until I reached the trail. I marched along it at a fast pace, looking over my shoulder from time to time, in case I was being followed.

It was while I was looking back that I hit a sharp rock with the big toe of my right foot, and cut it. Blood started to flow freely, blood that I could ill-afford to lose. I sat down holding the cut flesh together, in an attempt to stop the flow. I remember that my father often used sand to dry the ink on letters; there was no reason why I should not use the same technique to stem the flow of blood. There was plenty of it, and since it was baked by the sun almost daily, I reasoned that it was bound to be more sterile than binding it with any part of my clothing.

I hobbled a few yards away from the trail, scooped the bone-dry, fine top layer, and sprinkled it liberally over the cut. The sand absorbed the blood, and when the toe had become red again, I sprinkled some more over it. After a while the bleeding stopped.

It was rapidly becoming dark, so I scooped some sand to make myself a pillow and bedded down for the night. I was happy; there was no sound coming from anywhere, not even the slightest rustle of a desert rat, or the 'zing' of a mosquito. I felt free. I lay on my back looking at the stars. I found the Plough and the North Star, then looked towards the west, trying to visualize, some three thousand miles away, a little white cottage by the linden trees, and the red-bricked church with the stork's nest opposite the spire. It seemed to me that I had been away from it for at least a century.

I shut my eyes and went to sleep. I woke up frozen to the marrow before the sun began to light up the eastern sky. I licked the trace of dew that had formed on the side of my tin can, and made my way along the trail.

I spent a day or two picking cotton in Kolkhoz Nukus, and a few more days in the machine and tractor station, a ramshackle old barn with a number of very old and unserviceable machines, where I was employed as a cleaner. I lived with the people of the *kolkhoz*, and the ratio of men to women was just as out of proportion as it had been in other places, about seven or eight women to a man.

I never have discovered the reason for the disparity. My view was that the birth-rate certainly had something to do with it, coupled to the number killed in the war against the Communists in the early twenties, plus the number of men in prisons and labour camps. There might have been some in the Red Army as well, although I had never heard of any in the places I stayed.

My toe had healed almost completely, and I decided to return to Bukhara and my friend the *mullah*.

I started my trek along the trail, a caravan route across the desert leading to a place called Turt Kul, or Four Lakes, some two hundred miles away. I was hoping to encounter a caravan and perhaps continue my journey with it. I marched resolutely along the trail and by midday I found a piece of yellow pressing, normally fed to camels. I put it in my rucksack, had a piece of *obinon*, which I had begged earlier, and a sip of water, then continued the journey.

That night, I slept in the desert, and by late morning the following day a mountain range came into view, with a pass on its western edge. I came to the conclusion that it had to be the range I had seen on my way down river. My spirits rose considerably.

In the afternoon the trail split into two, one heading for the pass, the other veering west. I decided to make for the pass, reasoning that I would have a better chance of picking up a barge convoy if I went that way.

The sandy desert gave way to solid rock, and I began to climb. The desolate, barren rocks were completely devoid of vegetation,

217

but when I reached the top of the pass I had a magnificent view of the Amu Daria winding its way from the south. I ate a little of my remaining food, drank some water, then found a reasonably soft spot and settled down for the night contented with my achievement.

By mid-afternoon the following day, after crossing some paddy-fields, I reached a small hamlet. There seemed nobody about save a goat or two and a few sheep. I knocked at the door of the nearest hut but there was no reply. I had no luck at the next two either, and began to wonder whether it was a ghost settlement. I tried another hut and from inside I could hear the very deep, rhythmical sighs of a person suffering from pain. I was not sure what to do. I knew that custom forbade anyone to enter a hut without invitation, yet my instinct told me that I ought to go in. I knocked again, then plucked up courage and entered. There was a rope stretched right across the hut, about three feet from the floor. In the middle of the room there was a woman, kneeling, her arms over the rope right up to her armpits, swaying to and fro, exhaling painfully each time she pushed forward on the rope. Her face was contorted with pain.

I had never seen anything like it or ever heard such a ritual. The young woman looked at me for a split second, her eyes full of horror, yet pleading at the same time. She did not say anything but continued to sway, her sighs now becoming more like a cry. It was only then that I had noticed that her abdomen was swollen – she was about to have a baby! My first thought was to take the advice of my legs and run. I had no business to be there, I had never seen a baby being born, and, more to the point, I had not the slightest idea what actually happened when a woman gave birth. I turned to leave, but I was barely through the door, when I heard the weak cry: 'Don't go!'

I stopped in my tracks and returned. To say that my ideas as to what I was going to do were rather vague would be a gross understatement. I was scared to death.

As far as I knew all babies were born in beds, so the first thing to do, I thought, would be to take her off that rope and lay her flat on her back. She was of a different opinion, so I left her there. She kept heaving at the rope, her cries becoming more spine-chilling, and she began to sink her fingernails in her skirt. It seemed fairly obvious to me that the birth was imminent. It was only then that I realized that she was kneeling on the front of her skirt, and that the baby might suffocate if I did not do something about it quickly.

With one mighty heave I lifted the struggling woman off the rope, laid her flat on her back, lifted her skirt up, she yelled, spread her legs apart, and out popped a baby yelling his head off!

The young mother gave a sigh of relief, her face now relaxed and her eyes closed. I thought I would pick the baby up, a pink, fairly squashed object, and wash it. Lifting it up, I discovered to my horror that he was still attached to his mother by a cord. I knew about the umbilical cord, but was under the impression that it automatically broke off at birth. Thinking that something was wrong, I gave it a gentle pull, but all it produced was a grunt and a little cry from the young woman.

Clearly, that was not the way to do it, but the two had to be separated. I put my hand in my pocket, fished out my knife, dipped it in the hot water in the cauldron to clean it as much as possible, then cut the cord about a couple of inches from the boy's tummy. A red liquid started oozing out of it, so I tied a knot at each end and that stopped it. I was halfway through washing the baby when the mother came to. She sat down, putting her hands up, asking for the baby. I saw a clean-looking piece of cloth by the fireplace, wrapped the baby in it and gave him to his smiling mother. I was smiling too, but with relief, because both of them were still alive despite my clumsy efforts. So there was I, a mid-wife, at the tender age of eighteen and a half.

My own ordeal over, I thought it wise to leave the happy couple before anybody should arrive and get the wrong impression. The young mother pleaded with me to stay a little longer, and before I could explain my fears, three women appeared at the doorway. How much of the ensuing hullabaloo, waving of hands and non-stop chatter was due to my unexpected presence, and how much was to do with the new arrival, I shall never know. After a while, the women stopped looking at me belligerently and I was invited to stay. Two of the women left the hut, while the oldest began kneading dough, as though she were going to bake a cake to mark the occasion. That was not so: soon after, she made some sort of noodles out of it and left them to dry. An old man entered a hut carrying the carcass of a freshly killed sheep. That was promptly cut up into small pieces, and together with many chopped onions and other vegetables was put in the cauldron to stew. Later, the noodles were added to it as well, producing a delicious meal called *besbarmak*.

There were three types of alcoholic drinks in that part of the world, all made of fermented milk: *koumiss* made from mare's milk, *shubat* from camel's and *airan* from sheep's. They all tasted roughly the same, looked fairly similar, something like a buttermilk, the *koumiss* being the best and the sweetest, and they were all made in the same fashion. The milk was poured into a sewn-up goat skin, hung outside the door, and stirred occasionally with a wooden stick which was left in the skin, the handle protruding through the neck. About two weeks later the brew was ready to drink.

More and more people came to the party which was always arranged when a boy was born. The men stayed outside the hut, drinking and chatting, while women did the cooking. When it became dark, a lamp was hung outside the door, and when one goat skin was emptied, another appeared promptly. All the settlement took part in the celebration, and the scarcity of males was clearly visible.

It was after the meal that I discovered why the young woman had been left on her own in the hut. She was not expecting the baby for another week, and went to work. Not feeling very well, she returned to the hut to realize that the labour pains had begun. In accordance with the custom, she tied a rope across the hut and went through the ritual. Exhaling while pushing at the rope, and inhaling when pulling at it was supposed to help the birth. Normally when a baby is due, an aunt stays with the mother-to-be to act as a midwife.

In the eyes of the locals, being a wanderer, I was expected to know what was happening in the world, and I was asked several times how far away the German Army was. The last time I had heard anything about the war the Germans had taken Kiev, but that was weeks before. I judged it to be 2,000 miles away.

'You tell us when they come closer,' said one of the men, 'and we start killing,' at the same time cutting his throat with his finger.

'Killing whom?' I inquired.

'The Communists, of course!'

'Ha!' shouted everyone within earshot. 'Yes!'

Some of the younger men disappeared into the darkness,

returning with foot-long daggers, some with handles made of solid silver. They placed a log of wood some twenty yards away – it was barely visible – then threw their stilettos at it. Not one of them missed, the blade sticking in the wood every time. Considering that all of us were rather full of *koumiss, shubat* or *airan*, or most probably a mixture of the lot, it was not a bad example of their skills.

I told them I was trying to reach Bukhara. I learnt that in the old days the journey would have been simple, for there were many caravans going to Bukhara each week. Nowadays, apparently, it was different. However, the men told me there was no need to walk all the way because one of their people was going to Khiva. He was hoping to catch a barge at a settlement some ten miles away, so offered to take me with him.

The party broke up in the early hours of the morning. I was invited to stay in the hut of the new-born baby. The sun was well up in the sky when I woke up. I had a bit of a headache, but otherwise I felt fine.

'Aren't you going to work?' I asked the old man as we went to wash.

'In the old days,' he replied, 'each time a boy was born in the *aul* [a camp comprising several tents], we always had a party, and we never hunted the next day. No need to change things now!'

Both the baby and the mother were doing fine, and she even left the hut to wave goodbye as I left for the river the next morning. We had to stop several times as I developed diarrhoea, perhaps due to the over-rich food to which my stomach was not accustomed, the drinks, the water, or maybe the combination of all three. When we arrived at the hamlet, no one had heard anything of the convoy. Fortunately my fellow travelling companion introduced me to a *babai*, with whom I lived while waiting for the convoy. He had changed his mind about going to Khiva and so returned to his home.

While staying with the *babai* my job was to collect the *yantok*, also known as *titanak*, a silvery-grey, prickly shrub, for the camels' fodder. I also took charge of the camels when they finished for the day, tied them up, then brought them back the following morning ready for work. Camels are nasty beasts; they kick, bite, or spit their saliva all over one, for no reason at all. The most treacherous of their tricks which I experienced was the side kick, usually performed with a front leg. Considering I was the one feeding them, I certainly did not expect such treatment, but I learned fast!

One morning I could not find one of my charges, although I had tied his legs in the same manner as the others. I looked everywhere, but he was gone, or so I thought. I had collected a huge heap of *yantok*, maybe ten feet high, and walking round it, I thought I could hear the grunts of the beast. I ran to the other side, but he was not there. When I returned to the previous spot, I heard the grunts again. It was only then that I realized that the camel had buried himself under the heap of *yantok*, without disturbing a twig!

My stomach was still bothering me a lot, and I was passing blood. I came to the conclusion that it was not just simple diarrhoea, but dysentery. I cured it in a most mysterious manner: I was picking *yantok* in the steppe, when for some unknown reason I felt the urge to go up a small incline, the top of which was covered by sand. Clearly though, there would be no *yantok* there. I walked to the top of the crest, only to see more sand descending gently towards a shallow valley. At the bottom of it there was a row of half a dozen or so tall trees. My head was telling me that there was no point in going down there, that if there was any *yantok*, I would have to carry it all the way back, a distance of perhaps a third of a mile, but a feeling dictated that I must go down, so I went. The trees were the size of a fully grown cherry tree, the leaves like a cross between plum and cherry. The canopy was covered by a mass of small, red fruits similar to a rowan tree, but spread evenly all over like cherries.

Back home, we were told that when we saw fruit which we had never seen before, we must not eat it if it was red, had a bitter taste or white sap. When I tried one of the fruit it was precisely like that, so I spat it out. However, instinct, or whatever it was, was urging me to eat it, so I had a stomachful. When I could not eat any more, I broke a few branches and brought them back to the settlement. Within three hours I was as right as rain! As I have said before, when a man is in prison under the conditions we were in, or on the run as I was, he develops an animal instinct unknown to an ordinary mortal. He does what this instinct tells him to do and his logic is illogical to a normal, civilized human.

When I returned to the settlement, the *babai* was looking for me, as the convoy was not far away. I found that most of the passengers were Poles. I strolled up and down, looking for someone I might have known, but I was out of luck, so I settled down by a family of four. During the conversation it transpired that they, too, were suffering from dysentery. I gave them a branch of my 'medicine tree'. Within three hours they were solid too!

The convoy consisted of three barges, pulled by a tug. Going against the flow of the stream was obviously a much slower process, sometimes so slow that we barely traversed a mile in a day. It was alleged that this particular convoy was an organized affair, under the command of two Polish 'lieutenants'. We were given bread in the morning and I looked forward to an enjoyable voyage.

The morning of 9 December came but the bread did not. By midday, one of the 'lieutenants' made a statement to the effect that because the journey had taken longer than planned we had run out of bread. However, he assured us he was in touch with the tug captain who would stop at the next settlement to obtain some more. The next day came and went, but the only thing we saw was the sand of Kizil Kum. The following day was the same and many people were becoming desperate, especially those with small children. I turned my rucksack upside down and found a few grains of rice. These I gave to the family I was sitting next to for their children to nibble. To make matters worse, we picked up dysentery again, and had no choice but to relieve ourselves over the side each time the pains came. A number of people died on that journey, and their bodies were thrown overboard. There was little movement on the barges, people just sat with their heads between their knees waiting for the next convulsion to come.

On the morning of the twelfth, and three days without our bread ration, there was still no sign of any settlement.

Since I always ate the whole of my bread ration as soon as I received it in case it was stolen, I had had nothing to eat for four full days. I felt a little weak, and I had a feeling that my brain was parting company with the skull in the region of my forehead.

About midday news spread that bread had been discovered in the rear barge, in a locked hold allegedly containing freight. I rose and staggered to the stern of my barge, the middle one, examining the possibility of crossing the gap between the two, to investigate the rumour.

The barges were connected to each other by a thick steel hawser. At first, I thought I would walk along it with my arms outstretched, but then discarded this plan as a little too ambitious. In the end, I crossed that perilous gap using my hands and legs, my body dangling underneath the cable. The actual crossing was simple enough, but boarding the barge from that hanging position sapped the last ounce of my energy. Obviously the hunger had taken more out of me than I had imagined.

The commotion on the far end of the barge was a clear indication that the bread story was not just gossip. Walking along the side of the barge I saw a number of happy faces, their jaws moving. How I wished that I were one of them! It was impossible to get anywhere near the hatch of the hold, where the bread was supposed to be. Slowly, agonizingly slowly, I wriggled myself somewhere in the vicinity of that opening, but from there on, there was only a solid wall of human bodies. It was impossible to move further. To the right of me, there was a steel structure about ten feet high. I thought if only I could, somehow, climb it, I would get some idea where the hatch was, then run over people's heads to reach it. The problem was that the building had no projections of any shape or form, it was just flat sheet-metal.

During the many forceful pushes from the rear I wriggled myself upwards, until my knees were resting on somebody's shoulders. During the next surge I rose, stood on the next fellow's head, then leapt forward towards the roof of the building, about three feet away. I only managed to grasp the top of the flat roof with my fingertips, but I was not going to let go for all the caviar in the Kremlin! I pulled and heaved as though my life depended on it, until my chin was level with the top. Using it as an extra anchor, I got a better grip with my hands, and after what seemed an hour, I was on top. I collapsed, totally spent. When I got my wind back I surveyed the situation, and I did not like what I saw. The opening was about three yards from the roof, and was full of people trying to push themselves inside. They were prevented from doing so not only by sheer numbers, but also by the lucky ones inside trying to get out, their stomachs full, and their pockets filled with bread.

The stalemate ended when a head appeared in a hatch. What followed, happened in a second or two: several hands grasped that head, pulling it upwards, and before the man's feet had gone through the hatch, his clothing was pulled apart, his body thrown to one side, on top of people's heads, and all the loaves that he was carrying torn to pieces by hundreds of hands within reach. I was not impressed by what I had seen, but I was not there to admire the scenery, or pass moral judgements. During the split second while the men around the opening were tearing apart that precious food, and stuffing it down their throats, the hatch remained free. I did not think; I leapt forwards and downwards, feet first. Why I was not killed, or did not at least break my leg, can only have been luck. Not only did I go clean through the hatch without touching the sides, but I also missed the steel ladder, which I did not know was there, and which went down to the bottom of the hold. Had either of my feet touched any of the rungs of the ladder, my head would either have hit the mouth of the opening, or I would have been turned upside down, my head hitting the bottom of the hold, and I doubt if I would have been here to tell the tale.

The first notion I had of the ladder was when my back hit it, after my feet collided with the bottom of the hold. It was pitch black down there, and the air was foul. I was concussed for a time, but when I came to, I could smell the delicious aroma of bread, and hear the sound of chewing.

I groped in all directions, but all I could feel were bodies or faces. I moved away from the ladder, and I felt something with my bare feet, something which was oval and not too hard, something which I had not tasted for more than four and a half days.

I grabbed it with both hands, and sank my teeth in it. The best meal in the best restaurant in Paris could not possibly taste as delicious as did that first bite of stale bread. It did not take me long to gobble that loaf. I moved on, searching for more. I became aware that I was breathing heavily, that my lungs were running out of air, and that I was going to faint.

'Down, you fool, down!' I thought, 'oxygen is heavier than carbon dioxide, there is bound to be some of it down here!' so I went down on all fours, and carried on until my head hit the side of the barge. I turned right, and almost immediately my head touched something. It was bread, stacks of it, as far as I could feel.

There was nobody near me – perhaps the foul air had driven them out. I sat down on the floor, my back to the side of the barge, picked up another loaf and started chewing. I felt good: plenty of bread, nothing to do, nobody near me, lovely! I was trying to formulate a plan of exit, but I was in no hurry, not yet, anyway. I felt like going to sleep, but the thought of carbon dioxide descending to my level kept me awake, so I sat there, listening to the water rushing past the hull of the barge.

The idyllic situation did not last long. Listening to the water made me aware that I could easily drink some of it. As the time passed, the thirst became acute and I had to make a decision: do I leave all that bread for a drink of water, or do I suffer thirst and eat as much as I want? The water won, but I had to find a way of taking at least some for the family that I was sitting by. I had plenty of string round my middle, keeping my *fufayka* in place, so I measured the length, leaving enough for the knot, and chewed two pieces off with my teeth. I tied the bottom of my trouser legs, and stuffed them with pieces of bread. I tore apart a few more loaves and placed them behind my back, in the sleeves, and a lot in front of my chest. I looked towards the almost closed hatch, and crawled towards it. All I had to do now was to get out of the hold alive, with my clothing intact, and the family would not starve any more.

When I finally reached it, I sat a long time at the bottom of the ladder, thinking. One reason was that the air was cool and fresh there, and the other was that I did not want to finish up like that man I had seen; I did not want to die. I know now what a man facing execution feels like, because I have felt it. I also know now what a man who is prepared to give everything he possesses to save his life feels, because I felt it too. But unlike those two, I also know something entirely different: when I left the family, which I happened to sit beside on the barge, the man was sitting with his head between his legs, halfway between his knees and his ankles, too starved to move. His wife was also sitting, her back resting against the mid-structure of the barge, her eyes closed, holding a small child in each arm. The children, one about eight, the other about six years of age, were asleep, the younger dreaming about eating, I thought, because her jaws were moving as though chewing. I know now what a man feels like, or what he thinks about, when he has to make a decision whether or not to risk his skin in order to bring some bread to such a family, because I made such a decision. It was the picture of that little, innocent toddler, who had had nothing to eat for at least two days, to my knowledge, chewing away in her sleep that I had in mind when I started my climb up the ladder.

Walking up that ladder, I kept my head down. I did not want the eager hands waiting above to give me any help, by jerking me upwards, which was tantamount to hanging. When I felt the hands touching my neck, I stopped for a moment, throwing the pieces of bread I had in front of my *fufayka*, high in the air. The hands disappeared from the vicinity of the hatch, I ran up the remaining few steps, throwing bread in all directions. During the ensuing commotion, I slid past the immediate surroundings of the opening, then joined the fray as though I were one of the crowd.

I got rid of all the bread in my *fufayka*, save a piece or two I still had behind my back, but I also had the bread concealed in the bottom of my trousers, which was the object of the whole exercise. When I returned to my barge, and offered the bread to the family, the woman did not believe that it was real. I felt really good.

The hoard which was discovered in the rear barge was, in fact, a small one. However, a committee was formed to deal with the two crooks, and after a certain amount of 'persuasion', the main store was discovered in the forward barge. The bread was distributed throughout the community, by tossing each loaf from one barge to another.

Before midday on 14 December, the convoy reached Farab. The two thugs were handed over to the waiting NKVD while the rest of us were divided into groups and sent to different locations 'pending call-up'. Unfortunately, I had no chance of escaping as I had done in Nukus. There were several questions which remained unanswered regarding the stolen bread. If there were only two persons involved in the theft, how were they going to unload more than a ton of it without anyone noticing? And, even supposing they did manage to off-load it, how were they going to transport it a distance of about sixty miles to Kagan, the nearest big town, where they would have a chance to sell it on the black market? Farab, and the settlement on the other side of the river, Chardjui, were much too small to absorb such a large quantity.

I do not know the answer to those questions, but for the record the alleged names of the two 'lieutenants' were Olszewski, the leader, and Piotrowicz, his second-in-command. I kept a wary eye for those two gentlemen when I left the Soviet Union. Unfortunately, I never heard of them again.

Two other Poles and I arrived in the Red October Collective Farm later that day. There were two Polish lads already present and we slept together in a barn by a small pond. The community consisted mainly of Uzbeks, with one or two Turkmenistans. The women picked cotton, while the men dug a canal. In the morning we received a small piece of *obinon*, then went to work with the other men to help them with the digging. There was no machinery of any kind, each man using a huge, heart-shaped hoe, about two feet in diameter. With one blow they sank the blade of the hoe into fairly sandy soil, then in the next movement they tossed it on to a platform of the *arava* which was at a height of at least four feet. I tried the exercise only once. Although I could lift the hoe and swing it through the air without much difficulty, when it came to the tossing of the load on to the *arava* I was obliged to quit. Since I was no use as a digger I became a camel driver, taking the dug-up soil away. The little experience I had gained while waiting for the convoy came in helpful, and I soon became quite proficient in handling the beast.

The Poles were all *bezhentsy* like myself, caught by the frontier troops of the USSR on the way to Romania and Hungary, released from labour camps and looking for the Polish Army. One who had worked in the *taiga* was in a very poor state of health. He was as thin as a rake and so weak that he could hardly move. Needless to say he could not go to work and therefore received no food, so we shared our meagre *obinon* ration with him. I slept next to him in the barn, with the others on either side of us to keep warm. Some nights were so cold that in the morning the pond was covered with ice thick enough to walk on. When we awoke one morning he did not move. I gave him a shake to wake him up but he did not respond. He was dead.

The way of life of the Uzbeks was entirely different from the Karakalpaks'. Most of the households were surrounded by a wall about four feet high, and usually in the form of a square. As a rule the living quarters formed part of one wall, the barn and the animal shed forming the other two, the fourth wall having a gate.

The middle of the square was empty.

The barn where I slept belonged to the collective farm, and as such was not part of any household. I was invited several times into the compound, and even to the living quarters, perhaps because I was able to speak a little of the language. In the ones I visited, the living quarters consisted of a communal room – the only room to which a visitor was ever invited – and a private room, or sometimes two, where the women retired after supper. The cooking was done in an open shed with a roof on top, and the meals were taken in the communal room, or sometimes outside.

One evening I was invited by an Uzbek to his house. After supper, two more arrived and one of them produced a Russian newspaper. I was asked to read it, then tell them how far the Germans had reached. The newspaper was dated late November. I looked eagerly for a map but there was nothing except an article about the heroic Red Army pushing the Germans from Rostov, and fighting near Kharkov. The names of the other towns meant nothing to me. I knew only too well were Kharkov was, and I remembered from my school atlas that Rostov was at the mouth of the River Don where it enters the Azov Sea. The Uzbeks seemed to be pleased with what I told them, but I did not know how to interpret it. They removed any doubts I might have had soon afterwards. One of them cried: 'You tell us when they come a little closer, and we start.' He put his hand to his throat, moving it to and fro several times in a horizontal direction. I pleaded with them not to start anything silly, that the Germans still had to cross a big sea called the Caspian, then Kara Kum before they got close. I also suggested that if the Germans reached Baku, and the oil wells, they might not want to advance any further.

The answer came quickly: 'You tell us when they reach Baku, and we start . . .' He ended with the same movement as before!

Later they told me what it was like before the Communists came, and about the war they waged against them. I mentioned the film I had seen about that war. They all laughed, shaking their heads.

'Communism, the butcher of freedom!' exclaimed one of them. Yes! We all agreed in unison. No human being who was un-fortunate enough to sample the honey of Communism could ever disagree with that particular sentiment.

When the Communists began to win the war, the tribe's valuables were distributed among the trustworthy, so that when the Uzbeks became free again, they could be collected and used for the benefit of the community. My host led me to a dark, box-like piece of furniture standing by the wall, with big, brass hinges and other ornaments, unlocked the lid and lifted it up. I could not believe my eyes. That piece of furniture which I had seen before, standing in the common room for all to see, was lined with thick felt. It contained brooches of all sizes and shapes, made of gold, and studded with red and yellow stones, clasps and medallions made of gold and silver. All the stones looked like the real thing, and that was only a small part of the tribe's treasure!

Uzbeks, like their cousins the Kazakhs and the Karakalpaks, were Moslems. Although the Soviet government had closed all the mosques – I saw hundreds of them, but not one open for worship – the locals took that part of the Soviet constitution dealing with the 'anti-religious propaganda' with a huge pinch of salt, and prayed in the fields.

It wasn't long before my feet began to itch; I knew it was time to move on again. The other Poles decided to wait so I bade them goodbye, obtained directions from the Uzbeks, and left. I returned to Farab, then walked to the bridge crossing the Amu Daria, knowing that the trains had to slow down there. I jumped on the first freight train going east.

Once back in Bukhara, I had no trouble finding the *mullah*, but the news he had was not encouraging. Indeed, he had lost all hope of ever seeing me again, and therefore had made no arrangements for a caravan. I decided to return to Samarkand and see if I could find any trace of the army there. I slept in the snake pit and picked up a passenger train from Kagan in the morning.

I did not find any trace of the Polish Army in Samarkand, so I took a freight train going in an easterly direction. Arriving in Tashkent, I pounded the streets for a day or two, with an occasional visit to the market. I had no difficulty finding partners for thieving expeditions; those of the *bezprizornye* who were not in prisons or the Children's Working Colonies were there, spending the winter in the south.

I decided to go back to Bukhara, and wait for the caravan going in the direction of Afghanistan. I stopped in Samarkand just for a meal, then carried on westward. The freight train terminated at a place called Aktash, so I picked up a passenger train. When we arrived at Gizhduvan I jumped off the buffers, as at any other station, and nearly screamed with excitement. There on the short, raised platform stood a dapper, oldish man of about forty, wearing the uniform of the Polish Army with three bars of a platoon leader on his epaulettes! I ran up to him, introduced myself, then asked him if he knew where the Polish Army was forming.

'If you just wait a few moments I will take you to our unit,' he replied. 'I must wait until the train departs, in case there is someone else on it.'

About half a mile away, in the back streets of Gizhduvan, there was a small mud hut with a flat roof, the recruiting centre of the Polish Army. I doubt very much if I would have found it on my own.

The date was 7 February 1942, and I remember it vividly. It had taken me five months and two days from the date of my release from the labour camp to find the army recruiting centre and achieve my goal. During that time I had covered some 5,500 miles in Soviet Asia, travelling without an internal passport and with little money.

How, and why did I succeed where thousands of others failed? There were several reasons, leaving pure luck aside, a most important ingredient in such an exercise. First, I was brought up by my parents to be entirely self-reliant and positively encouraged to use my head and my hands to their full capacity. Second, at school I was expected to listen to and absorb what was being said. Consequently, I had an idea where some of the places were, and the likely distances involved, who the people were, and where the mountains and the deserts were. I was taught to learn things, rather than merely listen to political dogma, a most useless form of education. Third, there was instinct. The kind of instinct that a human being, incarcerated within the four walls of a crowded cell, rarely seeing the sun and never the outside world, develops when he reverts to nature and becomes an animal: the push that makes him do things, or go places, without a logical reason or explanation. Furthermore, I had the ability to speak Russian fluently, a factor which certainly helped in the initial stages of my captivity. The ability to pick up local languages also helped tremendously, and this talent, in my opinion, stemmed from my schooldays when I was taught to *listen* in order to learn things. However, there was another reason. To the east of the Urals the Communists had no friends, only enemies. This does not mean that they had many friends to the west of the mountains, or to the north for that matter, except perhaps Moscow, but to the east of the Urals there were only convicts: the convicts who toiled in the labour camps, and the convicts who guarded them, the convicts who administered the *sovkhozes* and *kolkhozes*, and the convicts who were sent there to work as 'free resettlers'. Being an ex-convict myself, I was among friends!

13

When we arrived at the Polish Army recruiting centre, a captain took a statement from me and asked me a number of questions. Then a medical chap took a quick look at me, I was pronounced alive, and the captain informed me that I was provisionally accepted. Naturally, I was delighted with the news.

At the crack of dawn the following day about twenty of us were assembled into some sort of order and instructed that we were going to join the main camp. We marched off in step like soldiers, hoping to arrive at our destination soon, and looking as though we had been in the army all our lives. We left Gizhduvan behind us, following a trail through the sands. After a couple of hours we were straggling a little, and a couple of hours later our squad of twenty trailed over a distance of a mile or more. I was somewhere in the middle, trying to puzzle out where we were going, and how far we were from the main camp. We were walking in an easterly direction and on occasion I could hear and see the trains thundering along the line I knew so well, only a few miles to the south. By afternoon we were ready for a drink but there was no water; there was nothing but sand. However, by late afternoon we slowly caught up with the leading group who had kindly waited for us. We were told to smarten up approaching the camp, and that we should march in like soldiers not vagabonds.

'What is the name of the place we are going to?' I asked the group leader while we were resting.

'Kermine,' he replied.

'Kermine?' I queried the name. 'It has a railway station, so why did we not go by train?'

'The simple answer is,' replied the leader, 'that we have no authority from the Soviets to travel on trains, and the Polish authorities have no money for such luxuries.'

'It is a pity that I didn't know we were going as far as that,' I continued. 'I would have taken all of us on the train.'

'And what would you use for tickets?' asked the leader.

'Tickets?' I responded. 'What are they?'

We all laughed. No doubt all of us at some stage had travelled on the trains without paying. But we were no longer vagabonds released from the various labour camps of the Communist empire. We were no longer capitalist pigs or bourgeois dogs, spies or saboteurs. To the Communist leaders, ex-bosom pals of Fascist Germany with whom they had raped our country only a few years before, we had suddenly become good boys and good boys did not travel on trains without paying! It was a strange feeling to realize that I must not do things like that any more, that I must not steal, cheat, or con people, that at last I was becoming a human being again. It seemed such a long time since I had been one. It was a strange feeling, but a nice one.

We marched into the camp in military fashion, tired out after our thirty-mile trek across the desert, but with our heads held high. We were given a meal, then told to find ourselves a place to sleep, that is anywhere in the camp except the tents. They were already occupied by men who had been vetted and medically examined. We were only provisional soldiers. The camp, comprising about a dozen tents, was situated on a sandy flat a mile or so from the settlement called Kermine. There was a building on the edge of the camp, with a roof projecting away from the wall. It was a good spot for the night in case of dew, so I found a place among the others and went to sleep. When I awoke, I noticed a man next to me with his back to the wall, his head resting on his knees. I moved gently away from him so as not to disturb his sleep. The leader of our group appeared soon after and instructed us to look for a number of his men who were still missing. Thinking that my sleeping partner might be one of them I returned to the spot where he sat, shouting at him to wake up. He did not move, so I gave him a shake. He fell to one side, still in his crouching position. He was dead.

I went back to my leader to report the fact. He told me that it was nothing unusual and that the burial party would take care of him. After breakfast, we were taken to the vicinity of the wooden building. The dead man was still there. One by one we were called inside. While I was awaiting my turn, two men with a stretcher appeared and carried the body away. They took it to a communal grave some distance from camp, placed it among other corpses, then sprayed them all with whitewash. More bodies were collected throughout the day, and eventually the grave was covered over with soil. Another party set about digging a fresh one ready for the next day.

I went through the questioning like the others, then had a medical check-up. This was followed by more questioning. Clearly, the people in charge were no fools, and they were making sure that no Communist bastard wormed his way into our army. Finally, five days after my arrival I was accepted, and to my great joy attached to the Air Force Group. On 16 February we became Number 5 Squadron of the Polish Air Force and I was now sleeping in a tent.

We were kept busy listening to lectures, digging graves and latrines, or filling them up. There was a big tent some distance away where people who reported sick were kept. They were not given any medical treatment because the doctors had no medicine to give except a friendly chat to keep their spirits up until they died. The disease they suffered from was endemic in that part of the world: typhus.

An old biplane landed and taxied to the edge of the camp. The pilot, dressed in typical leather jacket and trousers, jumped out, then took his helmet off to speak to one of the senior officers present. He turned out to be a she! When she returned to her aeroplane I watched her every move. I watched her taking off, bouncing on the uneven ground, then becoming airborne. When she disappeared beyond the range of hills, I sighed, hoping that in the not-too-distant future I might become a pilot, something I had wanted to be since I was a little boy.

One day a priest appeared in camp and the Commandant decided that we ought to have a thanksgiving Mass. The building was cleared of tables and benches, and an altar constructed. Somehow the news spread, bringing many of the locals, both Moslem and Russian Orthodox, to our camp. It also brought the NKVD. About twenty of the thugs arrived in a lorry and tried to discourage the people from attending, either by pushing them away from the door, shouting that the assembly was forbidden, or by taking pictures. A few of the locals obeyed, many did not. The Commandant arrived and tried to plead with the soldiers that they had no right to interfere, but they would not listen so he completely ignored them and led us to the church. There was not room for all of us in the building so the great majority had to remain outside. I managed to get in, as did the NKVD. With the exception of the Secret Police we all took our hats off. In a few simple words the priest told them that it was a place of worship and they were welcome, but if they wanted to stay they had to take their hats off, or else leave. There was a long silence, and the atmosphere electric, with all heads turned towards Stalin's henchmen. The upholders of Communism realized that those weather-beaten, haggard-looking faces meant business, and that they had better do what the priest suggested or they would be taken outside one by one, in small pieces! They took their hats off. The priest turned to the altar and all of us dropped to our knees. All, that is, except Stalin's thugs. They stood there for a while, sticking out like sore thumbs, but a little persuasion by some of the congregation soon made us equal. I had seen something that I had never imagined I would. There they were, the NKVD, Stalin's Secret Police, upholders of Communism and Stalin's constitution – one paragraph of which stated that the government had the right to indulge in anti-religious propaganda – in a church, with their hats off and on their knees. The priest delivered a strong sermon, chosing his words carefully. I do not know if any of the storm troopers understood Polish or not, but they did not interfere. The Mass over, we left the building, forming little groups to talk about the sermon or to tell others what had happened inside. The troopers tried to break up those little groups for a time but they soon realized their presence was no longer welcome and that we knew just as many swear words as they did. They boarded the lorry and left just as unexpectedly as they arrived.

Rumours started circulating that the first transport from Kermine was soon to leave the Soviet Union for Persia and Great Britain. There were lots of smiling faces, but I had nothing to smile about. I began to feel sleepy, shivery and I was running a temperature. I tried hard to shake the fever, but on 4 March I had to

236

give in and report sick. I knew very well what was wrong with me and was determined not to become one of those bodies in the communal grave. I reported to the sick tent and a day or so later we were transferred to a building in the village close to the railway station. There we were provided with beds, a great improvement on the sandy soil of the tent.

There was also a nurse in her twenties, who gave food to those who felt like eating, or a jab of morphine to those who were past recovery. She also used to take our temperatures. She would put a thermometer under my armpit and tell me to lie still so that it would not break. I used to take a quick peep at it to see what it read. It was thirty-nine degrees centigrade, then forty, then forty-one. I tried lowering it by lying very still and breathing slowly, but it did not help. I wanted to toss and turn, or stand on my head. The temperature kept going up and up and I did not know much about the next few days, except that I was perpetually climbing a wall, a wall that had no beginning or end, top or bottom, a wall that used to spin or rock about, but I had to climb it. I knew that once I reached the top of that wall I would be all right, so I kept on climbing. I felt very, very tired and I sweated a lot, but I kept on climbing.

I opened my eyes and the wall was gone. The nurse was standing by my bed, her hand on my forehead. I felt absolutely spent, and very, very hungry.

'You had a nice long sleep, laddie,' said the nurse, 'you will be all right now, just have a quiet rest.'

It was dark when I woke up again, and I noticed that the man on my right had not eaten his food – a small portion of semolina. I watched him for some time but he did not budge, so I decided to get up and have a look at him, and if he were dead to eat his food. The idea was excellent, except that my body refused to oblige. I was too weak even to sit down. I watched him for some time, but he did not shift his position, so I ate his food.

When two men came with semolina in the morning, they wanted to wake the man up for his breakfast, but I told them that he had had a very disturbed night, and he was better left alone. As soon as I had eaten mine, I quickly swapped plates and ate his portion of semolina.

I was worried that when the nurse came, she might realize that the last time she looked at the man, he was lying on his back. I lifted myself from my bed and turned him on his side. He was dead all right, and it took a hell of a lot out of me to do it. In all, I managed to swap the plates five times before my game was discovered and the stretcher-bearers arrived and took his body away.

I was getting a little concerned about missing the transport from the Soviet Union. I kept pestering the nurse about letting me out, but she insisted that I had to wait until I was seen by a doctor. He came one afternoon. The little red spots that I had had all over my body had turned brown and begun to fade. I was fairly confident that he would let me out, my confidence based on hope rather than on anything else.

He examined me, muttering to himself, then sat down on a chair on the far side of the room. He told me to get up, walk to the opposite wall and back. I did what he told me, but only just; the walls seemed to be swaying in all directions and my leg bones felt soft and when I turned around, the room spun a thousand times.

'How do you feel?' asked the doctor when I got to him.

'Great! Absolutely great!' said I, lying in his face. 'I am taking up a bed, needed much more perhaps by somebody else.'

'Hm, yes, very well. Back to bed now, the nurse will bring you your clothes.'

I thanked him, turning smartly about, then started running back to bed. I ran partly to impress the doctor, but mainly because I knew that if I did not lie down soon, I would collapse on the floor.

It was on 19 March that I finally left the hospital tent, fifteen days after reporting sick. It took me more than seven hours to cover the short distance to my tent because I had to stop and lie down many times on the way in order to regain my strength. I stayed in the tent for the next two days and in the early hours of 22 March we were woken up and told to prepare for marching out. I was still very weak and it was clear that we would be marching to the railway station. I informed my tent mates that I would start straight away, or else I would never make it in time.

The sun was well up when a column of happy, smiling men dressed in rags passed me, marching in a soldierly fashion. I tried to keep up with them but my legs would not oblige. I watched them with envy but was determined to join them before the train departed. I was not going to miss the golden opportunity of leaving the Soviet Union, even if the effort were to kill me. No sane man would forgo such a chance. When the column disappeared from view in the direction of the railway station, I lifted myself on all fours, my rucksack dangling from my neck, and followed their clearly defined tracks. With only a hundred yards to go, I had a good rest and joined the merry men on two legs.

We left Kermine in the afternoon. I was looking forward to seeing Farab and the other settlements again, but I was asleep when we passed through them. We stayed a long time in a place called Mary, and by this time I was strong enough to help carry the bread from the Red Army store. Later that night the train stopped at a station, and hordes of NKVD men boarded it.

We were told to shut all the windows and remain in our compartments while the NKVD patrolled the corridors. The train moved off and we were still going in a westerly direction. About an hour later the train stopped again, and the NKVD left just as suddenly as they had boarded. There was a simple explanation for the whole exercise. At one stage between the two towns the railway line ran fairly close to the border with Persia. So, to prevent the citizens of the USSR from using that railway line as a means of escape out of the country, the NKVD troops boarded each train on that route.

It was very hazy during the whole morning and we smelt the Caspian Sea a long time before we arrived in Krasnovodsk, the port on that vast lake. We alighted and sat on the quay near an old ship, the *Turkmenistan*, with a black hull and a dirty superstructure. Then the head counting began. We were counted, then counted yet again. Having become used to the inability of the comrades to count above three, we were not surprised. The soup arrived, the parting gift of our tormentors. Needless to say, it was *shchii*, the cabbage soup containing fish roes. It was not much different from the prison muck, except that the roes were more in evidence.

At last the counting stopped and the canvas belt across the gangway was removed. At the top of it stood two NKVD men who were busily counting for the last time on Soviet soil. The ship sounded its siren, the ropes were dropped and we were on our way. I watched the dreaded NKVD standing on the quay, hundreds of them, looking so powerless and insignificant. I did not let my exhilaration take over. We were on a Soviet ship and many things were still possible. I just felt happy. I was still a little weak but I knew I was gaining strength every hour.

The momentous day was 24 March 1942.

Early the next morning, the ship nosed its way into a small bay, then dropped anchor about a mile or two from shore. The little port was surrounded by hills, with large mountains behind. It was the Persian port of Pahlevi. A small boat arrived at the side and a few men came aboard. After about an hour they left, but the anchor was not weighed. Another boat heaved to, more men boarded the ship, then left as had the others. Judging by the expressions on their faces things were not going right.

Four or five agonizing hours passed with more visits by different people, before the ship weighed anchor and steamed into port. We were met by the Polish delegation, and after a most fabulous supper were accommodated for the night. After a morning banquet consisting of porridge, fried eggs and bacon, toast with butter and marmalade and magnificent coffee, we were told that we would be taken to the baths, then given new uniforms and underwear.

While waiting for my bath, my survival instinct took over. It occurred to me that once I entered, my clothes would be taken from me to be burned. There was money to be had for those rags of mine, money which I might need in the future! I broke ranks and within minutes I had found the market and sold my shirt for two tumans (about fifteen pence). I should have got double that amount but the buyer found it was infested with lice. On the way back I entered a shop and bought a notebook and an indelible pencil. I rejoined the ranks and started a diary, putting down all the dates and facts. Since then I have lost my yellow-coated pencil, but I still have the diary!

It was sheer bliss to take a shower. It was equally delightful to put clean underwear on, then the greenish uniform and to hear it rustle with every move. But it was hell, having put my boots on, to try to walk! I slid and skidded in all directions, falling on many occasions. It took me two days to get used to them.

In the evening we were addressed by a very high-ranking British officer, and on 28 March left Pahlevi for Teheran. That was the first transport of Poles from the USSR via Persia, and I was on it!

Considering the Communists had arrested and sent to Siberia and other such places some 1.5 million Poles, and the first transport consisted of some 500 men, my chances of being on that first transport were about 3,000 to 1!

I saw the magnificent scenery from the back of a lorry driven resolutely, and often much too fast, by a Persian driver. He stopped on occasions at solitary huts along the twisting route for a smoke of opium. We spent the night in Qazvin, a small town high in the mountains, and the next day, about twelve miles from Teheran, we passed through the last check-point manned by Soviet troops. It was only then that I breathed the clean air of freedom.

It is a heavenly feeling to be able to speak without first having to look round to see who might be listening; to be able to join a group of people and take part in a conversation, without the possibility of being accused of plotting anti-revolutionary this or that; to be able to laugh, without worrying that it might be taken as ridiculing the government or the Party; to be free of fear, the perpetual fear of arrest, the perpetual fear of a knock on the door, or a tap on one's shoulder. Only those who have lived under Communism, the alleged Paradise of the Working Class, know that precise, yet indescribable, feeling: the feeling of being a human being.

Marx had it all wrong. He produced a doctrine which abolishes the human race from the surface of the earth, and puts in its place a swarm of ants without any rights or purpose in life. The ants who kept on working for fear of being squashed by the gigantic steam-roller of the State Secret Police, which in turn is ruled by a band of ruthless terrorists who have reached that elevated position for no other reason, except that they were more ruthless than their competitors whom they annihilated on their way up, rulers whose authority – to quote one of my prison mates, himself a one-time Party member – 'ought never to have progressed beyond minding sheep in the fields'.

I spent my nineteenth birthday in Teheran and received an unexpected present. We were all given large tins of corned beef, butter, margarine, sugar and other goodies. We were told, to our great surprise, that from the moment of our arrival we had been fed on only one third of the British Army ration, for fear that our stomachs could not take the food. And we had thought that we

241

were being given special rations, that we were purposely being overfed!

I looked round the city of Teheran, including the Palace of the Shah. It was magnificent. I also saw a man selling *shashlik* on a street corner. Surveying the set-up with an expert eye, I came to the conclusion that I could easily steal a number of skewers without the vendor knowing much about it. However, I bought one instead; it tasted just as good as the ones I had stolen in Samarkand, Bukhara, or Tashkent, places that seemed so far away, places which I had left years before.

We left Teheran by train, passing through innumerable tunnels. We arrived in Ahvaz on 4 April, and camped outside the town. We had a medical inspection and the doctors discovered that my body, especially my hands, was riddled with scabies and I was therefore sent to hospital. Three days later, I realized that the duty doctor was more interested in parts of my anatomy other than my hands where most of the vermin were. The fool did not know that at the tender age of nineteen I had already lived a lifetime. I picked up my uniform and returned to camp. But it was a sad homecoming. My squadron had left, and I was attached to the army. On 1 May I was told it was my turn to do guard duty. At 10 p.m. I was posted outside the kitchen, and told to keep an eye on it and on the surrounding area. It was a beautiful night. The full moon illuminated the nearby mountains, and somewhere between them and me hyenas were laughing. I stood there, leaning on my rifle, enjoying it all. I thought about my past and realized that precisely a year before I had been in that horrible hole of Kharkov, together with 153 other human beings, standing by the smelly, overflowing *parasha*, while half of the inmates were lying on the floor. I sighed, took a deep breath of the clean, arid, desert air, wondering what had happened to my fellow prisoners.

On 16 May we left Ahvaz for Bandar-Shah-Pur and boarded the troopship, the *Devonshire*, arriving in Aden on the twenty-third. I had my first British cigarette there, a Gold Flake – it nearly killed me! It was like smoking hot air in comparison with the strong, Russian *kuroshki*. Early on 28 May we landed at Tewfik at the southern end of the Suez Canal, and by evening we were in tents at Heluwan in Egypt. I had a day out in Cairo, spending some time watching two Egyptians playing chess. I was invited to play a game and beat them both in quick succession.

We boarded the ship *Mauretania* on 5 June, leaving Suez the next day. When we were rounding the corner of Africa, a storm descended upon us. Many did not feel like having breakfast so I collected a number of ration cards and had four breakfasts one after another! We crossed the equator on the afternoon of the eleventh, arriving a few days later at the beautiful port of Durban in South Africa. We left by train for Pietermaritzburg, where we camped some distance from the town. I went to town one day, and instead of going along the trail to the main road to catch a bus, I decided to cut across the fields and walk there. About halfway between camp and the town there was a hollow and a copse. I was passing it when I saw a foolscap sheet of paper being blown by the wind. I ran after it and looked at its contents. It was written in some foreign language that I did not understand except for two words, 'Comrades' and 'Communism'. I knew only too well about the activities of the Comintern, the fifth column of the Communist empire, and I realized I had picked up one of the propaganda leaflets printed by those unscrupulous men. The fact that Great Britain was sending food, arms, and other supplies to the Soviet Union to help in their struggle for survival against the German invader – often at a great loss of men and ships – did not alter the principle of Communism that the end justifies the means. The comrades were not going to change their subversive activities on anyone's account.

I walked into the wind, in the direction of the hollow and the copse. There, partially covered by branches, I found a black crate about four feet long and two feet square. The lid was slightly ajar, so I opened it a little more, to find more of the literature. I hammered the lid back, then decided to report the find to the police. My problem was one of communication, I could not speak any English, and as it happened the policeman on duty did not speak any German. He made a phone call and a German speaker arrived at the station; I took him to the copse. He confirmed that it was indeed Communist propaganda and congratulated me on the find. I did not require any congratulations. I had not only seen Communism as presented in books, in flashy and often persuasive flowery phrases, but also experienced the doctrine in its ugly reality.

On 27 June we took part in a large military parade, marching with our heads held high through the streets of the town, our bones now covered by a healthy layer of flesh and muscle. Three weeks later we returned to Durban, received our rifles and escorted Italian POWs to the ship *Monarch of Bermuda*. A few days later we weighed anchor and, rounding the Cape of Good Hope, arrived at Cape Town. Table Mountain looked precisely as I remembered it from photographs in my geography books, except that it was a little lower than I had anticipated. I had a day out in town before leaving port on 4 August in the company of the battleship *Malaya*, and the *Queen Elizabeth*. I spent my time learning English or guarding the Italians. They called me the *bambino*, the child.

Our ship dropped anchor in Freetown, Sierra Leone, a very sticky, hot place full of palm trees and mosquitoes, and left the harbour in the afternoon of 16 August without any escort. Rumour had it that the liner was much too fast for any submarine to catch her. Early on the morning of 18 August, I came off guard duty and went up on deck for a breath of fresh air. I stood at the railings on the port side, watching the water passing by the hull far below. Without any warning, the ship turned abruptly, keeling over so far that I had to grab the rail for fear of sliding across the deck. The sailors ran to their gun positions, while the ship continued her awe-inspiring turns.

Clearly, there was a submarine about. I scanned the surface of the ocean but I could see nothing. About half an hour later, a big, four-engined flying-boat appeared from somewhere, flashed a message to the captain with a green light, then flew away. The ship stopped, and the engines were switched off, or throttled back, because I could not hear the usual throbbing. We drifted aimlessly for hours. Way ahead, the flying-boat appeared again, circling round and round. Then it dived towards the surface, we heard explosions and the flying-boat climbed away to continue circling. After some time the aeroplane flew towards us, flashed another message to the captain, the engines were started and we continued our voyage unharmed.

When I woke up early one morning, we were stationary. I went on deck to see what was happening, only to discover that we were moving, but very slowly. The ship was fogbound. Later that day,

27 August, we arrived at a port. The fog was so thick that I could hardly see the ground. We were told that we would disembark the next morning. We were in Great Britain.

The next day the fog was just as thick. I remembered reading about the fogs in Britain but I did not really believe that they could be so thick. A thought flashed through my mind: poor people, if that fog is here all the time they do not know what the world around them looks like! I need not have worried. The sun rose and the fog started to clear. We were ushered towards the gangway, clutching our kit bags, and I looked at my watch as I walked ashore.

It was 10 a.m. on 28 August 1942 when I finally stepped on British soil at Greenock in Scotland. Soon afterwards we boarded a train, leaving the quayside behind. The thick mist prevented my taking a good look at the country I had set out for, so full of hope, almost three years before.

We arrived in Auchtertool near Kirkcaldy and were accommodated in an old whisky distillery. A few days later I went for an interview with a selection board which was to decide which unit I would be assigned to. The chairman listed those available; none appealed to me. I wanted to join the air force and become a pilot but they did not mention it. I decided to take the bull right by the horns.

'Sir, I would like to join the air force and become a pilot.'

'Sorry, laddie,' said the chairman. 'The places have already been taken up.'

The board conferred for a while, then the chairman announced: 'I'll tell you what, laddie. Instead of flying them, you will be shooting them down. You will join the anti-aircraft artillery!'

'Very well,' I replied, feeling disappointed.

Early next morning lorries began arriving in the courtyard of the distillery to take us to our respective units. When my lorry reached its destination, the officer who met us discovered that he had one person too many. He called each man by name and they all took a few paces forward. When the officer came to the end of the list I was left standing on my own.

'What are you doing here?' he asked.

'I don't really know,' I replied, still trying not to look guilty. 'Isn't this the artillery unit?'

'No!' he replied, looking annoyed. 'This is an air force station!'

'I am sorry, sir. I must have boarded the wrong lorry!'

The officer thought for a moment, then made his mind up.

'Very well, then. Now you are here, you may as well join!'

So I joined. The town was Blackpool and I was billeted in one of the guest houses in the Tildesley Road. I joined as a ground mechanic under training. We were given blue uniforms and a day or two later I saw a notice requesting volunteers for air gunners. I put my name down and reported to the Winter Gardens for a test as the notice had requested.

When the list announcing the names of the successful applicants appeared on the board, we all ran to it. I quickly scanned the names, but mine was not there. I was a miserable failure! I looked at the list again, this time more carefully. I thought I had passed, the test had not been all that hard. No, I was right the first time, my name was not on the list of those who had been accepted. But it was not on the list of failures either!

My name was included at the very bottom of the notice, next to another's. It stated that he and I were posted on pilot's and navigator's courses. Later, I was to pass all the necessary examinations and qualify as a pilot. My childhood dream of flying aeroplanes did come true after all, and for the rest of the war I flew Spitfires and Mustangs on active service.

Epilogue

My brother Adam survived, too. Having collected ten years, he had been sent to a labour camp called Pechora in northern Siberia. Although he managed to escape he had been forced to give himself up, frozen and hungry. On his release he, too, found the Polish Army, was evacuated, then helped to chase Rommel and his Afrika Korps out of Africa and Italy. Unfortunately, he lost his hearing at Monte Cassino. We were reunited in Britain in 1946, six and a half years after our separation. He now lives in Scotland.

My mother died before she and my father could obtain permission from their Communist masters to spend a short holiday abroad. It was granted to my father eventually; we had to wait twenty-seven years to see him.

My father, then an old man of eighty-four, had to walk five miles to the passport office to inquire about the new procedures. He was told by the Communist official that he could read it all on a poster hanging on the wall. Having forgotten his glasses, he was told to fetch them. Another fifteen miles on foot. He then went to the capitalist British Embassy to apply for a visa. When the clerk discovered his age he told him not to trouble himself to return and said that the visa would be sent to him free of charge. As he told me later: 'I had read about English gentlemen. I met one there.'

He was overwhelmed by the courtesy of the British people during his stay with us. He returned to Poland and died soon afterwards, a happy man.

'I never expected to have my two sons under one roof again,' he told us. 'God is good.'

It took me three years to reach my destination in Britain, and in the process I travelled some 33,000 miles. I started my journey a boy and finished it a man; the going was often hard, but reaching freedom was worth that and more. Freedom, after all, is like health – only those who have lost it know how much it is worth. Communism, on the other hand, is like a cuckoo which lays its egg in another bird's nest. It is nothing more than the opium of the poor and the cancer of humanity. I should know, I lived in that oppressed land.